CW01263442

DAVID SELTZER

TRANSIT TOURISM

THE ICONIC ART AND DESIGN OF 22 SUBWAY
SYSTEMS AROUND THE WORLD

SCHIFFER
PUBLISHING

4880 Lower Valley Road • Atglen, PA 19310

Text Copyright © 2025 by David Seltzer
Photographs Copyright © 2025 by David Seltzer unless noetd in the image credits
About the Cover: Canary Wharf Station on London's Jubilee Line
Library of Congress Control Number: 2024942490

All rights reserved. No part of this work may be reproduced or used in any form or by any means—graphic, electronic, or mechanical, including photocopying or information storage and retrieval systems—without written permission from the publisher.

The scanning, uploading, and distribution of this book or any part thereof via the Internet or any other means without the permission of the publisher is illegal and punishable by law. Please purchase only authorized editions and do not participate in or encourage the electronic piracy of copyrighted materials.

"Schiffer," "Schiffer Publishing, Ltd.," and the pen and inkwell logo are registered trademarks of Schiffer Publishing, Ltd.

Designed by Carolyn Zalesne, The IT Girl, LLC
Cover design by Molly Shields

Type set in Quasimoda/Museo

ISBN: 978-0-7643-6903-2
ePub: 978-1-5073-0545-4
Printed in China

Published by Schiffer Publishing, Ltd.
4880 Lower Valley Road
Atglen, PA 19310
Phone: (610) 593-1777; Fax: (610) 593-2002
Email: info@schifferbooks.com
Web: www.schifferbooks.com

For our complete selection of fine books on this and related subjects, please visit our website at www.schifferbooks.com. You may also write for a free catalog.

Schiffer Publishing's titles are available at special discounts for bulk purchases for sales promotions or premiums. Special editions, including personalized covers, corporate imprints, and excerpts, can be created in large quantities for special needs. For more information, contact the publisher.

FSC
www.fsc.org
MIX
Paper | Supporting responsible forestry
FSC® C104723

THIS TRAIN MAKES THE FOLLOWING STOPS

ACKNOWLEDGMENTS VI | FOREWORD IX | ABOUT THE AUTHOR XII

INTRODUCTION 1

WHAT IS A SUBWAY? 7

A BRIEF HISTORY IN 20 STATIONS 11

NORTH AMERICA

BOSTON 21

CHICAGO 33

MEXICO CITY 41

MONTRÉAL 51

NEW YORK 61

PHILADELPHIA 77

WASHINGTON, DC 89

EUROPE

BRUSSELS 99

BUDAPEST 107

Dedicated to

Lisa, Jamie, and Evan

for putting up with my urban travel intransit-gence on family trips over the years

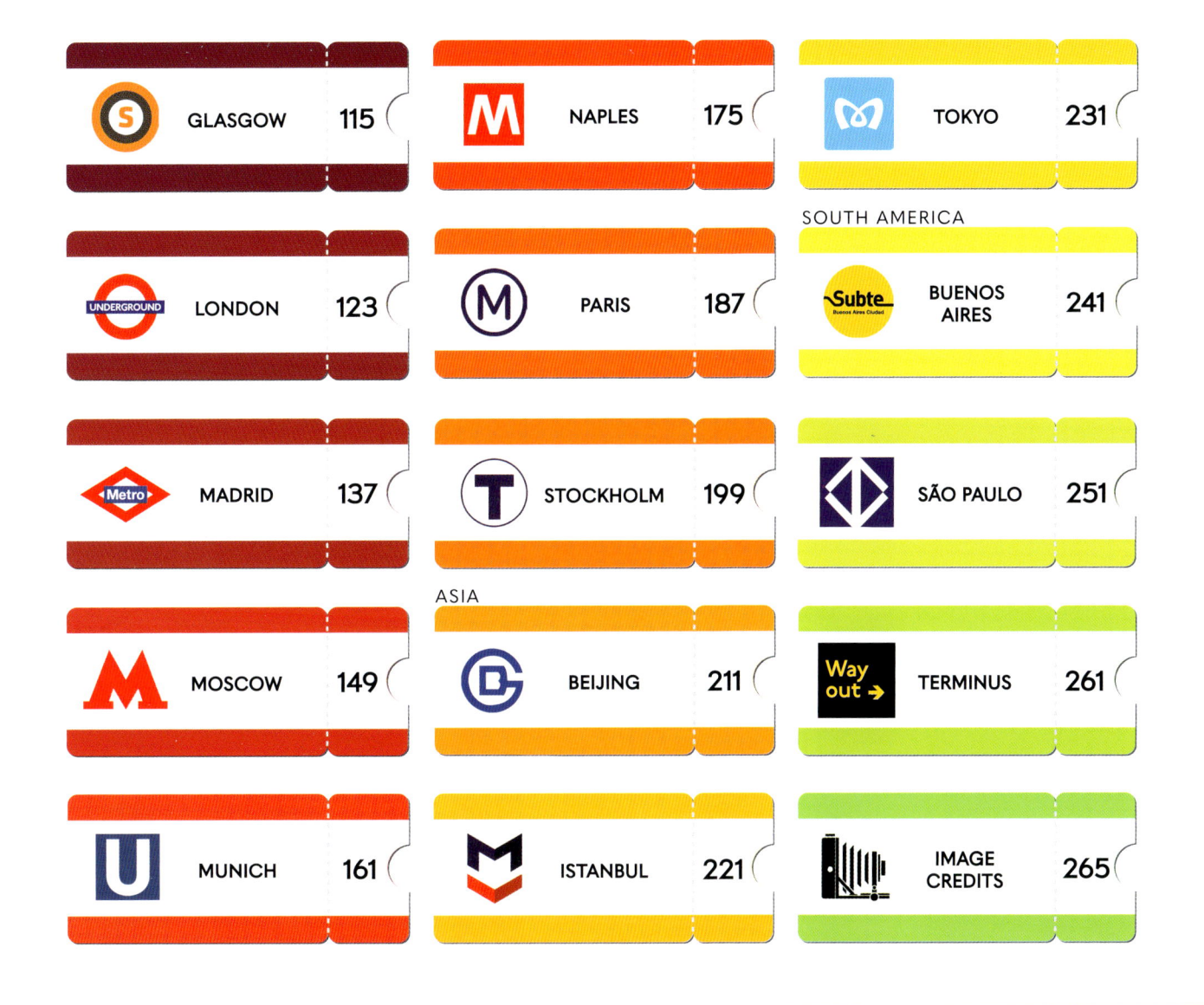

GLASGOW 115	NAPLES 175	TOKYO 231
		SOUTH AMERICA
LONDON 123	PARIS 187	BUENOS AIRES 241
MADRID 137	STOCKHOLM 199	SÃO PAULO 251
	ASIA	
MOSCOW 149	BEIJING 211	TERMINUS 261
MUNICH 161	ISTANBUL 221	IMAGE CREDITS 265

ACKNOWLEDGMENTS

Transit Tourism: The Iconic Art and Design of 22 Subway Systems around the World may come across as the result of a singular passion—even obsession—but I had many "fellow travelers" along the way assisting me on my journey. First and foremost, I must thank **Carolyn Zalesne**, who did a spectacular job as my book designer, publishing consultant, and spiritual advisor. She has made it possible for me to realize my vision of creating an attractively designed book that should appeal both to general readers and transit enthusiasts. **Maria Eife**, a gifted artist, jeweler, and digital-image wizard, was indispensable and infinitely patient in organizing and documenting the hundreds of photos and images appearing in this book, and finding work-arounds where a substitute image was needed. **Sarah Archer**, an accomplished author of several excellent books about midcentury and contemporary design, was a wonderful editor who brought greater clarity and immediacy to my writing. The late **Mort Downey**, who served as US deputy secretary of transportation, New York MTA executive director, and Washington Metro board chair, was a thought leader and tireless advocate for transit for decades, and I am deeply indebted to him for his insightful foreword to this book. I also must thank **Judy**

Zalesne, my CGO (chief grammatical officer), for her sharp-eyed review of the text, and only I am to be blamed for any remaining split infinitives or misplaced modifiers. I also wish to thank **Clémence Scouten**, **John Chesney**, and **John Foote** for providing guidance, review, and encouragement in the formative stages of the book.

While some of the images appearing in this book are from photos I had taken on my smartphone while touring subways, the vast majority are from third-party sources. I am deeply indebted to **Robert Schwandl**, a prolific author of over two dozen illustrated guidebooks about transit systems around the world, for granting me permission to reproduce a number of the excellent photographs from his superb website (urbanrail.net). **Bob Anderson** is a talented amateur architectural photographer, and I am grateful for his making available some of the striking architectural photographs of subway stations posted on his website (nabobswims.com/urban-rail-transport). **Brian Salter**, an expat Brit living in Hong Kong, graciously allowed me to use some of his images from his e-book *Underground Art in the Beijing Subway*. The sources of all the images in the book are listed in the "Image Credits" section.

I wish to thank my subway tour guides in various cities who arranged informative and entertaining exploratory trips or reviewed my chapter drafts (or both) for their respective cities: **Roberto Blanco** (Buenos Aires), **Andy Campbell** of Dress for the Weather Architects (Glasgow), **Crystal** of Remote Lands Tours (Beijing); **Ugur Ildiz** (Istanbul), **Pablo Alvarez de Toledo Müller** (Madrid), **Christian Denkman** (Munich), **Michael Herrman** (Paris), **Luísa Gonçalves** (São Paulo), and **Keiko Kamei** (Tokyo), among others. I also am greatly appreciative of those individuals familiar with specific cities who reviewed chapter manuscripts and offered helpful suggestions:

David and Andrea Gilmore (Boston), **Roberto Tchechenistky** and **Eduardo Ardiles** (Buenos Aires), **Inga Saffron** (Moscow), **Peter Angelides** (Naples), **Bonnie Mackay** and **Bob Eisenhardt** (New York), **Yolanda Robins** (Paris), **Jerry Silverman** (Philadelphia), **Josh Koplin** (Tokyo), and **Dene Garbow** (Washington), among others.

I have striven mightily to ensure the accuracy of all the information presented in this book, but any factual errors or omissions are "all on me," as they say in the professional sports world. If you wish to share thoughts, corrections, or suggestions about this book, please contact me at transittourismbook@gmail.com, and I will endeavor to incorporate them in any subsequent printing.

David Seltzer
Philadelphia
November 2024

FOREWORD

I want to thank David Seltzer for this contribution to the appreciation of subways and the role they play in making our great cities more livable for residents and visitors. Like him, I have the strange habit of making an extensive subway tour a part of any visit to a new city in the United States or overseas.

Throughout my long career, I've been a federal policymaker, a transit manager with the PATH system and the MTA in New York, and a board member of the Washington Metro. Something I learned early on with pleasure was that transit systems don't shield trade secrets from their competitors in the same way producers of consumer products do. Transit systems compete largely with automobile and other system operators who willingly trade ideas in the interest of improving the industry. There is no patent protection preventing a good operations or maintenance practice—or even a breakthrough in customer service—from being applied in another city. So, whether through industry conventions, through occasional study tours, or, in more-recent years, as a tourist, I've always hunted for ideas to bring home, and even those to avoid.

In Beijing, I found the passenger wayfinding signage to be outstanding. Every station on the main line is identical in design—center platforms with two exit stairs at each end. And within each station are English-language signs on the sidewalls indicating the station name, an arrow for the expected direction of the next train, and its last station of departure and next station of arrival. At the center of the platform there's a map designating the four exits as A through D, with identification of which one serves what landmark, as in "Take stairway C for Mao's Tomb." I had more confidence traveling in Beijing than I usually have in traversing the Washington Metro.

In London, I noted the London Underground's assurance that it will charge you a ride at a time but cap the charges if they reach the level of a daily pass. For a system hoping to attract tourists, that's a real plus in customer service.

I've also experienced ideas that don't travel well. I've always assumed that subway stations were not practical locations to do airport-like security screenings, but when I visited Beijing, I saw it working quite efficiently. Nevertheless, I concluded it would not work at home.

David's keen eye has made similar observations: ideas that are inspired and improved upon from city to city, as well as those more and less successful attempts to offer riders the ability to get from one place to another and do so with meaningful surroundings and helpful signage. David's journey is filled with a seasoned respect for the enormity and complex nature of transit systems, all told with a delightful sense of humor.

David and I also share the effort of trying to interest our wives in our strange habit; it was not always successful. My late wife, Joyce, may have been more accommodating than David's wife, Lisa (who prefers to shop aboveground while David rides the subway), but even Joyce drew the line when our Metro ride through Vienna (Austria, not Virginia) was interrupted by a several-block walk. I guess not everyone shares David's and my passion for adventure! (Apparently, the center section of that line was closed for the month of August for track repairs. I learned from other riders that day that they were willing to accept the delay and discomfort because they had been adequately notified and there was good signage offering alternatives. I took those comments back to my colleagues in Washington; good advice as we planned our Metro rehab program.)

If you are a transit executive or an advocate looking to collect ideas from other systems here and abroad, David's book is useful reading. But for everyone else—seasoned subway riders to first-timer adventurers—this book is an enlightening journey. By focusing on the key elements of each city system, especially the influence of local culture on its development, David provides the context you need to appreciate the all-important ties between the cities above and their subways below. Enjoy the ride!

Mortimer L Downey
1936–2023

Former senior manager at the NY-NJ PATH system, executive director of New York MTA, and board chairman of Washington Metro, as well as an eight-year incumbent as deputy secretary of the US Department of Transportation

ABOUT THE AUTHOR

David Seltzer hails from Philadelphia, a city more renowned for its railroad and streetcar legacy than its subways. He has worked as an investment banker and municipal financial advisor since 1976, advising state and local government agencies—including some of the nation's largest transit systems—in raising capital for major infrastructure projects and programs. He has had a lifelong interest in subways, possesses a library of over 450 books on the subject, and has toured 45 systems around the world (only 153 left to go).

David is active in civic affairs, serving on the boards of the Philadelphia Museum of Art, CraftNOW Philadelphia (which he cofounded), and the Philadelphia Youth Sports Collaborative. He previously chaired Philadelphia Gas Works (the nation's largest municipally owned gas company) and the Philadelphia History Museum. He and his wife reside in Center City, Philadelphia, along with their highly demanding cat, Mr. Waffles.

BEIJING	BRUSSELS	BUENOS AIRES	COPENHAGEN
STOCKHOLM	PHILADELPHIA	TOKYO	ISTANBUL
GLASGOW	LONDON	MILAN	MADRID
MEXICO CITY	MUNICH	SÃO PAULO	VANCOUVER

INTRODUCTION

Why on earth (or more aptly, why *under* earth) would anyone wish to read a travel book about riding subways? After all, isn't it a little dark for sightseeing in those tunnels?

On the contrary, riding the local transit system is essential to understanding a city's distinctive character. This book comprises a collection of personal and highly opinionated travel essays drawn from my experiences riding subway systems around the world. But this is not a technical, historical, or sociological account; rather, it is a generalist's armchair tour of twenty-two cities' subway systems located in eighteen countries on four continents, describing the rider experience and how each subway (or underground, metro, or U-Bahn) evinces something essential about the city it serves.

Cities build transit systems for various reasons. Improving mobility is obviously the primary objective, but oftentimes there are other motivations as well. A city may be competing for hosting rights for major international events, such as a world's fair (Lisbon) or the Olympic Games (Athens, Munich), and wish to demonstrate easy access. A city may seek to spur real estate development in fallow areas (New York's Hudson Yards, London's industrial Docklands). The subway could serve as a statement of civic pride and coming of age (Montréal). A subway could be built for the purpose of national defense (Beijing, Pyongyang) or even serve ideological goals (Moscow).

INTRODUCTION

Yet, to paraphrase Winston Churchill, we shape our subways, and afterward our subways shape us. (This is particularly the case for the hunched posture riders must assume squeezing into Glasgow's diminutive subway coaches.)

What interests me most are the particularities—the design, the feel, the personality—of each transit system. Most subways have their own distinct set of aesthetics, a unique *visual culture*. It starts with the station design, including the materials used, the lighting and fixtures, and the entry kiosks. But it's much more than the architecture. Each system has its own design language. Its **logo** serves as the brand identifier to the public. The **map** shows how the system presents itself and its city to its riders. Many subways even have their own bespoke **typeface** for signage, which is akin to the system's "handwriting." Further, some public transportation agencies have extensive "art in transit" programs, either inserting artwork into older stations to brighten them up or, more ambitiously, incorporating major art pieces into the design of new stations. Finally, there are the **vehicles**—the "rolling stock," in transit jargon. Many of the more recent railcar models are themselves triumphs of contemporary industrial design and often are decorated in a unique livery.[1]

Indeed, our recognition of a city's "brand" is often indelibly linked to the aesthetics of its public transport system. Even those who prefer taking an *Uber* to an *U-Bahn* probably recognize iconic transit symbols from various cities, such as those shown below. In short, the house style of a transit system can be thought of as part of each city's DNA.[2]

---

[1] In terms of the rider experience, I have focused on the stations rather than the subway cars. Why? As in automobile models, there has been a certain convergence in the style and design of subway cars in recent decades. The railcar industry is dominated by a limited number of international manufacturers. While each system may have its own distinct door chimes, it is increasingly difficult to differentiate railcars in Brussels from those in Beijing. I imagine my train-spotter readers will be appalled at this dismissive attitude toward rolling stock.

[2] Concerning logos, some countries use a standard symbol for a subway entrance (e.g., a white "U" in a blue box in Germany or a white "M" in a red box in Italy) that is separate from the corporate logo for the transit agency. In the US, the transit authority's logo typically is used to designate station entrances; there is no universally used symbol indicating "subway."

INTRODUCTION

Left: Boston's encircled T

Center: London's celebrated roundel

Right: Washington's stately pylon

Your Conductor

Tour guides should always start by sharing something about their personal backgrounds, explaining how it informs the tour we're about to take together. Well, for over forty years, I worked in public finance, raising capital for various transportation agencies around the country, including some of the nation's largest transit authorities. And it turns out that my vocation has also been my avocation, since I harbor a passion that dare not speak its name: *trains*. More specifically, urban passenger trains. I am not sure what prompted this interest, although I suspect it had something to do with my childhood bedroom window overlooking the Reading Railroad in suburban Philadelphia. While there are those who find it very soothing at night to hear the background sounds of a gurgling brook or trees rustling in the wind, for me it was always the Lansdale Local clattering by.

My lifelong interest in rapid transit was firmly established by elementary school. As sixth graders, my next-door neighbor, Tom Field, and I would sally forth on Saturday mornings to explore Greater Philadelphia via public transportation. With our twenty-three-cent token in hand, we would venture across the water as far east as Camden, New Jersey, by taking the Broad Street

TRANSIT TOURISM | 3

INTRODUCTION

subway and the Bridge Line, and as far west as Norristown—the Montgomery County seat—by taking the Market Street Elevated and the Philadelphia and Western (also known as the "Pig & Whistle") Red Arrow Line, one of the nation's last interurban trolleys. Who needs purple mountain majesties above the fruited plain when you can admire the Quaker City skyline from the El above the row-house roofs?

Ever since, on my domestic and international travels, I have made it a point to seek out a city's subway system. To date, I've ridden subways in nearly fifty cities and counting, ranging from the planet's northernmost subway (Helsinki) to its southernmost (Buenos Aires).[3]

To be sure, at times I have tested the limits of audience interest in this particular subject matter. In 1986, as newlyweds, my wife, Lisa, and I flew to London for our honeymoon. Upon our arrival at Heathrow the following morning, I told her the exciting news that we could take the new Piccadilly Line extension *directly* from the airport terminal to the very doorstep of our hotel in the West End! This suggestion was met with a withering Susie Essmanesque glare. The marriage surely would have been terminated before it could be consummated, had I not acquiesced and opted for the more private but much-pricier taxi drive into town. Ever since, on our overseas trips—in order to ensure domestic tranquility—we designate one day where Lisa goes shopping and I commandeer our tour guide to take me on a subway tour.

I continue to read every book about subways I can get my hands on. My personal collection on the subject now totals over 450 volumes. My favorite books deal with the artwork and architecture of subways. Mind you, I don't consider myself a "trolley jolly"—one of those flannel-shirted

---

[3] The complete list to date: Amsterdam, Atlanta, Baltimore, Barcelona, Beijing, Berlin, Bilbao, Boston, Brussels, Budapest, Buenos Aires, Chicago, Copenhagen, Fukuoka, Glasgow, Gwangju, Haifa, Helsinki, Istanbul, Kyoto, Lisbon, London, Los Angeles, Madrid, Mexico City, Milan, Montréal, Munich, Naples, Newark, Osaka, Oslo, Paris, Pittsburgh, Prague, Rio de Janeiro, Rome, Santiago, San Francisco, São Paulo, Seoul, Stockholm, Tianjin, Tokyo, Toronto, Washington, Vancouver, Vienna, and, of course, my hometown of Philadelphia.

foamers who record the train's clickety-clack for their future listening enjoyment. But I do save the official map of every system I've ridden.

Our Tour Route

This guidebook starts by trying to answer the surprisingly difficult question of "What is a subway?" I then give a thumbnail summary of key developments in rapid transit over the last 160 years, for those wanting a historical perspective. The city-by-city descriptions then follow, providing current metrics for each system (except for ridership, which reflects prepandemic data). The systems are arranged by continent. Except for the five American cities, I have rationed myself to one city per country.

I have personally ridden each of the subways described in this book.[4] There are some world-class subway systems that are missing from this book because I have not yet had the opportunity to visit those cities: Athens, Hong Kong, and someday, perhaps, Pyongyang. There are other top-quality systems I have ridden but didn't include in this initial volume because of space limitations. Disappointed readers will have to await the no-doubt eagerly anticipated volume 2 of *Transit Tourism* for essays on these additional cities' systems.

The reviews represent my own personal and highly opinionated views. I have gathered information from sources I deem reliable, including each transit agency's website, my personal library, and Wikipedia, but if there are factual errors, I would be grateful if you could notify me.

As noted above, the thesis of this guidebook is that each subway to a certain extent reflects the character of that city. But it is also useful to compare each transit network to its peer systems. One

---

4 Well, I have ridden all but one of them. But you'll have to read the book to find out which one, and why.

INTRODUCTION

could rank subways on physical characteristics, such as route length, ridership, or the number of stations; on operational metrics, such as frequency, speed and reliability; or on service features, such as fare levels and hours of operation.

Because this book is for the general urbanist rather than the confirmed train buff, I have developed a highly subjective rating system (the Seltzer Token Rankings) based on the *quality of the user experience*. Specifically:

> **Convenience**: How well does the system serve the user in getting around the city?
> **Ease of Use**: How readily can a newcomer understand how to use it?
> **Quality of Design**: How attractive is its architecture, artwork, and design language (system graphics, logo, maps, and wayfinding)?
> **Personality**: How emblematic is the subway system of the city it serves?

Based on my notes from the underground, for each system, I assign a grade from one to four tokens on the basis of these criteria. (I know, I know: by using "fungible" tokens in this digital era, I am hopelessly dating myself.) But while my scoring system may be highly personal, I hope you won't find it harsh, arbitrary, and inconsistent, like that of East German skating judges.

So, with this introduction, please stand clear of the closing doors, and off we go!

To the Trains →

WHAT IS A SUBWAY?[1]

According to a leading trade organization, as of 2021, a total of 193 cities in 61 countries around the world have urban rail transportation systems, or "metros," as they are generically termed. The cities range from Adana (Türkiye) to Zhengzhou (China) and operate over 10,000 route miles, have nearly 13,000 stations, and serve 58 billion riders each year.[2] And the number keeps expanding, with over thirty more cities around the globe expected to open subways in the next several years, nearly half of which are located in China and India. And this doesn't include the countless extensions of existing systems that are currently being constructed.

The transit industry uses the term "metro" to describe these urban rail systems, but it must be acknowledged that the terminology quickly gets a little squirrely. Although terms such as "subway," "underground," "metro," "urban rail," and "rapid transit" are used somewhat interchangeably, I have *very specific notions* of what types of public transportation services qualify as "subways" for the purpose of this guidebook.

---

1 What a subway most definitely is not, at least within these pages, is the Britishism referring to those pedestrian passageways crossing beneath the street.
2 World Metro Figures 2021, UITP (International Association of Public Transport). All the ridership data are prepandemic (generally 2019).

WHAT IS A SUBWAY?

First and foremost, I define a subway as a rapid-transit rail line within a major city where at least some portion of the routes run underground, serving multiple stations. There is something about the *undergroundedness* of a subway (as opposed to an entirely elevated or surface line) that makes it more impressive. Its subterranean stations disgorge thousands of commuters onto downtown city streets, seemingly from nowhere. The engineering challenges posed by constructing systems underground in densely populated areas are enormous. Subways invisibly wend their way beneath a city's buildings and streets, its buried water mains and power lines, its rivers and hills. You enter the subway at one station and emerge at another, in a completely different district, city, state, or—in the case of Istanbul—continent.[3] In fact, you'll find that the *subwayness* of each system is one of the metrics I list at the beginning of each city description.

The trains generally are electric powered, more commonly through a third rail rather than overhead wires and pantographs. But about a dozen systems have at least one line that uses linear induction motors (including Beijing, Kuala Lumpur, Osaka, Toronto). Happily, steam engines were phased out over a century ago.

Subways are a form of "rapid transit," a now-archaic mid-twentieth-century term, connoting multicar, high-capacity trains operating on a dedicated rail route (its "right-of-way") with multiple stations, high-level (no-step) platforms, frequent service, and reasonably rapid speeds (i.e., faster than local street traffic). By this definition, the term "subways" would exclude the Chunnel, or Japan's Honshu-Hokkaido rail tunnel, or other *intercity* subterranean passenger rail lines. It would similarly exclude an underground city *bus* tunnel with multiple stations, such as Boston's Silver Line. (Someday, if and when it is converted to rail, we can talk.)

---

[3] Well, technically, the trans-Bosporus Marmaray rail line is more akin to subterranean commuter rail lines such as Paris's RER and London's Elizabeth line than a true metro, but permit me this literary license.

WHAT IS A SUBWAY?

The definition gets further complicated, however, since a number of cities (including Munich, Tokyo, Istanbul, Stockholm, Paris, and London, with its new Elizabeth Line project) have built rail tunnels for suburban commuter trains running through the heart of the city with multiple underground stations. The commuter railways may even (shockingly!) cohabitate, sharing tunnels and tracks with the more conventional local "subways," as in Tokyo. But I place those transit services in the category of commuter railroads, which are of interest, but secondary to subways.

Now, most rapid-transit systems are not built entirely underground, oftentimes just in the central city because of the extremely high cost of tunneling. For example, over 85 percent of the Chicago Transit Authority's rapid-transit lines are elevated (the eponymous "L"), although portions of two lines do run underground through the Loop. Boston's Orange Line and Philadelphia's Market-Frankford Line both operate aboveground for the majority of their routes but run underground through their respective downtowns.

But it gets more complicated. Dozens of cities operate what are called "light rail" services, which are trams or streetcars that are shorter, smaller, and, yes, lighter than so-called "heavy" rail, or conventional subway trains. Light-rail lines may operate for some or all of their route on their own dedicated right-of-way or run underground in the central business district. (Think Boston's Green Line or San Francisco Muni's trolley routes.) In some cities, an underground route is initially built to handle only the lower-capacity trams or trolleys, with the option to be retrofitted to heavy rail in the future if demand warrants. (This larval stage is called "pre-Metro".) In my book (which *is* what we are talking about here, after all), these underground light-rail lines do qualify as subways.

In summary, while there may be no singular and indisputable definition of "subway" that satisfies everyone, let me borrow Justice Potter Stewart's famous observation about pornography and simply say about a subway: *I know it when I see it.*

Moscow Metro
rete metropolitana e tratte ferroviarie urbane
underground and urban railways map
2016-2018 OFFICIAL PUBLIC
Rapid Transit Map
Tokyo Metro Guide
with Subway
English
Plano de bolsillo
Pocket map
Metro
RIVER CLYDE
SEPTA
Railroad & Rail Transit Pocket Map
Chicago Transit Authority
Rail 'L' MAP
August 2015
MVV
London Underground
Tube map
December 2014
MAYOR OF LONDON
TRANSPORT FOR LONDON
Paris poche
Metro & CHRONO
Métro & CHRONO
01.09 2011
Subway Map
MTA
SISTEMA DE TRANSPORTE COLECTIVO
Red del Metro
Metrorail Pocket Guide
RIDER INFORMATION
METRO SYSTEM MAP
POINTS OF INTEREST
RD
OR
BL
GR
YL
SV
SL
Spårtrafik
Stockholm · Rail network
SL Trafikupplysningen
08-600 10 00
İSTANBUL
Raylı Sistemler
Ağ Haritası
İstanbul Rail Network Map
Gratuit
RÉSEAU DU MÉTRO
2013
stm
Subte

A BRIEF HISTORY OF SUBWAYS

A BRIEF HISTORY OF SUBWAYS IN TWENTY STATIONS

For those interested in the history of subway development, I've provided an overview in twenty stations—each station represents a significant innovation in the evolution of urban rapid transit.

1863—PADDINGTON (Metropolitan/Circle Line, London): The world's **first underground urban railway** was opened in 1863, running 3¾ miles through central London from Paddington Station to Farringdon. The carriages were pulled by steam locomotives, which were ill "sooted" to underground service. The lines gained greater popularity after being electrified in 1907.

1868—29TH STREET (IRT 9th Avenue Elevated, New York): The **first elevated rapid transit line** started operations from Lower Manhattan to the Upper West Side, running above 9th Avenue in New York. The line was originally cable powered, converted to steam several years later, and ultimately electric powered. This line served as a model for New York's other elevated railways built over 2nd, 3rd, and 6th Avenues, as well as lines in Boston, Chicago, and Philadelphia. Following the opening of the 8th Avenue subway in the 1930s, the Manhattan portion of the 9th Avenue El was demolished in 1940.

TRANSIT TOURISM | 11

TWENTY STATIONS

1890—ELEPHANT & CASTLE (Northern Line, South London): This station in the London borough of Southwark is part of the **first electrified subway**. It is a "tube" line (bored tunnel) using a third rail for power, which set the pattern for all future London Underground lines. Originally opened as part of the City and South London Railway in 1890, it was subsequently amalgamated into the Underground's Northern Line. The successful application of this new, "clean" technology allowed conversion of the steam-engine trains on the Metropolitan and District Lines a decade and a half later.

1896—DEÁK FERENC SQUARE (Line 1, Budapest): This line, known locally as the Földalatti (Underground), is the **first powered subway in Continental Europe.** It originally consisted of electric-powered trams running for 2.5 miles and six stations from the heart of downtown (Deák Square) to the fairgrounds for the Budapest Millennium Exposition in 1896. It is the only transit operation listed by UNESCO as a World Heritage Site.

1897—PARK STREET (Green Line, Boston): **America's first subway** opened with five (now four) surface streetcar routes serving inner suburbs west and south of Boston, entering a tunnel beneath congested Tremont Street in downtown Boston. Park Street Station is located on the eastern edge of Boston Common. With the completion in 1912 of the first portion of the "Red" Line to Harvard Square in Cambridge, a new lower interchange station was added, named Park Street Under.

A BRIEF HISTORY OF SUBWAYS

1897—ROOSEVELT (originally 12th Street, Chicago South Side Elevated): The **first use of multiple-unit train control** from a single car, allowing elimination of locomotive engines. This propulsion system is now the standard for most metros worldwide. This completely elevated service now operates as Chicago Transit Authority's Green Line.

1900—LOUVRE-RIVOLI (Line 1 Paris): Beginning of the **first multiline city subway network.** The primary sponsoring company—La Compagnie du Chemin de Fer Métropolitain de Paris (the Metropolitan Railway)—became known as the "métro" for short. This term is now used worldwide to denote rapid-transit lines running above or below ground. By the end of that decade, seven other metro lines had opened, crisscrossing Paris. The Louvre-Rivoli station entrance was designed by Hector Guimard in a flamboyant art nouveau style.

1904—CITY HALL (IRT, New York): When it was opened by the Interborough Rapid Transit Company, this station originally served as the southern end of **New York's inaugural subway line.** It ran 9 miles from Lower Manhattan to Harlem along a route that subsequently became parts of the #3, the #6, and the S crosstown shuttle lines. While the oldest extant subway service in New York, it is not actually the first: in 1870, Alfred Beach clandestinely built an experimental subway running 100 yards under Lower Broadway. The single car was propelled forward and back by a large fan.

TRANSIT TOURISM | 13

TWENTY STATIONS

1913—PLAZA DE MAYO (Line A, Buenos Aires): Downtown terminus of the Subte, this is the **first subway line in Latin America**. Plaza de Mayo station is adjacent to the Pink House, Argentina's Presidential Palace. The stations are exquisite period pieces, and its original cars remained in operation for a century, until retired in 2013. The line has been extended twice and received a gentle makeover in the mid-1990s.

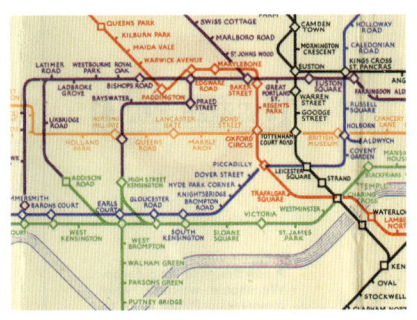

1933—PICCADILLY CIRCUS (Piccadilly Line, London): Introduction of Harry Beck's **iconic London Underground map**. It has served as the model for most transit maps worldwide ever since. London Transport CEO Frank Pick promoted the novel map along with the redesign of Piccadilly Circus and forty new stations designed by Charles Holden to brand the Underground in the 1930s. The station ticketing hall contains an exhibition about Pick.

1952—KOMSOMOLSKAYA (Koltsevaya Line, Moscow): Located beneath a square surrounded by three major railway termini, the Komsomolskaya station is not only one of the Moscow metro's busiest stations but also **its most ornate.** Since the opening of the first metro line fifteen years earlier, dictator Josef Stalin directed that the stations be designed as "Palaces of the People." With its glittering chandeliers, decorative molding, and lavish marble finishes, no station is more palatial than Komsomolskaya!

14 | BRIEF HISTORY

A BRIEF HISTORY OF SUBWAYS

1964—SAN BABILA (Line 1, Milan): Introduction of **trendsetting station graphics**, wayfinding, and Helvetica font by the renowned Dutch-born graphic designer Bob Noorda. Milan's crisp "House Style"—color-coded station sign stripes, clear graphics, and clean typeface—served as the standard for many other subway systems around the world over the following decades (and the inspiration for this book's design as well!).

1966—BERRI-UQAM (Green, Blue, and Yellow Lines, Montréal): Inauguration of the world's **first rubber-tire Metro system**, followed two years later by Mexico City. The rubber tires give a quieter and smoother ride and allow steeper inclines than steel-wheel-on-steel-rail operations. Today, over two dozen cities have at least one line with rubber-tire metro service; the first individual line had opened in Paris in 1956.

1968—WALTHAMSTOW CENTRAL (Victoria Line, London): This was the northern terminus of the world's **first Automatic Train Operation subway line.** Philadelphia's Lindenwold Line followed suit the following year, and San Francisco's BART became the first multiline subway system to operate automatically. These "ATO" systems have attendants in the cab of the front car, for safety. The first truly driverless underground line commenced service in 1983 in Lille, France. There are now fully automated metro lines in forty-five cities worldwide.

TRANSIT TOURISM | 15

TWENTY STATIONS

1971—TIANANMEN EAST (Line 1, Beijing): Opening of the **first subway line in China.** China far and away now leads the world in subways, with systems operating in forty-five cities, including the four largest systems in the world, and seven of the top ten. Another six cities will be opening new systems by 2025. As of this writing, Beijing (505 route miles) edges out Shanghai (498 route miles) for the longest system.

1972—12TH STREET–OAKLAND CITY CENTER (Red–Orange–Yellow Lines, BART): One of the initial stations for the **first completely new US system** in half a century, redefining how Americans perceived subways. Bay Area Rapid Transit (BART) introduced new technologies such as magnetic far cards, automatic train control, and the world's then-longest submersible tunnel—the TransBay Tube—connecting San Francisco and Oakland (3.6 miles). The system has an unusually wide track gauge (a foot wider than most US systems), with cars that are 10½ ft. wide and 75 ft. long, and used a "space-age" design aesthetic for vehicles and stations.

1977—CHÂTELET-LES HALLES (Metro Lines 1, 4, 7, 11, 14; RER Lines A, B, D; Paris): The **largest, most complex transit hub in the world,** this sprawling underground complex serves five Metro lines and three suburban train (RER) routes. Hundreds of thousands of passengers use the station daily. The site was the former nineteenth-century glass-ceilinged Paris food market Les Halles.

A BRIEF HISTORY OF SUBWAYS

1987—TOA PAYOH (North-South Line, Singapore): This station and line segment was the **first metro to use platform screen doors** (barriers between platform edge and tracks). Platform screens are considered safer, quieter, and more efficient than open platforms in terms of climate control. They are now becoming increasingly common and have been installed in parts of eighty-six metros worldwide, of which nearly half are in China.

1987—SADAT (Line 1, Cairo): **First metro system opened on the continent of Africa.** This station is on the underground portion of what is now a three-line subway system serving Egypt's capital. Algiers launched Africa's second metro service in 2011.

2023—SAN FRANCISCO STATION (Line 1, Quito): Ecuador's capital is the **most recent city to open a metro system,** as of this writing. The 14-mile, fifteen-station, all-underground Metro makes Quito the 194th city worldwide with a subway. At an elevation of 9,300 feet, it is the highest elevation subway (and capital) in the world. The station under Plaza San Francisco is in the historic center, a UNESCO World Heritage site.

CITIES OPENING SUBWAYS
LISTED BY DECADE

Until the 1950s, only seventeen cities worldwide had subways. Since then, the number has grown elevenfold, to over 190. Nearly half of today's systems opened in the twenty-first century. In the last decade, cities in China and India have accounted for most of the expansion, as this infographic illustrates.

Located in China **Located in India** • Chapter in Book •

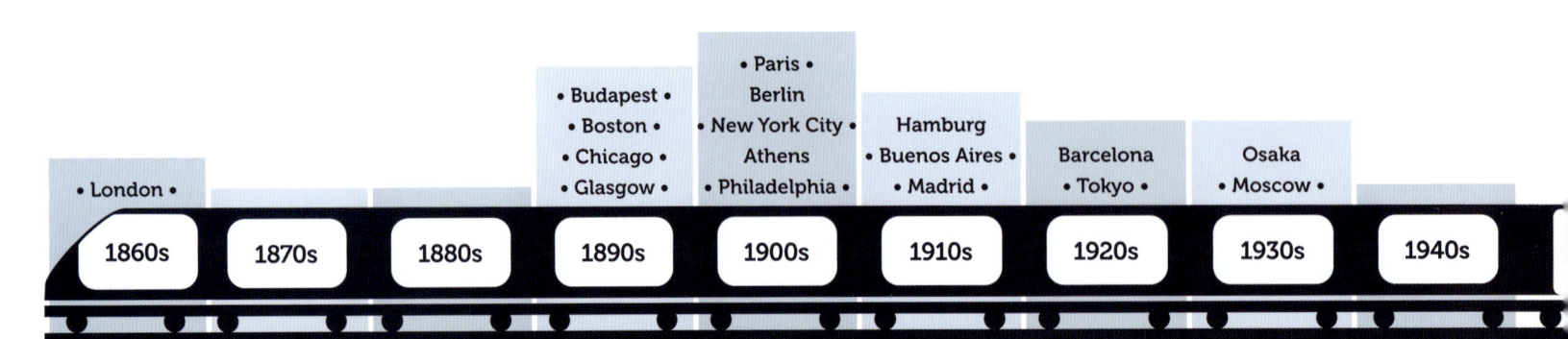

1860s	1870s	1880s	1890s	1900s	1910s	1920s	1930s	1940s
• London •			• Budapest • • Boston • • Chicago • • Glasgow •	• Paris • Berlin • New York City • Athens • Philadelphia •	Hamburg • Buenos Aires • • Madrid •	Barcelona • Tokyo •	Osaka • Moscow •	

CITIES OPENING SUBWAYS (BY DECADE)

1950s
- • Stockholm •
- Toronto
- Rome
- St. Petersburg
- Cleveland
- Nagoya
- Haifa
- Lisbon

1960s
- Kyiv
- Milan
- • Montréal •
- Tbsli
- Oslo
- Baku
- Rotterdam
- • Mexico City •

1970s
- • Beijing •
- • Munich •
- Sapporo
- Nuremburg
- Yokohama
- San Fransisco
- Pyongyang
- • São Paolo •
- Prague
- Seoul
- Santiago
- Kharkov
- Vienna
- • Brussels •
- • Washington •
- Marseille
- Kobe
- Amsterdam
- Liverpool
- Tashkent
- Lyon
- Rio de Janeiro
- Hong Kong
- Bucharest
- Atlanta

1980s
- Newcastle
- Yerevan
- Fukuoko
- Kyoto
- Helsinki
- Lille
- Baltimore
- Caracas
- Minsk
- Tainjin
- Kolkata
- Manila
- Miami
- Porto Alegre
- Recife
- Vancouver
- Busan
- Nizhny Novgorod
- Belo Horizonte
- Novosibirsk
- Cairo
- Sendai
- Samara
- Singapore
- • Istanbul •

1990s
- Genoa
- Monterrey
- Yekterinaburg
- Shanghai
- Toulouse
- • Naples •
- Los Angeles
- Hiroshima
- Medellin
- Warsaw
- Bilbao
- Dnipro
- Kuala Lumpur
- Taipei
- Guangzhou
- Daegu
- Ankara
- Sofia
- Catania
- Incheon
- Manila
- Bangkok

2000s
- Tehran
- Izmir
- Brasilia
- Ottawa
- Copenhagen
- Rennes
- Delhi
- Bursa
- Dalian
- Shenzu
- Wuhan
- Gwanju
- San Juan
- Chongqing
- Nanjing
- Kazan
- Turin
- Daejeou
- Lausanne
- Kaohsiung
- Santo Domingo
- Adana
- Dubai

2010s
- Chengdu
- Foshan
- Shenyang
- Algiers
- Changchun
- Xi'an
- Bengaluru
- Mashad
- Almaty
- Lima
- Hangzhou
- Kunming
- Suzhou
- Harbin
- Zhengzho
- Gurgaon
- Brescia
- Salvador
- Changsha
- Ningbo
- Wuxi
- Mumbai
- Shiraz
- Panama City
- Nanchang
- Qingdao
- Chennai

2010s (continued)
- Jaipur
- Isfahan
- Tabriz
- Dongguan
- Fuzhou
- Hefei
- Nanning
- Guiyang
- Shijiazhuang
- Xiamen
- Hyderabad
- Kochi
- Luknow
- Taoyuan
- Ürümqi
- Sydney
- Changzhou
- Hohhot
- Jinan
- Langzhou
- Wenzhou
- Xuzhou
- Ahmenabad
- Nagpur
- Noida
- Jakarta
- Doha

2020s
- Guadalajara
- Lahore
- Taiyuan
- Luoyang
- Taichung
- Wuhu
- Kanpur
- Hanoi
- Jinhua
- Pune
- Quito

TRANSIT TOURISM | 19

Massachusetts Bay Transportation Authority
Rapid Transit/Key Bus Routes Map
LOWELL LINE
HAVERHILL LINE
NEWBURYPORT/ROCKPORT LINE
OL
OAK GROVE
Malden Center
Wellington
Assembly
Sullivan Sq
Community College
West Medford
GL E
MEDFORD/TUFTS
Ball Sq
Magoun Sq
Gilman Sq
East Somerville
GL D
UNION SQ
Lechmere
Science Park/West End
North Station
RL
ALEWIFE
Davis
Porter
Harvard
Central
Kendall/MIT
Charles/MGH
Park St
Downtown Crossing
State
Haymarket
Gov't Center
BL
BOWDOIN
Aquarium
Maverick
Airport
Wood Island
Orient Heights
Suffolk Downs
Beachmont
Revere Beach
WONDERLAND
Lynn
WOODLAWN
Revere Center
Box District
Eastern Ave
SL3
CHELSEA
Bellingham Sq
Charlestown Navy Yard
SL1
AIRPORT TERMINALS
Logan International Airport
Rental Car Center
Logan Ferry Terminal
Long Wharf (North)
Long Wharf (South)
Rowes Wharf
South Station
Courthouse
World Trade Ctr
Silver Line Way
Harbor St
Tide St
SL2
DESIGN CENTER
HULL FERRY
HINGHAM FERRY
FITCHBURG LINE
Waltham
Waverley
Belmont
ARLINGTON HEIGHTS
WATERTOWN SQ
WATERTOWN YARD
Union Sq (Allston)
WORCESTER LINE
Newtonville
Boston Landing
Harvard Ave
Griggs St
Allston St
Warren St
Washington St
Sutherland Rd
Chiswick Rd
Chestnut Hill Ave
South St
BOSTON COLLEGE
GL B
Packard's Corner
Babcock St
Amory St
BU Central
BU East
Blandford St
Kenmore
Hynes Convention Ctr
Copley
Arlington
Boylston
Kent St
St. Paul St
Coolidge Corner
Hawes St
St. Mary's St
Summit Ave
Brandon Hall
Fairbanks St
Washington Sq
Tappan St
Dean Rd
Englewood Ave
CLEVELAND CIRCLE
GL C
Fenway
Longwood
Brookline Village
Brookline Hills
Beaconsfield
Reservoir
Chestnut Hill
Newton Centre
Newton Highlands
Eliot
Waban
Woodland
RIVERSIDE
GL D
Lansdowne
Prudential
Symphony
Northeastern
Museum of Fine Arts
Longwood Medical Area
Brigham Circle
Fenwood Rd
Mission Park
Riverway
Back of the Hill
HEATH ST
GL E
Tufts Medical Center
Chinatown
Chinatown Gate
Back Bay
Mass. Ave
Ruggles
Roxbury Crossing
Jackson Sq
Stony Brook
Green St
FOREST HILLS
Herald St
East Berkeley St
Union Park St
Newton St
Worcester Sq
Mass. Ave
Lenox St
Melnea Cass Blvd
NUBIAN
SL4
SL5
Newmarket
Uphams Corner
Kane Sq
Grove Hall
Four Corners/Geneva
Franklin Park
Talbot Ave
Morton St
Blue Hill Ave
Codman Sq
Broadway
Andrew
JFK/UMass
Savin Hill
Fields Corner
Shawmut
ASHMONT
RL
Cedar Grove
RL M
MATTAPAN
Capen St
Valley Rd
Central Ave
Milton
Butler
Fairmount
FAIRMOUNT LINE
North Quincy
Wollaston
Quincy Center
Quincy Adams
BRAINTREE
RL
GREENBUSH LINE
KINGSTON LINE
MIDDLEBOROUGH/LAKEVILLE LINE
NEEDHAM HEIGHTS
Needham Center
Needham Junction
NEEDHAM LINE
Hersey
W. Roxbury
Highland
Bellevue
Roslindale Village
OL
Hyde Park (Cleary Sq)
Readville (Wolcott Sq)
FRANKLIN LINE
PROVIDENCE/STOUGHTON LINE
Legend
RL RED LINE
M MATTAPAN LINE
OL ORANGE LINE
BL BLUE LINE
SL SILVER LINE and branches
GL GREEN LINE and branches
B Terminates at Gov't Ctr
C Terminates at Gov't Ctr
D Terminates at Union Sq
E Terminates at Medford/Tufts
COMMUTER RAIL
KEY BUS ROUTE Frequent service
FERRY
*Boylston: Accessible for Silver Line only
Accessible station
All MBTA and Massport bus and ferry services are accessible
Rapid Transit transfer station
Commuter Rail transfer station
Free Logan Airport shuttle bus
Amtrak service Back Bay, North & South Stations
@MBTA
/TheMBTA
@TheMBTA
/MBTAGM
@TheMBTA
Customer Communications & Travel Info
617-222-3200, 800-392-6100,
TTY 617-222-5146, www.mbta.com
MBTA Transit Police: 911
TTY 617-222-1200
Elevator/Escalator availability: 617-222-2828
©MBTA 2022 v.37
Not to scale

BOSTON
Massachusetts Bay Transportation Authority

System Length	53 route miles[1]
Number of Lines	5 (2 are light rail)
Number of Stations	94[1]
Year Opened	1897
Year of Last Expansion	2022 (2 Green Line extensions)
Annual Ridership	200 million (2019)
Subwayness	38% of stations underground

Boylston Head House (Green Line)

To me, Boston has always seemed the most European of American cities: its charmingly winding streets, its evocative British place-names, its cosmopolitan flavor, and—not least importantly—the centrality of transit in its civic psyche. Boston has always been highly transit oriented, and it remains one of my favorite rail systems. As a high school student, I used to visit my aunt and uncle in Cambridge; they were proper Bostonians who lived a few blocks from Harvard Square. I enjoyed going to see them, especially the *going* part, since the trips afforded me the opportunity to ride not one, not two, but *three* different

---

1 System and station data exclude light-rail service operating on local streets.

MASSACHUSETTS BAY TRANSPORTATION AUTHORITY

subway lines. From Logan Airport I would take the Blue Line, the Green Line (or, depending on my mood that day, the Orange Line), and, finally, the Red Line to reach Harvard Square.

Boston built the nation's very first subway in 1897, allowing the trolleys to avoid gridlocked traffic on Tremont Street. By 1920, four subway lines converged in a downtown parallelogram from north, south, east, and west.[2] The combined effect of Boston's disorderly street pattern (apocryphally based on colonial cow paths), the meandering routes of its four subway lines, and the "wicked" local patois of many station cashiers made it exceptionally challenging for out-of-towners to navigate the system.

But in the mid-1960s, the renamed regional transit agency, the Massachusetts Bay Transportation Authority (MBTA for short), did a remarkable thing: it sponsored a complete design makeover, the first and arguably the best one ever done on these shores. This system-wide rebranding is captured brilliantly in a catalog, *Design in Transit,* I saved from a 1967 exhibition at the Boston Institute of Contemporary Art. Showing the design work of the architectural and design firm Cambridge Seven Associates, the exhibition illustrated how superior graphics could completely transform an aging and confusing subway system into an attractive and understandable traveling environment. The redesign appears to be influenced by the groundbreaking work that Dutch graphic designer Bob Noorda fashioned for Milan's then-new Metro in the early 1960s. (A few years later, he collaborated with Massimo Vignelli on redesigning the wayfinding and signs for the New York City subway.)

With this plan, the MBTA introduced to American transit systems a number of transit design features that were highly innovative at the time and now have become standard. First, they

---

[2] There was previously an elevated line with several stops running along the waterfront above Atlantic Avenue, but it was demolished in the late 1930s. I am not counting the Silver Line bus rapid transit service, launched in 2002, because even though it has several underground stations in South Boston, "I don't do buses."

BOSTON

color-coded each line so that riders wouldn't need to know station termini names in order to navigate the system. These colors appeared consistently on maps and vehicles and along station walls in four bright primary colors. Second, they simplified the unwieldy interchange station names. "Devonshire-State-Milk" became "State"; "Summer-Winter-Washington" became "Washington" (and subsequently "Downtown Crossing"); and "Union-Friend-Haymarket" became "Haymarket." Third, the MBTA applied a complete new set of graphics, starting with a fresh logo (T) (inspired by Stockholm's Tunnelbana marker) as the symbol for all transit services. It became synonymous with the MBTA itself and gave the system its eponymous nickname of the "T." The MBTA's streamlined typeface and graphics for wayfinding and signage was one of the earliest applications of the now-ubiquitous Helvetica typeface in the United States. And finally, the MBTA produced a series of detailed neighborhood maps and attractive, high-contrast photo murals of local landmarks, which they posted on station walls to orient riders to their surroundings.

The illustration below shows the combined effect of these design features on the pilot project of renovating Arlington Station in Back Bay.

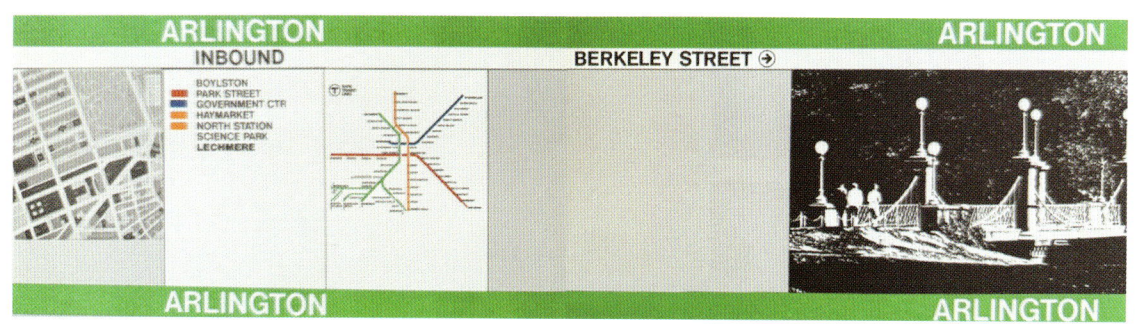

Rendering of 1965 Arlington Station makeover

TRANSIT TOURISM | 23

MASSACHUSETTS BAY TRANSPORTATION AUTHORITY

To see just how radical the transformation in Boston was, simply compare the shambolic earlier map from the mid-1950s to the simplified and elegant color-coded schematic diagram from 1965.

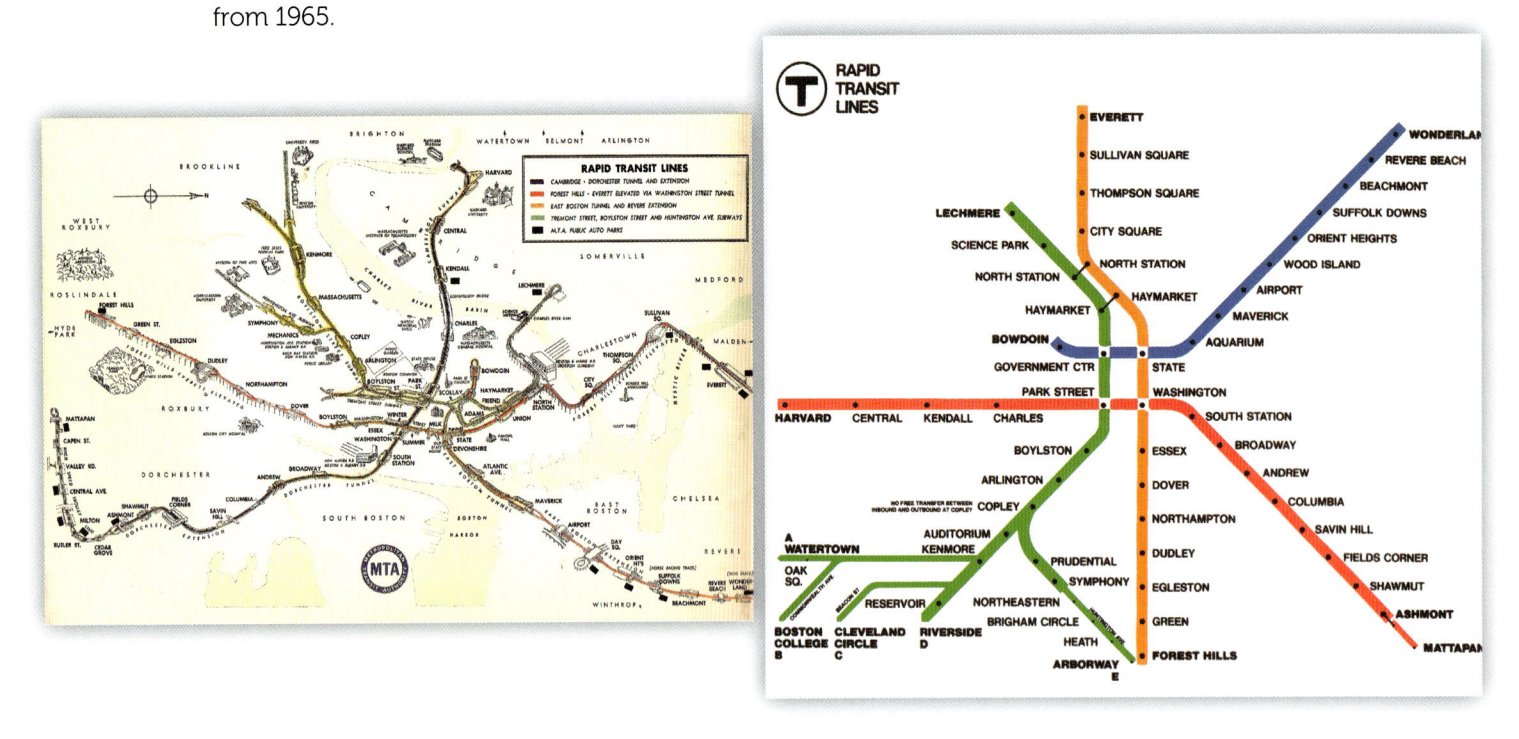

The map's transformation was inspired by the revolutionary redesign of London's even more complicated Underground lines by Harry Beck in 1933. The result was a graphically pleasing and clear display of Boston's complex transit network. So greatly impressed was I by this superb graphic

24 | NORTH AMERICA—USA

BOSTON

that I decided to paint a full-scale replica of it on the wall of my freshman dorm at Trinity College in 1970. Somewhat less impressed was Trinity's Facilities Services Department, who assessed a damage charge against my room security deposit for defacing college property.

Sadly, over the years, Boston has allowed the pristine 1960s redesign to become cluttered. The route map, once a model of clean, sophisticated design, is now encumbered not just with commuter rail lines but—*I ask you!*—bus routes as well. Much of the clarity, symmetry, and beauty of the original map has been lost.

In riding the "T" today, it's clear that the map is not the only design element that has deteriorated. On my most recent visit, the entire system seemed run down. Much of the railcar fleet looks and feels very beat up, having suffered one too many long Boston winters. Many of the stations look tired as well, with peeling paint, unkempt platforms, and the incursion of advertisements onto the wall spaces formerly reserved for the colored line stripes, station names, and wayfinding signage. Some stations have lost their very attractive Inbound (red-orange) and Outbound (blue-green) brick checkerboard walls at the platform ends. This diminished condition reminded me of another landmark of underground infrastructure I had seen: the Catacombs of Rome, where Roman civilization's decline can be instantly grasped by comparing the highly refined carvings on caskets from Rome's Classical period with the jumbled lettering and crudely chiseled figures on sarcophagi from the Dark Ages.

But in Boston, not all is dark: there have been several shining exceptions to the design decline in recent years. The new entrance to the Government Center Station is a striking glass cube on the stairwell structure, with multihued LED lighting that shifts from blue green to purple to red—a very attractive beacon at the foot of Beacon Hill. It has happily replaced the squat brick ziggurat entrance on City Hall Plaza, which was reminiscent of the portal to the Morlocks' subterranean world in the 1960 film *The Time Machine*.

MASSACHUSETTS BAY TRANSPORTATION AUTHORITY

And through it all, the "T" has retained some of its eclectic and noteworthy legacy design features. For starters, there is the glorious view of Back Bay as the Red Line emerges from Cambridge to cross the Charles on the "salt-and-pepper-shaker" Longfellow Bridge en route to Park Street, which is the heart of the system.

Boston-bound train crossing Longfellow Bridge

Park Street *Over* (the Green Line station above the Red Line's Park Street *Under*) is as charmingly chaotic as ever. Screeching trolleys from four different routes careen around the sharp

BOSTON

turns under Tremont Street, an underground bumper car free-for-all. Nearby is the State Street Station entrance, built incongruously right into the ground floor of the historic Old State House, constructed in 1713. How many national historical landmarks contain a working subway station? And that unstately State Street portal could not be more different than the refined Copley Square kiosk in Back Bay, or the resolute granite headhouses of Park Street and Boylston stations on Boston Common.

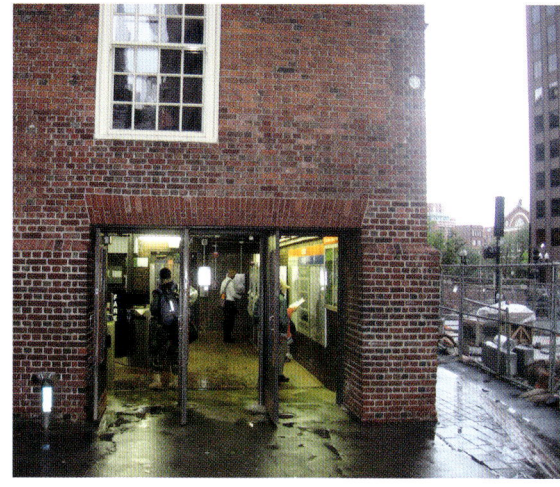

Top:
Subway entrance beneath Old State House

Left:
Copley Square

Right:
Park Street headhouse

TRANSIT TOURISM | 27

MASSACHUSETTS BAY TRANSPORTATION AUTHORITY

One stop away from State Street is the very Parisian-looking Aquarium Station, with its gently vaulted ceiling and column-free vista. *Merveilleux!*

Inset:
Anvers station
(Line 2, Paris)

Aquarium Station
(Blue Line, Boston)

28 | NORTH AMERICA—USA

BOSTON

And last but not least is the internationally beloved icon of the Harvard Square entry kiosk from 1928, which for nearly four decades housed the Out-of-Town Newsstand, selling papers and magazines from around the world. Although the newsstand regrettably is gone now, the nearly century-old headhouse remains.

Old Harvard Square entry kiosk

MASSACHUSETTS BAY TRANSPORTATION AUTHORITY

Boston has continued to make investments in expanding its system. A 4-mile, six-station surface extension of the Green Line with two branches to the near northern suburbs of Somerville and Medford opened in 2022, and the new South Coast commuter rail line to New Bedford is underway. The "T" continues to roll.

From 1966 MBTA Capital Expansion Plan

there's a new Ⓣ rolling your way

Red Line train at Harvard Square

30 | NORTH AMERICA—USA

BOSTON

SUMMARY

The "T" is a lot like Boston itself: quirky and tradition bound, yet investing in the future; proudly local, but at the same time self-aware of its international renown. Despite the frustrations and shortcomings of the system, Bostonians seem to retain a stubborn affection for the "T." They even have their own Subway System Anthem, "Charlie on the MTA," which has given its name to the transit agency's fare pass—the CharlieCard. Few probably recall that this originally was a political protest song from 1949 decrying the advent of the nickel transfer charge between lines that allegedly prevented Charlie from ever getting off the train. Now, the song is a source of regional pride, and the long-ago protest is all water under the (Longfellow) Bridge.

SELTZER TOKEN RATINGS (SCALE 1–4)

CONVENIENCE	4
EASE OF USE	3
QUALITY OF DESIGN	2
PERSONALITY	3

TRANSIT TOURISM | 31

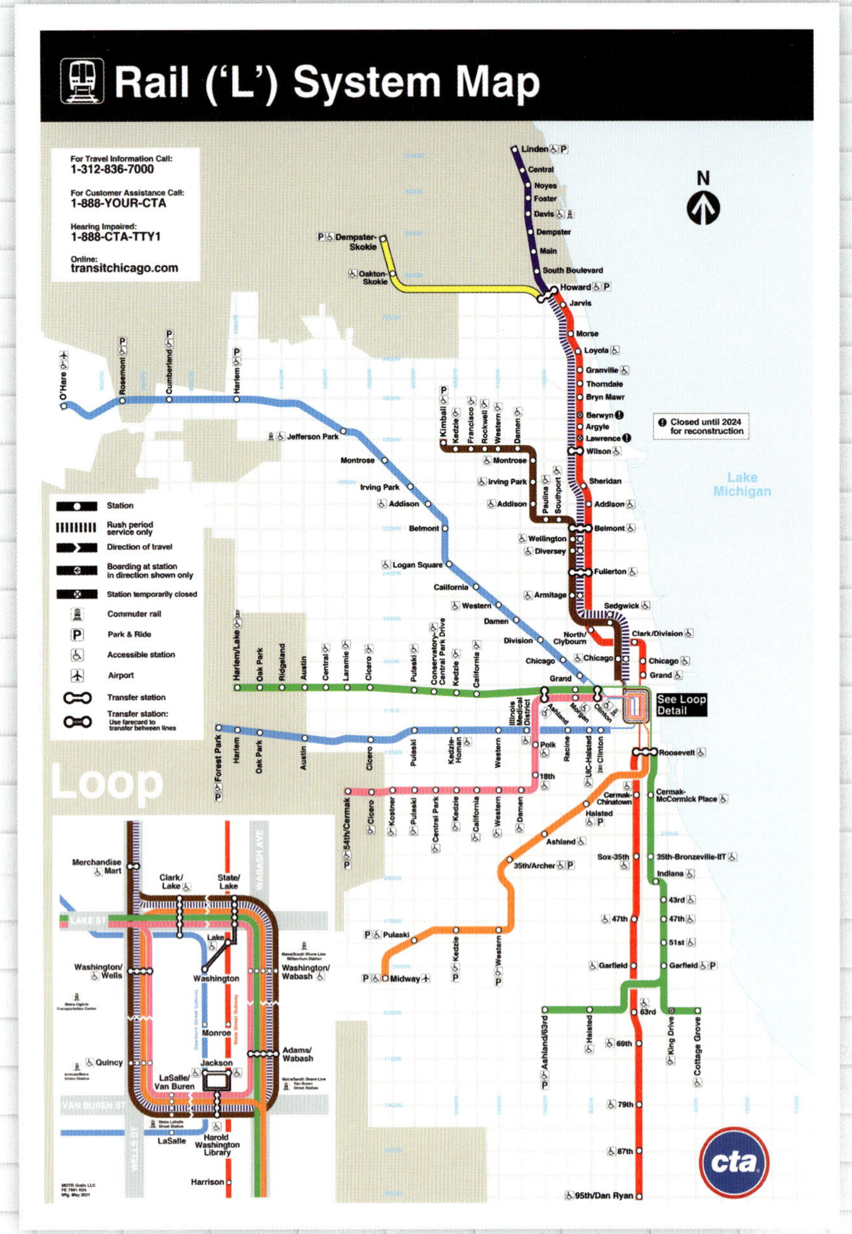
Rail ('L') System Map
For Travel Information Call:
1-312-836-7000
For Customer Assistance Call:
1-888-YOUR-CTA
Hearing Impaired:
1-888-CTA-TTY1
Online:
transitchicago.com
N
Lake Michigan
Closed until 2024 for reconstruction
Station
Rush period service only
Direction of travel
Boarding at station in direction shown only
Station temporarily closed
Commuter rail
Park & Ride
Accessible station
Airport
Transfer station
Transfer station: Use farecard to transfer between lines
Linden
Central
Noyes
Foster
Davis
Dempster
Main
South Boulevard
Howard
Dempster-Skokie
Oakton-Skokie
Jarvis
Morse
Loyola
Granville
Thorndale
Bryn Mawr
Berwyn
Argyle
Lawrence
Wilson
Sheridan
Addison
Belmont
Fullerton
Sedgwick
Clark/Division
Chicago
Grand
See Loop Detail
Roosevelt
Cermak-McCormick Place
35th-Bronzeville-IIT
Indiana
43rd
47th
51st
Garfield
63rd
King Drive
Cottage Grove
Ashland/63rd
Halsted
Cermak-Chinatown
Sox-35th
69th
79th
87th
95th/Dan Ryan
O'Hare
Rosemont
Cumberland
Harlem
Jefferson Park
Montrose
Irving Park
Logan Square
California
Western
Damen
Division
Grand
Clinton
UIC-Halsted
Racine
Illinois Medical District
Kedzie-Homan
Pulaski
Cicero
Austin
Oak Park
Forest Park
Kimball
Kedzie
Francisco
Rockwell
Southport
Paulina
Wellington
Diversey
Armitage
North/Clybourn
Harlem/Lake
Ridgeland
Central
Laramie
Conservatory-Central Park Drive
Ashland
Morgan
Polk
18th
54th/Cermak
Kostner
Central Park
35th/Archer
Midway
Loop
Merchandise Mart
Clark/Lake
State/Lake
LAKE ST
WABASH AVE
Lake
Washington/Wells
Washington
Washington/Wabash
Monroe
Adams/Wabash
Quincy
Jackson
LaSalle/Van Buren
VAN BUREN ST
LaSalle
Harold Washington Library
WELLS ST
Harrison
cta

CHICAGO

CHICAGO
Chicago Transit Authority

System Length	103 route miles
Number of Lines	8
Number of Stations	145
Year Opened	1897
Year of Last Expansion	2015
Annual Ridership	219 million (2019)
Subwayness	11% of stations underground

Entrance to L in the Loop

Chicago is arguably the most emblematic of American cities, with its soaring skyscrapers, its rectilinear street plan, and especially its patriotic street names: patriotic figures such as Washington, Adams, Madison, and Jackson, along with resolutely mid-American names such as Dearborn, Wabash, State, and Lake.

With notable buildings by Louis Sullivan, Frank Lloyd Wright, Ludwig Mies van der Rohe, and other famous architects, Chicago is a mecca of innovative architecture. Yet, as synonymous as Chicago is with high-quality building design, its transit architecture demonstrates—as Mies *might not* have put it—that "less is less." Where is

CHICAGO TRANSIT AUTHORITY

Top:
1926 Chicago Rapid Transit Co. poster reproduced for L's Centennial in 1997

Bottom:
Train at State/Lake Station

the swashbuckling Burnhamesque spirit of making no little plans with the magic to stir men's blood? Chicago's transit architecture is decidedly flat, like the Chicago landscape, or, for that matter, the Chicago accent.

Chicago's 103-mile-long rapid-transit system, owned and operated by the Chicago Transit Authority (CTA), consists of six principal lines and two outlying shuttle extensions. It is known in the local vernacular as the "L" (distinct from the "El" as applied to elevated train lines in New York and Philadelphia). Yet, only a third of the system is actually on elevated trestles: half is at grade or on an embankment, and just 11 percent is underground, mostly downtown. In radial fashion, CTA's subway and surface lines fan out from Chicago's central business district every which way but east (Lake Michigan intrudes).

The eponymous Loop has the riveting and riveted retro appearance of a giant steampunk mechanism—albeit an electrified one. Five of CTA's elevated lines trundle around the 2-mile Erector Set structure, with some routes running clockwise and others counterclockwise. Four out of the five lines complete a full circuit around the Loop and return whence they came. But—stay with me on this—one route, the Green Line, traverses only *half* the Loop and runs in both directions, adding to the confusion.

34 | NORTH AMERICA—USA

CHICAGO

The CTA map heroically (but not entirely successfully) attempts to decipher this mixing bowl with the detailed map to the right. Perhaps a roulette wheel would be a more appropriate metaphor than a mixing bowl, since the trains zip around the Loop in seemingly random fashion before settling upon an exit to outlying neighborhoods. Be forewarned: if you board a train in the Loop, you could end up *anywhere* in the city: northbound to Evanston, northwest to Kimball, westbound to Harlem, southwest to Midway, or far South Side to 95th Street.

Yet, Chicagoans seem to love the Loop, since it is so inextricably tied to the Second City's (well, technically today, *Third* City's) self-image. Think of all the Hollywood films where the Loop might get an Oscar for Best Supporting Structure, such as The Sting, The Blues Brothers, The Fugitive, and Risky Business.

Back in the 1970s, the city gave serious consideration to replacing the Loop with an underground circle line. But such was the public outcry (and such was the price tag, *oy!*) that the scheme was abandoned, and the trains have continued to rumble overhead.

Yet, not all of CTA's rapid transit lines actually circuit the Loop. Two of the lines, Red and Blue, run as subways through the central business district, transecting it north–south via

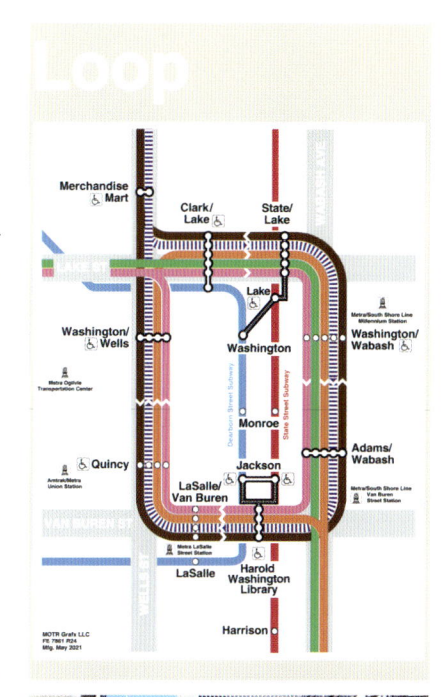

Top:
Map of the Loop roulette

Bottom:
The "L" rumbling through downtown Chicago

TRANSIT TOURISM | 35

CHICAGO TRANSIT AUTHORITY

parallel tunnels under Dearborn Street and State Street. And very strange subways they are: the two lines run a block apart through downtown, and within the Loop the platforms extend almost the entire half-mile length from Randolph to Jackson Streets. If so inclined, one could walk rather than ride between those stations, using the extended platform.

The long expanse of platforms at the Monroe stations on the Blue and Red Lines

The design of Chicago's underground segments is 1940s industrial-functional, with lots of exposed girders, barrel vault ceilings, and minimal ornamentation. At least the Loop L stations hovering over the central business district display occasional architectural flourishes, such as Quincy, which boasts a restored *fin de siècle* design, and a few other elevated stations that have been retrofitted with dramatic new rooflines (Cermak-McCormick and Washington-Wabash).

While most of the transit architecture is strictly functional in style, CTA has sponsored an impressive public art program that perks up its stations considerably. As of this writing, some fifty stations (about one-third of the system) have art installations, many by local artists. CTA has

CHICAGO

Washington-Wabash Station (on the Loop)

published a beautiful book in which the installations are presented: *Elevated: Art and Architecture of the Chicago Transit Authority.* At 450 pages and weighing in at over 4 pounds, it is the heftiest volume in my collection of four-hundred-plus subway books, and thus perfectly suited for residents of the City of Broad Shoulders.

Both of Chicago's airports, O'Hare and Midway, are served directly by transit. The L ride from Midway to the Loop is convenient enough, twenty-five minutes on the Orange Line. However, the ride from O'Hare into town tests even a transit enthusiast's stamina, as it proceeds in a very leisurely fashion for three-quarters of an hour and makes over fifteen stops before finally reaching the Loop. As an alternative, there is sporadic commuter rail service from a nearby station via Chicago's regional rail system, Metra, and perhaps someday Elon Musk's proposed underground hyperloop will whisk passengers from downtown to O'Hare Airport in twelve minutes flat. We shall see.

CHICAGO TRANSIT AUTHORITY

I recall back in my investment-banking days at EF Hutton, I underwrote a debt offering for the Chicago Transit Authority. For the closing, I chartered a 1920s-era L car and had a catered cocktail tour of the system before it deposited well-hydrated CTA officials, bond attorneys, and bankers at a station directly above the near North Side restaurant where we would enjoy our closing dinner. It was a memorable and (I thought) highly appropriate way of celebrating CTA's first public debt offering in decades. Alas, since the mid-1990s, it has been considered Rather Bad Form to hold lavish, wine-laden bond-closing dinners, and such a boondoggle today would be unthinkable. But let's not forget, investment bankers are people too, and they have feelings, just like you and me.

For Chicago enthusiasts, CTA's online gift shop sells lots of attractive branded merchandise, and the Chicago Architecture Center gives a wonderful guided tour of the Loop called "Elevated Architecture." The walking/riding tour allows you to see not only the transit architecture but also a wide variety of building ornamentation at the L's third-floor level that normally would be difficult to view (largely because the L itself is in the way). A quintessentially Chicagoan excursion is to take the L to Wrigley Field or New Comiskey (Guaranteed Rate) Park for a ballgame. I have found that the CTA baseball crowds are much mellower than, say, the "footie" fans taking the Tube to watch Chelsea or Arsenal, where wearing the wrong-hued jersey could invite unwelcome comments about your maternal heritage—or worse.

In addition to its rapid transit, Chicago historically has been (and continues to be) the rail hub for the country. For over a century, it has served as the nation's center for freight rail, and it still has four major passenger rail terminals: Union Station, which is being renovated by Amtrak, Northwestern Station, LaSalle Street Station, and Metra Millennium Station, née Randolph Street. Sadly, all except Union Station have been reduced to humdrum low-ceilinged commuter terminals; they must have missed the Burnham memo about making magic to stir men's souls.

CHICAGO

SUMMARY

As the nation's only remaining downtown elevated line, Chicago's clattering Loop is an anachronism. Despite or perhaps because of this, it is an iconic feature of both the city's landscape and its psyche, much like the ivy-covered outfield walls of Wrigley Field, or the dyed-green waters of the Chicago River on St. Patty's Day. CTA's eight lines serve the city effectively, but from a design viewpoint they are minimalist and charmless, and not up to the same standard as Chicago's first-rate architectural heritage. Yet, although the system lacks the signature style (and appeal) found in other cities, circumnavigating the Loop by L still ranks up there as a quintessential way of experiencing the Windy City.

SELTZER TOKEN RATINGS (SCALE 1–4)

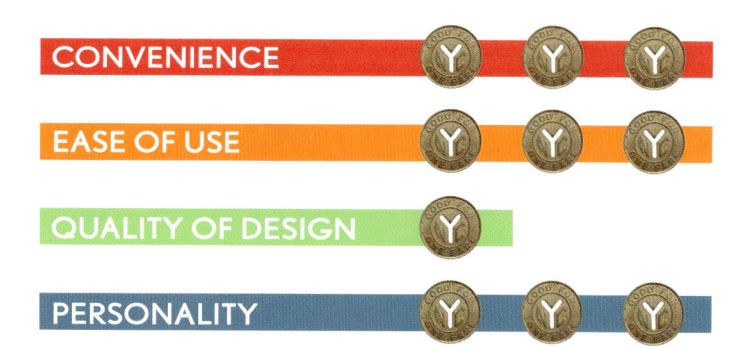

Category	Rating
CONVENIENCE	3
EASE OF USE	3
QUALITY OF DESIGN	1
PERSONALITY	3

TRANSIT TOURISM | 39

Red del Metro

MEXICO CITY

MEXICO CITY
Sistema de Transporte Colectivo (STC)

System Length	125 route miles
Number of Lines	12
Number of Stations	195 (incl. interchange)
Year Opened	1969
Year of Last Expansion	2012
Annual Ridership	1,655 million (2019)
Subwayness	59% of stations underground

No subway better reflects the history and heritage of the metropolis it serves than Mexico City's Metro. Sprawling and complex yet folksy and boisterous, the Sistema de Transporte Colectivo (STC) serves the mobility needs of 22 million inhabitants in the metropolitan area.

It is a metro with both attitude and altitude: At over 7,000 feet, it is the world's highest-elevation subway—or at least it was for half a century until the first line in Quito, Ecuador (9,350 feet), opened in 2023. Its *attitude* is one of frenetic but festive functionality. With 4.5 million daily riders, it has quite a crush hour during the long morning and evening commutes. To put it in perspective, the Metro carries

Entrance at Revolución station (Line 2)

SISTEMA DE TRANSPORTE COLECTIVO

passengers equal to 90 percent of New York City's ridership on a system with only 40 percent as many stations, making Mexico City the most densely packed subway system in the Western Hemisphere. Like Tokyo's subway, a car or two in each train is reserved for women and children.

The metro has a dozen lines. Ten are rubber tired, making it by far the largest of the pneumatic tire systems in the world.[1] The lines are numbered 1–12, except Lines 10 and 11, which are labeled Lines A and B because they run beyond the boundaries of the Federal District of Mexico City into the suburbs and were originally separate fares. Most of the expansion occurred in the 1970s and '80s. Tragically, the newest route—Line 12, which opened in 2012 and carries over 350,000 daily passengers—suffered a catastrophic collapse of an elevated portion in May 2021, causing over two dozen deaths and nearly a hundred injuries.

The routing of new subway lines (not just in Mexico City, but everywhere) is based on factors such as soil conditions, demographics, travel patterns, and politics. In the case of Mexico City, one could add history as well, since Line 2 follows the exact same path as the pre-Columbian causeways that linked the Aztecs' lake-island capital of Tenochtitlán—now the heart of the city—to the mainland. So, your six-stop metro trip from Villa de Cortés station to Zócalo directly retraces the footsteps of the conquistador Hernán Cortés. And coincidentally, my most recent visit in 2021 to ride the Metro happened on the date marking the five hundredth anniversary of the fall of the Aztec capital to the Spaniards.

Most of the stations are functional, low-ceilinged boxes excavated in the marshy soil only about 20 feet below street level. This makes for a sharp contrast with the subway systems of Moscow, St. Petersburg, and Pyongyang, which have stations as deep as 300 feet—the equivalent of a twenty-story building.

---

1 Approximately two dozen cities now have rubber-tired trains on single or multiple lines. Two of Mexico City's Lines (12 and A) use steel wheel on steel rail.

MEXICO CITY

The station architecture for the most part is unnoteworthy, but what the system lacks in architectural drama it makes up for with vivid colors and graphics. The trains on the numbered lines are painted a lively Aztec Orange, brightening up the stations if not the mood of the riders. The entire system has a folk art aesthetic, with warm earth tones and pictorial signage, in contrast to the cold, super-sleek styling of many other midcentury and more recent systems. It is the exact opposite of Washington Metro's formal, austere, and colorless appearance.

But at the half-century mark, the Metro is showing its age. The beautiful colors and graphics have faded in many of the stations, and walls and steps have deteriorated, reminiscent of Boston. Yet, while faded, the Metro is far from unpolished. In fact, a standout feature of the stations is their immaculate platform floors, which are made of highly polished marble and are kept spotlessly clean. I didn't see a single piece of litter in my most recent expedition.

La Villa-Basilica station (Line 6)

TRANSIT TOURISM | 43

SISTEMA DE TRANSPORTE COLECTIVO

The Metro's bold brand identity, including its logo, typeface, and map, was developed by Lance Wyman, the same New York graphic designer who created the memorable visual identity for Mexico City's 1968 Olympic Games. He has written that the stylized "M" logo he designed is derived from the three initial Metro lines contained within a box, representing the Zócalo (Plaza de la Constitución), the city's massive central square where Moctezuma's palace previously stood. Boldly, Wyman chose magenta for the color of Line 1, followed by aquamarine and guacamole green for Lines 2 and 3, all reflective of the Indigenous color palette. None of your predictable primary colors here!

Many of the station names are based on major streets, monuments, and civic and historical sites, capturing the rich urban fabric of Mexico City.[2] And, perhaps inspired by the Indigenous Aztec writing symbols, Wyman developed clever pictograms for each of the station names. Each of the icons is color-coded to the line it serves, and appears on the exterior totems (pylons) and in the stations. This was the first system where pictograms were assigned as identifiers for station stops.

While some of the official literature suggests that pictograms accompanying station names were used to make navigation easier for foreign visitors, it was also the case that in the mid-1960s, over a third of the adult Mexican population was illiterate. Nowadays, there is almost universal literacy, but the pictograms are still in use—some 163 different ones and counting, plus those on Mexico City's seven bus rapid-transit lines. Mexico City's reliance on a continuing supply of

---

[2] In the US, we have seen a disturbing trend of corporations buying naming rights for stations and eliminating any local "sense of place." However, the most extreme example of nongeographic station names can be found in Pyongyang, North Korea. All the stations on its two subway lines have uplifting revolutionary identifiers such as "Glory," "Triumph," and "Rejuvenation." And if I may offer a cautionary note for single women riding Pyongyang's metro: Be wary of a local suitor's intentions if he offers to take you on a ride from "Comrades in Arms" to "Paradise"...

MEXICO CITY

pictograms for its expanding transit network must effectively represent a Full Employment Act for graphic designers.[3]

One can see a thematic link between the Aztec symbols from half a millennium ago (*on the left*) and the Metro pictograms (*on the right*). Taken together, the pictograms vividly evoke the history and culture of North America's largest city.

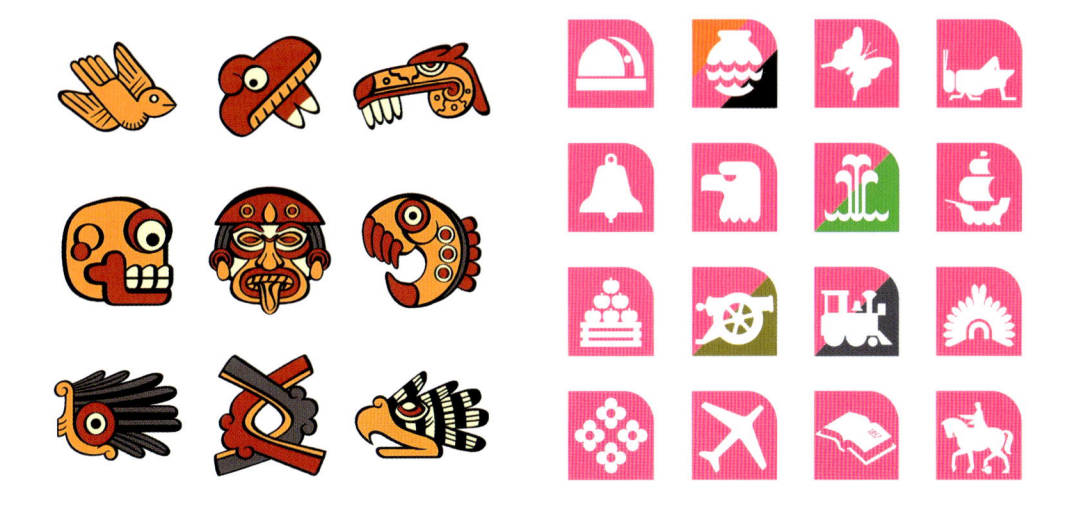

---

[3] Wyman's pictorial imagery for each Olympic sport has influenced graphics used at subsequent Olympic games, but his transit pictograms have not proven as popular. Among world transit systems, I am aware only of nearby Monterrey using pictograms to label its transit stations. In the early 1970s, Wyman had designed a set of pictograms for the proposed subway in Washington, DC. While Washington Metro did not end up using his station symbols, it did adopt his system map—the only colorful element in DC's otherwise bland subway!

SISTEMA DE TRANSPORTE COLECTIVO

Left: Typical Line route map

Right: pylon for Bellas Artes station

Wyman also designed a new typeface—*Tipo Metro*—for all the signage. Very much a product of the 1960s, it resembles the Microgramma lettering one sees in sci-fi movies such as *2001: A Space Odyssey* and *Star Trek*—what people in the mid-twentieth century thought the future would look like. If the *Johnston sans serif* type used on the London Underground is said to be the "handwriting of London," then *Tipo Metro* is surely the calligraphy of Mexico City. Both typefaces are indelibly associated with their respective cities.

The famed Tipo Metro typeface

ABCDEFGHIJKLM
NOPQRSTUVWXYZ

46 | NORTH AMERICA—MEXICO

MEXICO CITY

The system map shown at the beginning of the chapter, on the other hand, is a bit of a head-scratcher. Unlike most other cities' subway maps, it eschews the typical right angles and diagonal lines and instead shows irregular twists and turns. It's as though a crisp schematic map were laundered and put through the dryer on high heat but left unironed. Still, the map's irregularity has a certain appeal. To me, it makes the system seem less intimidating, despite its complexity and crowds.

Mexico City is widely known as a city of murals and is home to numerous works by famous muralists such as Diego Rivera and José Clemente Orozco. This legacy is reflected in the thirty stations that feature murals, many based on cultural and historical themes. Shown below on the left is Guillermo Ceniceros's *From the Codex to the Mural*, depicting the mythical founding of Mexico City up through the Aztecs. At Bellas Artes, Rino Lazo has painted a reproduction of famous eighth-century Mayan wall murals.

Left:
Tacubaya station
(Line 1)

Right:
Bellas Artes station mural
(Line 2)

TRANSIT TOURISM | 47

SISTEMA DE TRANSPORTE COLECTIVO

During the excavations downtown for the Pino Suárez station (interchange for Lines 1 and 2), an ancient Aztec temple to Ehécatl, the god of wind, was discovered and was incorporated into the station's design. It has been called the most popular cultural site in Mexico City, since some twenty million passengers pass through this interchange station every year!

Pino Suarez Metro station (Lines 1 and 2)

A number of stations mount temporary art exhibitions, and La Raza station by the Science Museum, serving Lines 3 and 5, includes wall exhibits along its extremely lengthy concourses. (Commuters definitely get their daily "steps" in when changing trains at the Metro's interchange stations, which often are hundreds of feet apart.) Starting in 2017, a dozen designated "Emblematic" or themed stations (half of them along Line 3) have been decorated with photomurals, painted murals, and other artwork celebrating famous Mexican athletes, Mexican authors and composers,

MEXICO CITY

and other regional subjects. STC operates a Museo de Metro at the Mixcoac station on Line 12, describing many of these historical and design features. Regrettably, it had been closed following the suspension of operations on that line after the trestle collapse in 2021, so I wasn't able to visit it.

SUMMARY

The Mexico City Metro is a large, busy system serving a large, busy city, and no other subway system better embodies its local history. The system shows influences of the city's pre-Columbian, colonial, post-Independence, and modern culture through station names, colors, and iconography. The station pictograms themselves present what amounts to a "graphic novel" visualization of Mexico's storied and tumultuous history. Bright, crowded, and exuberant, the Metro captures the vibrant personality of this amazing metropolis.

SELTZER TOKEN RATINGS (SCALE 1–4)

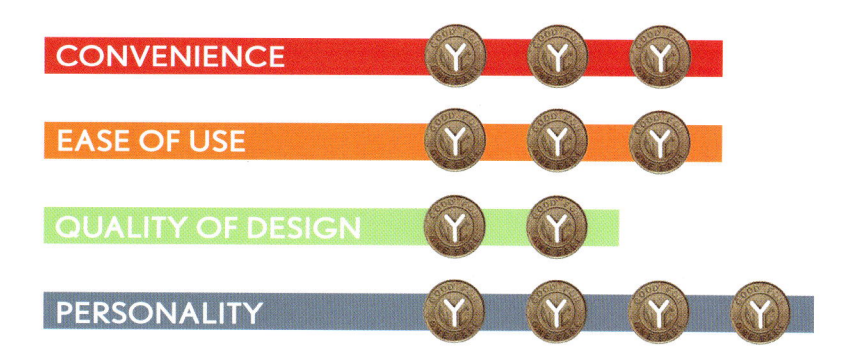

CONVENIENCE	3
EASE OF USE	3
QUALITY OF DESIGN	2
PERSONALITY	4

TRANSIT TOURISM | 49

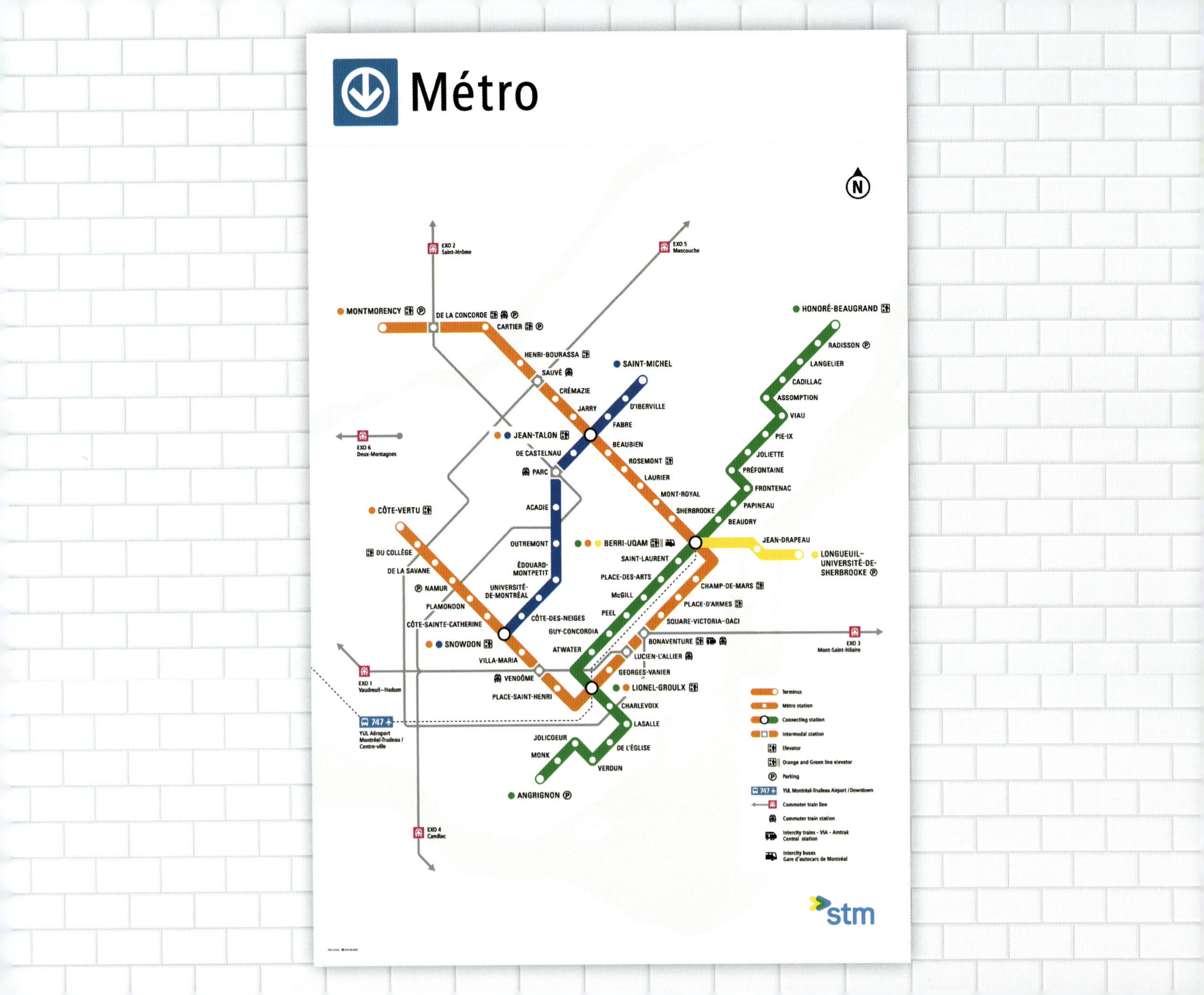
Métro
N
EXO 2
Saint-Jérôme
EXO 5
Mascouche
MONTMORENCY
DE LA CONCORDE
CARTIER
HENRI-BOURASSA
SAUVÉ
SAINT-MICHEL
CRÉMAZIE
JARRY
D'IBERVILLE
FABRE
JEAN-TALON
BEAUBIEN
DE CASTELNAU
ROSEMONT
PARC
LAURIER
MONT-ROYAL
EXO 6
Deux-Montagnes
HONORÉ-BEAUGRAND
RADISSON
LANGELIER
CADILLAC
ASSOMPTION
VIAU
PIE-IX
JOLIETTE
PRÉFONTAINE
FRONTENAC
PAPINEAU
BEAUDRY
SHERBROOKE
CÔTE-VERTU
ACADIE
DU COLLÈGE
DE LA SAVANE
NAMUR
PLAMONDON
CÔTE-SAINTE-CATHERINE
OUTREMONT
ÉDOUARD-MONTPETIT
UNIVERSITÉ-DE-MONTRÉAL
CÔTE-DES-NEIGES
SNOWDON
VILLA-MARIA
VENDÔME
PLACE-SAINT-HENRI
BERRI-UQAM
SAINT-LAURENT
PLACE-DES-ARTS
McGILL
PEEL
GUY-CONCORDIA
ATWATER
JEAN-DRAPEAU
LONGUEUIL-UNIVERSITÉ-DE-SHERBROOKE
CHAMP-DE-MARS
PLACE-D'ARMES
SQUARE-VICTORIA-OACI
BONAVENTURE
LUCIEN-L'ALLIER
GEORGES-VANIER
LIONEL-GROULX
CHARLEVOIX
LASALLE
DE L'ÉGLISE
VERDUN
JOLICOEUR
MONK
ANGRIGNON
EXO 3
Mont-Saint-Hilaire
EXO 1
Vaudreuil–Hudson
747
YUL Aéroport Montréal-Trudeau / Centre-ville
EXO 4
Candiac
Terminus
Métro station
Connecting station
Intermodal station
Elevator
Orange and Green line elevator
Parking
YUL Montréal-Trudeau Airport / Downtown
Commuter train line
Commuter train station
Intercity trains - VIA - Amtrak
Central station
Intercity buses
Gare d'autocars de Montréal
stm

MONTRÉAL

MONTRÉAL MÉTRO
Société de transport de Montréal (STM)

System Length	43 route miles
Number of Lines	4
Number of Stations	73
Year Opened	1966
Year of Last Expansion	2007
Annual Ridership	400 million (2019)
Subwayness	100% of stations underground

Beaudry station (Green Line)

Jaunty, sophisticated, even sexy: these are the words that spring to mind in describing Montréal's marvelous Métro. It arguably offers the most consistently high quality of design—a combination of architecture, artwork, and graphics—of any subway on the planet. The blue train sets themselves are triumphs of industrial design, with an elegant, almost svelte shapeliness. There are very few other subway systems that can evoke an "Ooh-la-la!"

I remember first visiting Montréal in 1969, thinking that the architectural highlights would be seeing Buckminster Fuller's famed geodesic dome from Expo 67 and Moshe Safdie's innovative Habitat

TRANSIT TOURISM | 51

SOCIÉTÉ DE TRANSPORT DE MONTRÉAL

residential complex of stacked modular units. Instead, I found myself enthralled by the architecture of the Métro. It demonstrated that subways could be stunning rather than Stygian. Looking at the stations on my most recent visit several years ago, I was amazed that the subway, while over half a century old, still seemed very fresh, dynamic, and *au courant*.

Ranked tenth among North American systems in terms of route miles, the system stands fourth in ridership after New York, Mexico City, and (just barely behind) Toronto. As Montréal's population grew rapidly in the postwar period, the Métro was conceived in the early 1960s to be as much a coming-of-age civic statement as a transportation investment. The then mayor, Jean Drapeau, convinced the citizenry that Montréal couldn't really be considered a world-class city unless and until it had a world-class metro—and that's exactly what he delivered.

The system was designed around three principles: all lines should be underground in order to avoid the perils of Montréal's winters; all train cars should be entirely rubber tired, allowing for tighter turns, steeper gradients, and smoother, quieter rides; and each station should be architecturally distinct. Three of the four lines—blue, green, and orange—are automated. Only the shortest line—yellow, which serves Ile-St. Hélène (the site of the Expo 67 World's Fair)—is manually operated. With the Green and Orange Lines opening concurrently in late 1966, and the Yellow Line commencing operations shortly thereafter—*voilà*: Montréalers had an instant citywide subway network. (Typically, new subway lines are phased years apart, due to financial and logistical constraints.) The three original lines interchange at the trilevel station Berri-UQAM, the system's busiest, in the heart of downtown.

The decision to use pneumatic rather than steel wheels was informed by the successful conversion of Paris Métro's Line 1 from steel wheels to tires a decade before.[1] Because the rubber-tired cars can turn corners more tightly and climb steeper inclines (6 percent gradient) than

---
[1] Other rubber-tired systems in this mode include Lausanne, Lyon, Marseilles, Mexico City, and Santiago.

MONTRÉAL

conventional "steel on steel" systems, the city realized it could achieve substantial construction cost savings on the tunneling. And with tracks that slope upward toward stations and downward away from them, gravity assists in both braking and accelerating the trains, reducing operating costs. As a famous non-Canadian once never said, "A Loonie saved is a Loonie earned."

Société de transport de Montréal (STM), the public agency responsible for building and operating the system, had the great foresight to retain different architectural firms for the initial three-line, twenty-six-station system. This first phase of the Métro introduced open and sleekly modern station designs, incorporating natural light wherever possible. Starting with construction of that original network through to today, over three dozen different architectural firms have designed the seventy-three stations on the four lines, ensuring a varied portfolio of styles, but all following the consistent philosophy of grand, unobstructed spaces; natural light; and bold use of different materials. This same architectural approach is guiding a 3.7-mile, five-station extension of the Blue Line getting underway in 2022 and anticipated to open in 2029.

While the system gives a "tip of the beret" to the Paris Métro in some respects (quiet rubber tires, slender physique of its cars, and gently vaulted tunnels), it is very much its own creation. There is no uniform system "look" to the stations as there is in Paris, London, or Washington. However, each station is being retrofitted with a compass rose embedded in the floor, indicating true north and pointing toward nearby streets, to give passengers a sense of direction when they alight from the trains.

The first generation of stations, built in the mid-1960s, set the high level of design standard for all subsequent extensions. Moreover, the stations appear well maintained, in contrast to the Mexico City Metro, of similar vintage, which is looking decidedly peaked (see chapter on Mexico City). Papineau station bears a strong resemblance to the archetypical Parisian metro stations, such as St. Sebastien-Froissart, both shown on the next page.

SOCIÉTÉ DE TRANSPORT DE MONTRÉAL

Left:
Papineau station
(Green Line)

Right:
Saint Sebastien-Froissart
station (Line 8, Paris)

But most of the stations have their own, unique modernist form. McGill station still looks very smart, notwithstanding the earth tones and its sixth decade of town and gown service.

McGill station (Green Line)

MONTRÉAL

Other stations from the 1970s and 1980s exhibit a bold range of architectural styles.

Left:
Outremont station (Blue Line)

Right:
Radisson station (Green Line) achieves dramatic effect with muscular forms of poured concrete

Place-St. Henri station (Orange Line) with colored glazed brick

TRANSIT TOURISM | 55

SOCIÉTÉ DE TRANSPORT DE MONTRÉAL

The diverse architectural designs illustrated in the photos on the previous page are works of art in their own right. Separate artwork installations were not incorporated into the initial station design of the first lines, but starting with the extensions in the mid-1970s, art pieces have been planned concurrently with engineering and architecture as each new station is designed. Today, over fifty stations have major artworks in, around, or above them.

Left:
Peel station
(Green Line)

Right:
Place-
des-Arts station
(Green Line)

From street level, most of the Metro entrances are either nondescript concrete boxes or stairways tucked into the ground floors of commercial buildings, giving little hint of the architectural splendors lying below. Many of the downtown stops are connected to underground shopping malls and adjacent major buildings through an elaborate concourse system, sheltering Montréalers from the long, harsh winter climate. But several of the portals are absolute knockouts, including Square-Victoria (Orange Line), featuring an original Hector Guimard *fin de siècle* kiosk bequeathed by the City of Paris to Montréal, and De la Concorde (Orange Line), whose glass box is tinted with a supergraphic of Métro's logo (see next page).

56 | NORTH AMERICA—CANADA

MONTRÉAL

Left:
An original Hector Guimard fin de siècle kiosk

Right:
De la Concorde station (Orange Line)

    Clean, modern graphics have always been a hallmark of the Montréal Métro. The very crisp Métro logo (a white directional arrow in a circle within a cyan square) along with signage, maps, and wayfinding were devised by Jacques Roy of the local firm of Guillon Associates in 1963. Over the decades, these designs have kept up appearances reasonably well. However, the signage and the friendly route map have benefited from a gentle makeover in recent years as part of Métro's refreshing its brand identity. Among the enhancements is a bespoke typeface called *Transit* that has improved legibility, a revised and simplified system map, and enhanced pictograms for wayfinding, all while maintaining the original station signage at the platform level as a nod to Métro's mid-twentieth-century heritage.

SOCIÉTÉ DE TRANSPORT DE MONTRÉAL

Although I don't generally dwell on rolling stock (with one exception: see Glasgow chapter), I do want to comment on Montréal's stylish subway cars. I think of them as having a lovely feminine character; they are considerably shorter (56 vs. 75 feet) and considerably narrower (8 vs. 10 feet) than most American subway cars, and of course much quieter, because of the rubber tires. Over the last several years, STM, the operator, has replaced the original cars with new "Azur" train sets painted in the characteristic soft-blue-and-white exterior colors that match the flag of Québec.

Angrignon station (Green Line)

MONTRÉAL

SUMMARY

Montréal has a beautiful subway that befits a beautiful city. The three original lines, opened in anticipation of Expo 67, set the design and performance standards for the later extensions and new line to come. With its comprehensive service coverage, first-class architecture, appealing artwork, and handsome graphics, Montréal has established the gold standard not just for North American transit systems, but for metros worldwide. *Merveilleux!* The Montréal Métro gets a perfect score in my book!

SELTZER TOKEN RATINGS (SCALE 1–4)

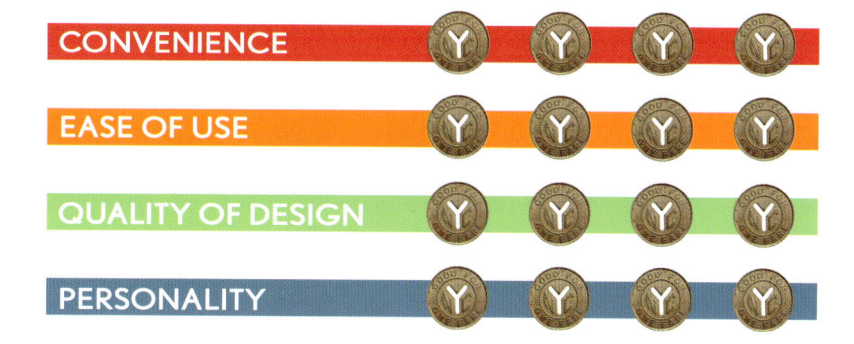

CONVENIENCE	4
EASE OF USE	4
QUALITY OF DESIGN	4
PERSONALITY	4

New York City Subway
with railroad and airport connections
Service Alert
No E M Service via 53 St
December 26-31, 2022
E will make F stops between W 4 St and Jackson Hts-Roosevelt Av
M will run between Metropolitan Av and Essex St (and via J Z to/from Chambers St, Tue to Fri)
For detailed info click here
Legend
The subway operates 24 hours-a-day, but not all lines operate at all times.
For more service information visit mta.info, call our Travel Information Center at 511 for help in English or Spanish (24 hours), or ask an agent for help in all other languages (6:00am to 10:00pm).
This map depicts typical weekday service.
On weekends and late nights, these routes change:
Weekends
Late nights (12:00 midnight to 6:00am, daily)
The Bronx
Manhattan
Queens
Brooklyn
Staten Island
Staten Island Railway
Hudson River
Central Park
December 2022

NEW YORK

NEW YORK
New York City Transit Authority
a subsidiary of the Metropolitan Transportation Authority

System Length	248 route miles[1]
Number of Lines	25
Number of Stations	472
Year Opened	1904
Year of Last Expansion	2017
Annual Ridership	1.7 billion (2019)
Subwayness	61% of stations underground

Station entrance at Broad and Wall Streets in the heart of New York's Financial District (J and Z Trains)

Star of song, stage, and screen, the New York City subway is probably familiar to most readers, even if they've never ridden it. It's an indispensable and iconic element of the nation's largest city. Scads of books have been written about it; I have at least eighty

---

[1] The data do not include the PATH transit lines of the Port Authority of New York and New Jersey—the seventh-busiest rail transit system in the US.

TRANSIT TOURISM | 61

in my own collection dealing with its history, politics, operations, design, rolling stock—even track layout.[2]

For many years, New York City's subway system was "the world's biggest"—with 472 stations, 22 separate lines, and 3 short shuttles. However, it has been far surpassed by other cities, many of them in East Asia. Tokyo, Shanghai, Beijing, and Seoul (along with Moscow) all handle greater ridership, and a dozen cities, including Shanghai, Beijing, Seoul, and London, today boast more system route miles. Still, by any measure, the scale of New York's transit system is impressive.[3] Over eight thousand trains carry five million passengers every weekday, and it is one of only four subways worldwide to run on a 24/7 basis. Its five major trunk lines running north–south through Manhattan are quadruple tracked for express-local service, a virtually unique feature for subways.[4]

Aboveground, many of the entries still sport the subway "globe" lights, which were originally intended to indicate which station stairways have cashiers vs. exit only. But with the advent of fare cards and automatic turnstiles, that distinction no longer strictly applies.

I became familiar with the Manhattan segments as an investment banker, visiting New York for business meetings over several decades. However, because my destinations were generally in the Financial District or Midtown, rarely did my travels take me to the more exotic reaches of the

---

[2] For a good general guide, see Oscar Israelowitz, *Secrets of the New York City Subway*. For artwork, décor and graphics, see Sandra Bloodworth and Cheryl Hageman, *Contemporary Art Underground*; Joseph Giovanni and Andrew Garn, *Subway Style: 100 years of Architecture and Design on the New York City Subway*; and Phillip Coppola's magisterial two-volume set containing his meticulously rendered line drawings of station tile and terra-cotta decorations, *Silver Connections: A Fresh Perspective on New York City Area Subway Systems*. And for those who are irremediable subway aficionados, don't miss Peter Dougherty's *Tracks of the New York City Subways: 2021 Edition*, diagramming every siding, switchback, and rail yard.

[3] I say "transit" rather than "subway," since nearly 40 percent of the system operates on tracks at ground level or on elevated structures, plus there are spectacular East River crossings on the Williamsburg and Manhattan Bridges. Manhattan itself used to have major elevated lines looming above 2nd, 3rd, 6th, and 9th Avenues, but all had been demolished by the mid-1950s.

[4] Philadelphia's Broad Street Line is reportedly the world's only other underground four-track subway.

NEW YORK

New York subway entrances:

Left:
14th Street at 8th Avenue
(A, C, and E Trains)

Right:
14th Street at 7th Avenue
(1, 2, and 3 Trains)

four outer boroughs (the Bronx, Brooklyn, and Queens, all served extensively by the subway, and Staten Island, which has its own, orphaned surface transit line).

New York's subway truly reflects the city's distinct personality: it is brusquely efficient, chaotic, cacophonous, and teeming with people from all walks of life. I say "cacophonous," but that is not entirely accurate. Between the roar of arriving trains, one sometimes hears melodious interludes, courtesy of buskers performing at midtown stations and sponsored by MTA's Arts for Transit program. Too many times, I've been induced to buy CDs from those wonderful Peruvian folk bands playing in the sonorous acoustics of the 5th Ave. Station, only to be utterly disappointed after returning home and hearing the group's thin, tinny sound from the recording studio.

The chaotic nature of the system can be experienced firsthand as you try changing trains using the rabbit warren of passageways at the major interchange stations, such as Times Square, Grand Central, and Fulton Street. A glance at the map shows the system layout is similarly confusing.

NEW YORK CITY TRANSIT AUTHORITY

The Brooklyn Subway Spaghetti Bowl—hold the ragù

Lower Manhattan's subways look like the tangled bundle of computer power cords under your desk, although the lines sort themselves out as they proceed uptown in more or less orderly fashion under the regular street grid north of Canal Street. Downtown Brooklyn's indecipherable knot of subway routes is even more bewildering. Over a dozen subway lines contort themselves in a subterranean game of Twister, touching (but not necessarily interconnecting) in the vicinity of the Dekalb, Jay Street, and Atlantic Avenue stations.[5] Try figuring out how to change from the 2 and 5 Nostrand Avenue Line in Brooklyn to the A and C Fulton Street Line. As the borough's informal motto proudly proclaims, *Fuhgeddaboudit!*

What perverse mindset conceived of such a helter-skelter system? Unbridled capitalism, of course! In the first two decades of the twentieth century, two competing private companies

---

[5] For the record, the jumble of lines in downtown Brooklyn consists of the 2, 3, 4, 5, A, C, B, D, G, N, Q, R, and W.

NEW YORK

E Train at Times Square-42nd Street (8th Ave. Line)

built or leased from the City of New York their own lines under the municipal "Dual Contract" franchises: the Interborough Rapid Transit (IRT) and Brooklyn-Manhattan Transit (BMT). In the thirties, a third system within a system emerged: the municipally owned and operated Independent (IND) lines.

For decades, these three operators separately ran their services and published maps barely acknowledging the others, with no free transfers between them. You can still hear older New Yorkers give directions referencing those long-defunct network names (IRT, BMT, IND) rather than the line numbers and letters—not particularly helpful to an *Ausländer* like me, from Philadelphia. The seven former IRT lines are numbered 1 to 7, and the fifteen former BMT and IND lines have letter names from A to Z, with some gaps. The IRT tunnels are too narrow to accommodate the larger trains running along the former BMT and IND lettered routes.

NEW YORK CITY TRANSIT AUTHORITY

Although the three networks were brought under common city ownership in 1940 and officially unified in 1953, navigating New York's system remains a challenge. In the early 1970s, the MTA invited famed Italian graphic, branding, and product designer Massimo Vignelli to develop a new map and wayfinding graphics in an attempt to make order out of chaos. Vignelli had come up with memorable brand designs for everything from American Airlines to Bloomingdales. For the subway, he produced an artistically elegant but largely inscrutable schematic map of the system. Rolled out in 1972, it was much admired by design aficionados but disliked by the riding public, who found its abstraction confusing. It works much better as artwork, and in fact the Museum of Modern Art has installed an exhibition describing Vignelli's subway design contributions along the platform walls of the 5th Ave. Station, around the corner from MOMA.

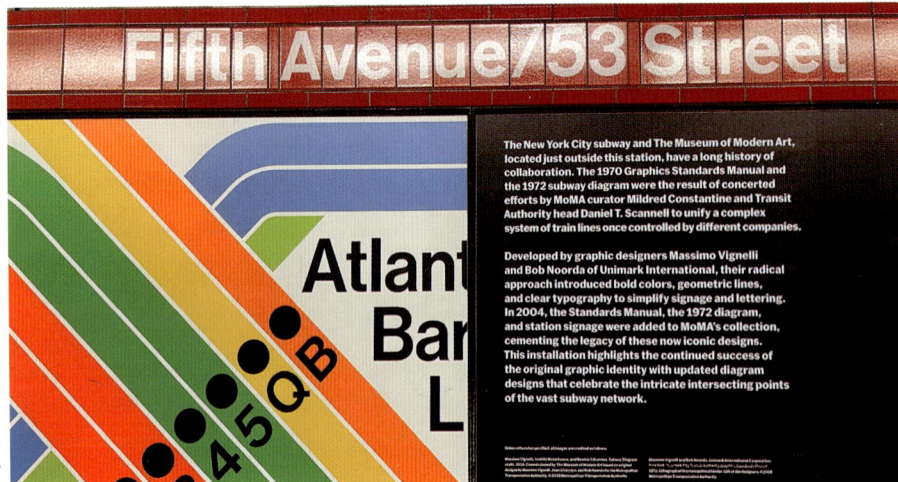

5th Ave. Station, E and M Trains

66 | NORTH AMERICA—USA

NEW YORK

The 1979 replacement map, drawn up by graphic designer Michael Hertz, lacks the sophistication of Vignelli's map but is clearly more user-friendly, since it shows principal geographic features, roadways, and other public transportation routes along with the subway lines. But even on this more legible route map, Lower Manhattan and downtown Brooklyn still remain a dog's breakfast of complicated crossovers and interchanges.

Left: Vignelli map

Right: Hertz map

Although Vignelli's map was abandoned, his wayfinding graphics have proven much more durable, since they continue to be used throughout the network to this day. His train and station signage in Helvetica typeface is seen everywhere, and its clean, easy legibility and hierarchy of information do provide *some* sense of order. You could write a book about it. (In fact, somebody did: Paul Shaw's *Helvetica and the New York City Subway System*.)

NEW YORK CITY TRANSIT AUTHORITY

MTA New York City Subway

Logos, of course, are another central design feature, expressing how organizations wish to present themselves to the public. The MTA's logo is unusual in transitdom: rather than a frontal view of the letter M or a symbol, it is an oblique view of the Metropolitan Transportation Authority's disc symbol mounted on the side of each railcar, appearing to show the departing train you just missed. Only in New York!

While the system's engineering is indeed a marvel, much of the station architecture is a mess. The overwhelming impression is one of unadorned I-beams, gum-stained cement platforms, and soiled, white tile walls—utilitarian in the extreme.

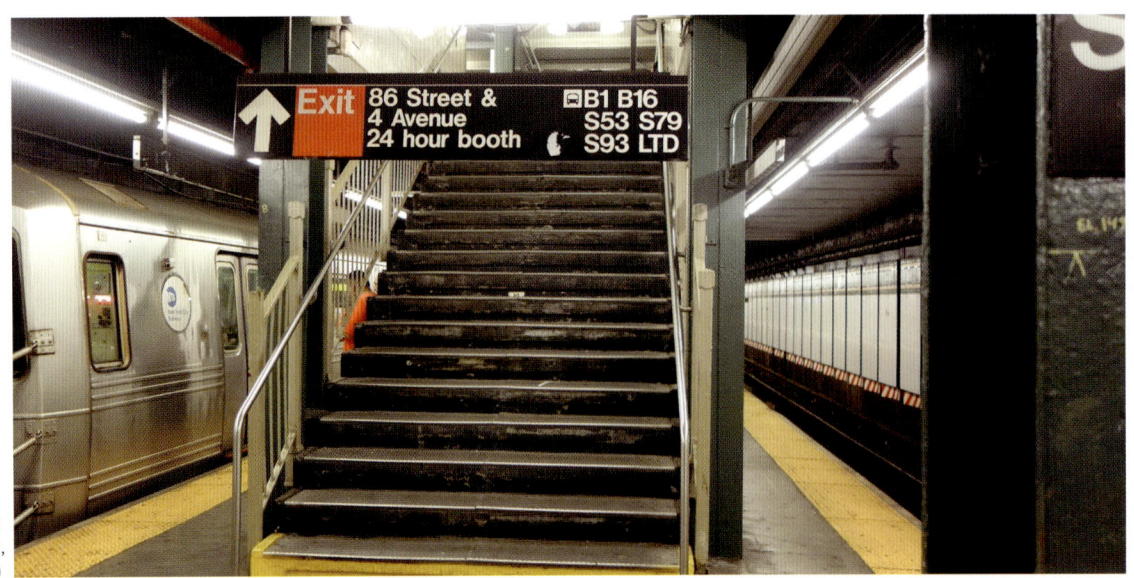

86th Street Station (Brooklyn, R Train)

NEW YORK

However, to the patient eye, there are nuggets of gold to be found in them thar stations. Many of the older stations still retain their arts and crafts style of decorations of glazed ceramic plaques and mosaic tile images, along with tessellated tilework displaying the station names in a dignified serifed face. The faience plaque images tell a story about each station: Columbus Circle shows the Santa Maria, Fulton Street shows Robert Fulton's steamboat, and Astor Place depicts, of all things, not a star, but a beaver, since John Jacob Astor's fortune was built on the beaver pelt trade.

Left: Station plaque on Seventh Avenue Line (1 Train)

Right: Astor Place Station, Lexington Ave. (6 Train)

Some of the new and newly rebuilt stations do indeed have spectacular architectural features, such as Nicholas Grimshaw's Fulton St. Transit Center with its off-kilter atrium, and the recent Hudson Yards Station adjacent to the Convention Center.

TRANSIT TOURISM | 69

NEW YORK CITY TRANSIT AUTHORITY

Left:
The atrium at the Fulton Street Center in the Financial District, where four trunk lines intersect

Right:
Ceiling mural at Hudson Yards Station, Flushing Line (7)

70 | NORTH AMERICA—USA

NEW YORK

And there is one exquisite gem of an old station: City Hall, a loop off the Lexington Avenue Line downtown. It is no longer in service because its short, curved platforms can't accommodate today's longer trains, but it is occasionally open for special tours.[6] If it looks reminiscent of the Oyster Bar at Grand Central, there's a good reason: the graceful vaulted arches were designed by the same Spanish-born engineer, Rafael Guastavino.

Old City Hall Station, Lexington Ave. Line

---

6 A nearby station also on a tight roundabout loop—South Ferry—used quaint retractable "connectors" that would be extended to close the gap between the car doors and the platforms. Because the platform was too short for today's longer trains, this idiosyncratic station from 1904 was replaced in 2009 with a more efficient but—let's call it as it is—completely boring straight-line platform. (The old South Ferry was briefly pressed back into service for several years during remediation from Superstorm Sandy.) Great gain in productivity, but tremendous loss in character: *Sic Transit Gloria Ferry!*

TRANSIT TOURISM | 71

NEW YORK CITY TRANSIT AUTHORITY

Since the 1980s, New York has had an ambitious and highly successful Arts for Transit program, installing over three hundred pieces of artwork throughout the system. Except for the most-recent subway extensions, the art pieces are largely add-ons to existing stations, many of which are otherwise austere tile-and-girder boxes. The art installations therefore are not so much transformative as palliative in nature. However, some of the new stations display superb tile decorations, hearkening back to the tradition of the original IRT tile mosaics from 1904. Shown below are the life-size tile portraits of New Yorkers at the 72nd Street Station of the newest line, the Second Avenue Subway, which opened in 2016.

Tile mural by Vik Muniz and close-up at 72nd Street Station, 2nd Avenue (Q Train)

In downtown Brooklyn (the nation's fifth-largest city, as its residents are proud to claim), off a nondescript street and down some steps, you'll find the marvelous New York Transit Museum. It is housed in the decommissioned Court Street subway station. The museum displays nineteen

NEW YORK

vintage subway cars, mounts permanent and rotating exhibitions, and hosts a gift shop that will meet all of your subway shopping needs. A surprising number of cities have transit museums, including London, Madrid, Mexico City, Paris, Shanghai, and Tokyo. The New York Transit Museum ranks right up there with the London Transport Museum in Covent Garden as perhaps the best.

And though it's not formally a part of the New York City subway system, the Port Authority Trans-Hudson (PATH) tubes comprise a major transit system in their own right, serving New York. Dating back to 1908, the PATH system connects Newark, Hoboken, and Jersey City to the Financial District and Midtown through two pairs of tunnels under the mighty Hudson. Although only 14 miles long, PATH carries over 300,000 daily riders, making it the nation's seventh-busiest rapid-transit system (just behind Philadelphia).

Much of the PATH line in New Jersey is aboveground, affording a fascinating view of both the Lower Manhattan skyline and the

Calatrava's Oculus at PATH's World Trade Center Transportation Hub

cloacal landscape of early-twentieth-century industrial America in the Meadowlands, before the trains plunge under the Palisades and the Hudson. One branch of the line terminates at the World Trade Center, surmounted by Santiago Calatrava's cathedral-like Oculus (see previous page). It leads to PATH's underground train loop four stories below, and this nearly $4 billion project surely is the world's most grandiose terminal for such a short trip. One could understand the rationale for building a monumental gateway to provide a sense of occasion for airline departures to far-flung destinations such as Hong Kong or Nairobi. But subway commutes to Hoboken and Newark?

Finally, while not a subway *per se*, the East Side Access project deserves mention. It is a new underground commuter rail extension giving the Long Island Railroad a second passenger station in Manhattan underneath Grand Central Terminal. The project should alleviate overcrowding at LIRR's Penn Station's facility and ease capacity limitations on the existing East River rail tunnels shared by LIRR and Amtrak. This approximately $11 billion project opened in 2023 after fifteen years of construction. The project consists of 2 miles of new tunnel and utilization of the long-dormant lower level of the 63rd Street subway tunnel connecting Queens and Manhattan's East Side. After running underneath the East River, the tracks make a hard left turn at Park Avenue, running below the existing rail tunnel used by Metro-North commuter trains. The extension terminates in a cavernous bilevel eight-track station fourteen stories below street level (Grand Central Madison). When I toured this massive cave-like space, it was under construction and workers were busily scurrying around performing assorted tasks. It reminded me of one of those secret underground lairs of a James Bond archvillain. At something like $3.5 billion per mile, it represents the world's most costly rail project, surpassing even the Second Ave. subway ("only" $2.5 billion/mile) and the Hudson Yards subway extension (a mere $1.5 billion/mile). Not that anyone's counting.

NEW YORK

SUMMARY

Even though New York can no longer lay claim to being the world's longest or busiest subway system, it is still unparalleled in terms of its number of stations, incredible engineering, operational complexity, and around-the-clock availability. Beautiful it isn't, but the subway's more than two dozen lines blanket most of New York City and provide a swift, cost-effective way to get around town—provided there aren't service delays. (For New Yorkers, the six most dreaded words in the English tongue are the conductor's announcement alleging, "This train should be moving shortly.") The New York subway is certainly not for the faint of heart, but once you have mastered it, riding any other city's subway is a piece of cake. To paraphrase Frank Sinatra's signature song, "*New York, New York*," if you can take it *there*, you can take it *anywhere*.

SELTZER TOKEN RATINGS (SCALE 1–4)

CONVENIENCE	4
EASE OF USE	2
QUALITY OF DESIGN*	2
PERSONALITY	4

*Quality of Design would have been rated one token only, except for the extensive art installations, which mitigate the drabness of many stations.

TRANSIT TOURISM | 75

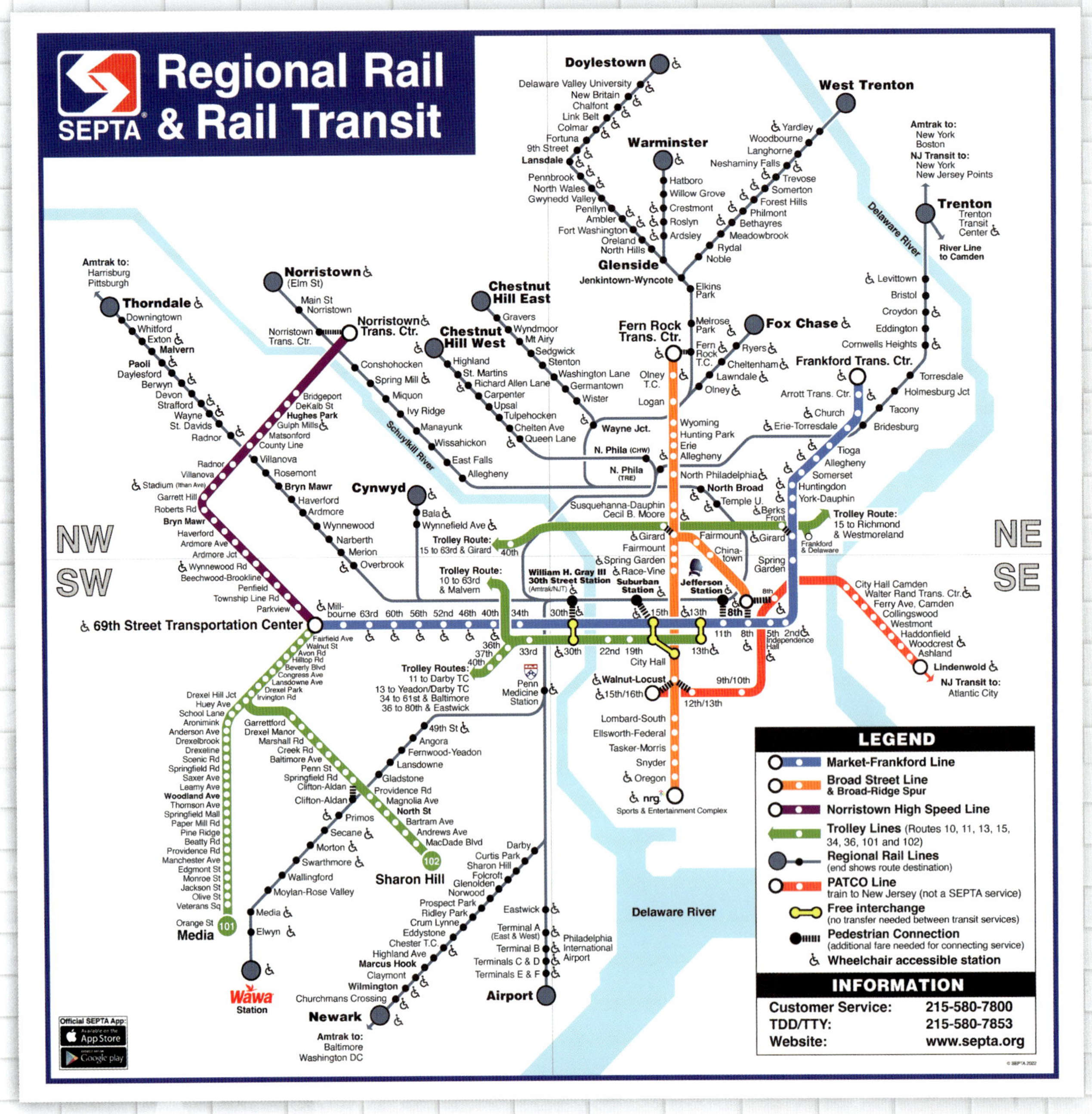
SEPTA
Regional Rail & Rail Transit
Doylestown
Delaware Valley University
New Britain
Chalfont
Link Belt
Colmar
Fortuna
9th Street
Lansdale
Pennbrook
North Wales
Gwynedd Valley
Penllyn
Ambler
Fort Washington
Oreland
North Hills
Glenside
Jenkintown-Wyncote
Warminster
Hatboro
Willow Grove
Crestmont
Roslyn
Ardsley
West Trenton
Yardley
Woodbourne
Langhorne
Neshaminy Falls
Trevose
Somerton
Forest Hills
Philmont
Bethayres
Meadowbrook
Rydal
Noble
Elkins Park
Melrose Park
Fern Rock T.C.
Amtrak to: New York Boston
NJ Transit to: New York New Jersey Points
Trenton
Trenton Transit Center
River Line to Camden
Delaware River
Levittown
Bristol
Croydon
Eddington
Cornwells Heights
Torresdale
Holmesburg Jct
Tacony
Bridesburg
Fox Chase
Ryers
Cheltenham
Lawndale
Olney
Frankford Trans. Ctr.
Arrott Trans. Ctr.
Church
Erie-Torresdale
Tioga
Allegheny
Somerset
Huntingdon
York-Dauphin
Berks
Front
Trolley Route: 15 to Richmond & Westmoreland
Frankford & Delaware
Girard
Spring Garden
Fern Rock Trans. Ctr.
Olney T.C.
Logan
Wyoming
Hunting Park
Erie
Allegheny
North Philadelphia
North Broad
Temple U.
Susquehanna-Dauphin
Cecil B. Moore
Fairmount
China-town
Chestnut Hill East
Gravers
Wyndmoor
Mt Airy
Sedgwick
Stenton
Washington Lane
Germantown
Wister
Wayne Jct.
N. Phila (CHW)
N. Phila (TRE)
Chestnut Hill West
Highland
St. Martins
Richard Allen Lane
Carpenter
Upsal
Tulpehocken
Chelten Ave
Queen Lane
Norristown (Elm St)
Main St
Norristown
Norristown Trans. Ctr.
Conshohocken
Spring Mill
Miquon
Ivy Ridge
Manayunk
Wissahickon
East Falls
Allegheny
Schuylkill River
Amtrak to: Harrisburg Pittsburgh
Thorndale
Downingtown
Whitford
Exton
Malvern
Paoli
Daylesford
Berwyn
Devon
Strafford
Wayne
St. Davids
Radnor
Villanova
Rosemont
Bryn Mawr
Haverford
Ardmore
Wynnewood
Narberth
Merion
Overbrook
Cynwyd
Bala
Wynnefield Ave
Bridgeport
DeKalb St
Hughes Park
Gulph Mills
Matsonford
County Line
Radnor
Villanova
Stadium (Ithan Ave)
Garrett Hill
Roberts Rd
Bryn Mawr
Haverford
Ardmore Ave
Ardmore Jct
Wynnewood Rd
Beechwood-Brookline
Penfield
Township Line Rd
Parkview
Trolley Route: 15 to 63rd & Girard
Trolley Route: 10 to 63rd & Malvern
NW
SW
NE
SE
Fairmount
Girard
Spring Garden
Race-Vine
William H. Gray III 30th Street Station (Amtrak/NJT)
Suburban Station
Jefferson Station
69th Street Transportation Center
Millbourne
63rd
60th
56th
52nd
46th
40th
34th
30th
15th
13th
8th
11th
5th Independence Hall
2nd
Fairfield Ave
Walnut St
Avon Rd
Hilltop Rd
Beverly Blvd
Congress Ave
Lansdowne Ave
Drexel Park
Irvington Rd
36th
37th
40th
33rd
22nd
19th
City Hall
Trolley Routes: 11 to Darby TC 13 to Yeadon/Darby TC 34 to 61st & Baltimore 36 to 80th & Eastwick
Penn Medicine Station
Walnut-Locust
15th/16th
12th/13th
9th/10th
City Hall Camden
Walter Rand Trans. Ctr.
Ferry Ave, Camden
Collingswood
Westmont
Haddonfield
Woodcrest
Ashland
Lindenwold
NJ Transit to: Atlantic City
Lombard-South
Ellsworth-Federal
Tasker-Morris
Snyder
Oregon
nrg
Sports & Entertainment Complex
Drexel Hill Jct
Huey Ave
School Lane
Aronimink
Anderson Ave
Drexelbrook
Drexeline
Scenic Rd
Springfield Rd
Saxer Ave
Leamy Ave
Woodland Ave
Thomson Ave
Springfield Mall
Paper Mill Rd
Pine Ridge
Beatty Rd
Providence Rd
Manchester Ave
Edgmont St
Monroe St
Jackson St
Olive St
Veterans Sq
Orange St
Media
101
Garrettford
Drexel Manor
Marshall Rd
Creek Rd
Baltimore Ave
Penn St
Springfield Rd
Clifton-Aldan
Providence Rd
Magnolia Ave
North St
Bartram Ave
Andrews Ave
MacDade Blvd
102
Sharon Hill
49th St
Angora
Fernwood-Yeadon
Lansdowne
Gladstone
Clifton-Aldan
Primos
Secane
Morton
Swarthmore
Wallingford
Moylan-Rose Valley
Media
Elwyn
Wawa Station
Darby
Curtis Park
Sharon Hill
Folcroft
Glenolden
Norwood
Prospect Park
Ridley Park
Crum Lynne
Eddystone
Chester T.C.
Highland Ave
Marcus Hook
Claymont
Wilmington
Churchmans Crossing
Newark
Amtrak to: Baltimore Washington DC
Eastwick
Terminal A (East & West)
Terminal B
Terminals C & D
Terminals E & F
Philadelphia International Airport
Airport
Delaware River
LEGEND
Market-Frankford Line
Broad Street Line & Broad-Ridge Spur
Norristown High Speed Line
Trolley Lines (Routes 10, 11, 13, 15, 34, 36, 101 and 102)
Regional Rail Lines (end shows route destination)
PATCO Line train to New Jersey (not a SEPTA service)
Free interchange (no transfer needed between transit services)
Pedestrian Connection (additional fare needed for connecting service)
Wheelchair accessible station
INFORMATION
Customer Service: 215-580-7800
TDD/TTY: 215-580-7853
Website: www.septa.org
Official SEPTA App:
App Store
Google play
© SEPTA 2022

PHILADELPHIA
Southeastern Pennsylvania Transportation Authority (SEPTA)

System Length	41 route miles[1]
Number of Lines	4 (1 is light rail)
Number of Stations	75[1]
Year Opened	1907
Year of Last Expansion	1973
Annual Ridership	101 million (2019)
Subwayness	63% of stations underground

Just as the host country for soccer's World Cup is guaranteed a bracket regardless of its performance in the qualifiers, I have reserved a chapter for the subway in my hometown of Philadelphia. One might be hard-pressed to argue that its subway system is Premier League caliber, but in certain surprising respects, Philadelphia can compete with the "top division teams."

---

1 System and station data include Lindenwold High Speed Line, operated by Port Authority Transit Corporation (PATCO), and that portion of five SEPTA light-rail routes accessing Center City via tunnel.

Broad Street Line entry

TRANSIT TOURISM | 77

SOUTHEASTERN PENNSYLVANIA TRANSPORTATION AUTHORITY

Situated between the Delaware and Schuylkill Rivers, the "Quaker City" follows William Penn's orderly geometric plan of 1681; in fact, it was the first planned city in America. The original east–west streets generally were named after trees—Chestnut, Walnut, Locust, Spruce, Pine—and north–south streets were numbered. Visiting in 1842, Charles Dickens observed: "It is a handsome city, but distractingly regular. After walking about it for an hour or two, I felt that I would have given the world for a crooked street." Crooked politicians the city has had in abundance over the years, but crooked streets, eh, not so much.

Market Street Elevated in West Philadelphia

PHILADELPHIA

Center City (downtown) Philadelphia is laid out as a Cartesian plane, with the two principal thoroughfares as its axes: Market Street, running east–west, and Broad Street (14th), running north–south. The point where they meet (analogous to the axes' origin) is Centre Square (now City Hall), the civic and geographic epicenter of Philadelphia.

Originally privately operated, Philadelphia's subways, trolleys, and buses have been managed since the mid-1960s by the Southeastern Pennsylvania Transportation Authority, better known as SEPTA. Today, SEPTA operates a wide array of public transportation services: subway-elevated trains, subway-surface cars, commuter rail, streetcars, interurban trolleys, trackless trolleys, not to mention buses—as varied a transit fleet as in any American city. For its first five decades, SEPTA was handicapped by parsimonious governmental funding, with more system contraction occurring than expansion. The authority's hangdog reputation was epitomized by its low-aspirational marketing motto: "We're Getting There" (might as well just have said, "SEPTA: *Now Offering Same-Day Service!*").

The city's two principal subway lines conform to and reinforce this rectilinear plan: the Market-Frankford Subway-Elevated, which opened in 1907, and the almost entirely underground Broad Street Subway, which opened in 1928. Philadelphia's population had been growing by upward of 250,000 people per decade in the late nineteenth and early twentieth centuries, and the city's extensive streetcar network—the largest in the nation—was at capacity. These two transit lines were the core of an ambitious master plan in 1913 that proposed half a dozen lines fanning out to all corners of the city, as well as a minicircle line in Center City. The Broad Street Line was built as the only subway outside New York with four tracks, to accommodate express and local trains serving the various branch lines that were planned to sprout from it. Sadly, only one small twig was ever built: the 1.5-mile three-station Ridge Avenue Spur off Broad Street, which surely qualifies as the most forlorn subway line in the world.

SOUTHEASTERN PENNSYLVANIA TRANSPORTATION AUTHORITY

Left: Forlorn Fairmount Station on the Ridge Avenue Spur

Right: The Lindenwold Line crossing the Delaware River on the Ben Franklin Bridge

While SEPTA has not expanded its transit system in recent decades, there actually has been one "new" transit line launched, though by a different public agency. The Lindenwold High Speed Line runs between Center City Philadelphia and suburban southern New Jersey and is operated by the Port Authority Transit Corporation (PATCO), a subsidiary of the bistate Delaware River Port Authority. Starting in the late 1930s, it had operated as a short line between the Center City shopping district and downtown Camden, New Jersey, over the Ben Franklin Bridge. PATCO extended the line a dozen miles into South Jersey, and it was the nation's first driverless automated transit line.

PHILADELPHIA

The Lindenwold Line made its inaugural run at the crack of dawn on February 15, 1969, leaving from Lindenwold, New Jersey. My next-door neighbor, Tom Field, and I desperately wanted to ride on the very first train, but our learner's permits didn't allow us to drive in the wee morning hours. We put a notice out to a local radio station that we were seeking a ride, and a college student listener who lived nearby and was already planning to go agreed to give us a lift. It was a memorable experience, and we were mentioned in an article appearing the next day in the *Evening Bulletin*. Fast-forward fifty years later: while on a *Hidden City Philadelphia* tour of the city's subway system, I got into an animated debate with the tour guide about who rode on the first PATCO train. We eventually established that he (one Jerry Silverman) was the very same bloke who gave me a lift back in 1969, and we had ridden on the first train *together*. He also happens to live a few blocks from me today. So, a "transitory" acquaintanceship from the late '60s has been renewed as a long-term friendship!

Unlike in New York or Boston, where the residents maintain a stubborn affection for their subways, Philadelphians have never truly embraced the subway as part of their civic identity. Maybe it's because Philly has always been more of a railroad town. The Baldwin Locomotive Works was the world's largest manufacturer of steam engines for decades, and the Budd Company was a leading fabricator of stainless-steel passenger railcars for much of the twentieth century. Philadelphia also was the home of the Reading Railroad, with its magnificent iron train shed and ground-floor farmers' market, still going strong to this day. And Philadelphia served as headquarters for the mighty Pennsylvania Railroad, which for many years was the nation's largest corporation. The "Main Line" of the Pennsy, running to Pittsburgh and beyond, gave its name to Philadelphia's tony western suburban towns, and a certain segment of the population residing there to this day still speaks in lockjaw fashion like Thurston Howell III from *Gilligan's Island*.

While Philadelphia's subway system lacks a signature or emblematic look like that of London and Paris, it has some features worthy of remark. The 1920s-era stations along the Broad Street

SOUTHEASTERN PENNSYLVANIA TRANSPORTATION AUTHORITY

Line have an unassuming, art deco–inspired, two-tone tile pattern against an allegedly white background. It's not over-the-top art deco styling, but perhaps a Quaker-restrained version of it: art Quāko? The station entrances originally had impressive Jazz-Gothic iron portals, but sadly, only a couple still remain. They have been replaced by a mishmash of portal styles and signage, with no unifying look.

Left:
City Hall Station
(Broad Street Line)

Right:
One of the last remaining Jazz-Gothic entrances to the Broad Street subway (Lombard-South Station)

While the Broad Street stations could hardly be characterized as picturesque, some of the station names derived from the cross streets are undeniably evocative: Hunting Park, Spring Garden, Fairmount, and Susquehanna all conjure up images of sylvan surroundings. And speaking of rural flavor, one can indeed take the subway from Wyoming to Oregon: it's seventeen stops along the Broad Street Local, no transfer required.

PHILADELPHIA

In contrast, the Market Street Line stations are more prosaically named after the numbered streets. I recall a high school math test I took when we were studying numerical series. A bonus question was "List the next item in this sequence: 40, 46, 52, 56, 60, 63. . ." The answer? *Millbourne*, of course, for these are the westbound stops on the Market Street El.

Notwithstanding the overall plainness of the system, I am pleased to report that there are faint stirrings of design aesthetics cautiously emerging, like the first forsythia of spring. In 2014, the Philadelphia-based architecture firm of Kieran Timberlake designed striking new glass head-houses for the reconceived Dilworth Park at City Hall / 15th Street Station, where three transit lines interchange. Previously, it had been a brutalist granite plaza with dark and malodorous passages beneath it. Now, it is a civic centerpiece.

Dilworth Park subway entrance

SOUTHEASTERN PENNSYLVANIA TRANSPORTATION AUTHORITY

Installed in the hardscaping pavement fountain of Dilworth Park is a brilliantly conceived, illuminated water spray sculpture by artist Janet Echelman. It is illuminated by different-colored lights corresponding to the "Orange," "Blue," and "Green" Lines, and activated by the trains passing underneath. The water spray calls to mind not only the subways passing below, but also City Hall's location on the site of the original city waterworks at Centre Square. The spray mist also recalls the Pennsylvania Railroad's steam engines idling at the long-gone magnificent Broad Street Station that once stood directly across the street.

Center City Philadelphia is honeycombed with concourses that wend their way several miles beneath the city streets, connecting ten subway stations with principal buildings and the underground Suburban and Market East commuter rail stations. One hears mysterious rumblings of subway trains trundling through the tunnels beneath the concourse passageways. These concourses, too, are gradually being remodeled. And over on the PATCO line, Franklin Square—a "ghost station" closed since 1979—is being completely refurbished with a glass box entrance and will reopen in 2024.

Left:
Ben Franklin tilework at City Hall Station

Right:
South Penn Square concourse at City Hall Station

PHILADELPHIA

Perhaps the most impressive makeover of all is at 5th Street–Independence Hall Station, adjacent to Independence Hall and the recently excavated foundations of the young nation's first "White House." In remodeling the station, SEPTA held an artist competition and selected local painter Tom Judd, who has created a remarkable painted mural laminated along both 200-foot-long platform walls. The work deftly interweaves historical portraits, landscapes, and images suggesting the contradictions inherent in American ideals of freedom with the reality of the civil rights struggles of Black Americans. Aesthetically and conceptually, it definitely steps up SEPTA's transit design game.

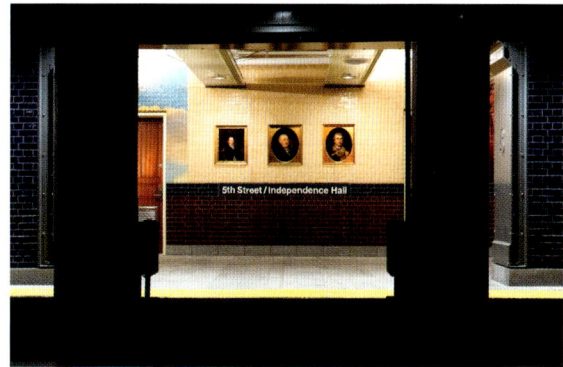

Tom Judd murals at 5th Street–Independence Station (Market–Frankford Line)

TRANSIT TOURISM | 85

SOUTHEASTERN PENNSYLVANIA TRANSPORTATION AUTHORITY

Shown below are views of Philadelphia's four principal rail transit services: (clockwise from upper left) the Subway Surface Trolleys (13th Street), Lindenwold High-Speed Line (9-10th Street), Market-Frankford Subway-Elevated (52nd Street), and Broad Street Subway (Spring Garden).

PHILADELPHIA

SUMMARY

So, returning to the World Cup analogy, it is doubtful from a design viewpoint that Philadelphia's subway would make it out of its bracket to the knockout round, given the heady competition shown by other cities elsewhere in this book. Nonetheless, the subway system has its own modest character befitting a city with Quaker roots, and it remains an important asset for getting around town. SEPTA historically has been so cash-strapped that it has been a struggle just to keep its current system running, let alone expand or enhance rider amenities. But SEPTA is now embarking on a complete rebranding of its rail transit services as SEPTA Metro, with new wayfinding, maps, and graphics. On the basis of the promising precedents of the 5th Street–Independence Station and at Dilworth Park, SEPTA—to invoke its former corporate catchphrase—may indeed be on its way to "getting there" at long last.

SELTZER TOKEN RATINGS (SCALE 1–4)

CONVENIENCE	2
EASE OF USE	2
QUALITY OF DESIGN	1
PERSONALITY	2

TRANSIT TOURISM

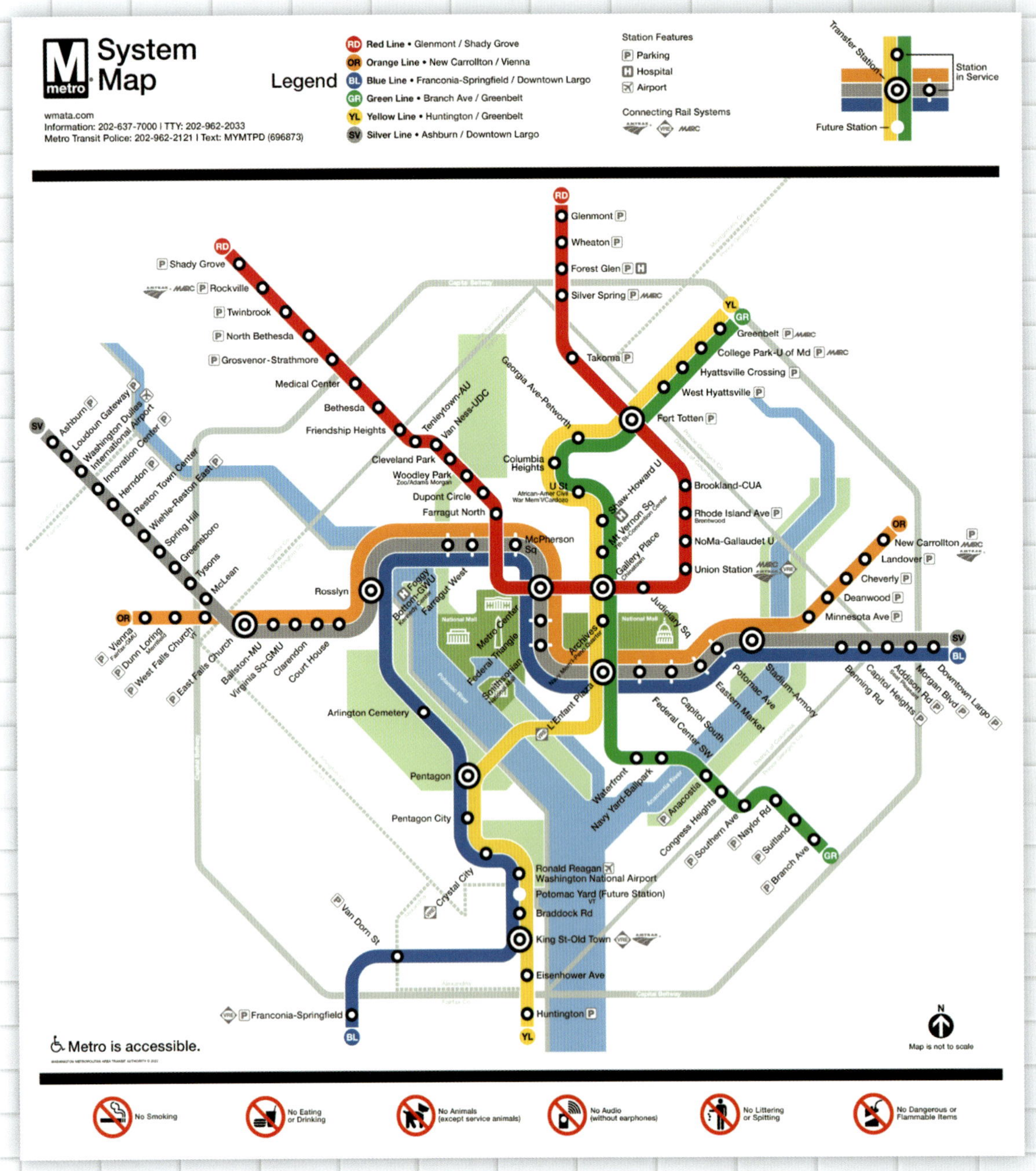

M metro
System Map
Legend
RD Red Line • Glenmont / Shady Grove
OR Orange Line • New Carrollton / Vienna
BL Blue Line • Franconia-Springfield / Downtown Largo
GR Green Line • Branch Ave / Greenbelt
YL Yellow Line • Huntington / Greenbelt
SV Silver Line • Ashburn / Downtown Largo
Station Features
Parking
Hospital
Airport
Connecting Rail Systems
Transfer Station
Station in Service
Future Station
wmata.com
Information: 202-637-7000 | TTY: 202-962-2033
Metro Transit Police: 202-962-2121 | Text: MYMTPD (696873)
Glenmont
Wheaton
Forest Glen
Silver Spring
Takoma
Fort Totten
Brookland-CUA
Rhode Island Ave
NoMa-Gallaudet U
Union Station
Shady Grove
Rockville
Twinbrook
North Bethesda
Grosvenor-Strathmore
Medical Center
Bethesda
Friendship Heights
Tenleytown-AU
Van Ness-UDC
Cleveland Park
Woodley Park
Dupont Circle
Farragut North
Greenbelt
College Park-U of Md
Hyattsville Crossing
West Hyattsville
Georgia Ave-Petworth
Columbia Heights
U St
Shaw-Howard U
Mt Vernon Sq
Gallery Place
Judiciary Sq
McPherson Sq
Ashburn
Loudoun Gateway
Washington Dulles International Airport
Innovation Center
Herndon
Reston Town Center
Wiehle-Reston East
Spring Hill
Greensboro
Tysons
McLean
Vienna
Dunn Loring
West Falls Church
East Falls Church
Ballston-MU
Virginia Sq-GMU
Clarendon
Court House
Rosslyn
Foggy Bottom-GWU
Farragut West
Metro Center
Federal Triangle
Smithsonian
Archives
L'Enfant Plaza
National Mall
New Carrollton
Landover
Cheverly
Deanwood
Minnesota Ave
Benning Rd
Capitol Heights
Addison Rd
Morgan Blvd
Downtown Largo
Stadium-Armory
Potomac Ave
Eastern Market
Capitol South
Federal Center SW
Waterfront
Navy Yard-Ballpark
Anacostia
Congress Heights
Southern Ave
Naylor Rd
Suitland
Branch Ave
Arlington Cemetery
Pentagon
Pentagon City
Crystal City
Ronald Reagan Washington National Airport
Potomac Yard (Future Station)
Braddock Rd
King St-Old Town
Eisenhower Ave
Huntington
Van Dorn St
Franconia-Springfield
Capital Beltway
Metro is accessible.
Map is not to scale
No Smoking
No Eating or Drinking
No Animals (except service animals)
No Audio (without earphones)
No Littering or Spitting
No Dangerous or Flammable Items

WASHINGTON, DC

WASHINGTON, DC
Washington Metropolitan Area Transit Authority

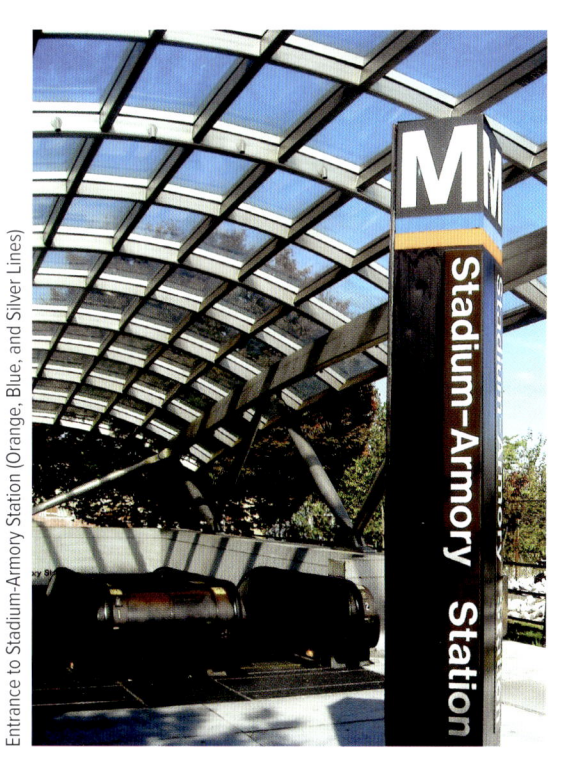

System Length	129 route miles
Number of Lines	6
Number of Stations	101
Year Opened	1976
Year of Last Expansion	2022 (Silver Line–Phase II)
Annual Ridership	238 million (2019)
Subwayness	48% of stations underground

Entrance to Stadium-Armory Station (Orange, Blue, and Silver Lines)

With its stately low buildings, wide thoroughfares, and immense greensward of the National Mall plunked right in the heart of downtown, Washington, DC, could be considered a city designed for people wary of cities. In the same way, Washington's transit system, with its spacious stations, plush car interiors, and trendy "Metrorail" name, could be considered a subway designed for people wary of subways.

When it first opened, Washington's Metrorail and the contemporaneous Bay Area Rapid Transit system in San Francisco did much to dispel the American negative stereotype of subways as dirty, dismal, and dangerous places, with the then-beleaguered New York City

TRANSIT TOURISM | 89

WASHINGTON METROPOLITAN AREA TRANSIT AUTHORITY

subway serving as the poster child. One of the nation's newer systems (the first 4-mile segment opened in 1976), Metrorail was billed by its Great Society promoters as "America's Subway." It blended the features of an urban transit system (closely spaced underground stations downtown and frequent service) with those of a suburban commuter rail line (upholstered seating and carpets in cars serving widely spaced surface stations in outlying areas).

Of course, Metrorail is not Washington's very first subway. *That* distinction belongs to the Capitol Subway, a curious shuttle just a few blocks long, with three branches connecting Senate and House office buildings to the United States Capitol.[1] The first leg, linking the Capitol Building to the Russell Senate Office Building, opened in 1909. Additional branches were added to the Senate Dirksen and Hart Office Buildings (1960, 1982) and the Rayburn House Office Building (1965). It is interesting to note that the Senate, with just one hundred members, is served by *two* lines and *three* stations, while the House of Representatives, with 435 members, has only *one* station. Even underground, the Senate is still very much the Upper Chamber.

Left: View of subway serving the Senate

Right: Capitol Subway map

---

[1] This miniature shuttle pales in comparison to the only other subway I'm aware of designated for government officials: Moscow's so-called Metro-2, a four-line supersecret metro allegedly extending from beneath the Kremlin to military bases and underground shelters on the outskirts of Moscow, for use in event of nuclear attack.

WASHINGTON, DC

As for the "real" subway, the original authorized Metrorail system was constructed in stages, opening between 1976 and 2001, and is operated by the Washington Metropolitan Area Transit Authority (WMATA). It now encompasses 6 lines, 101 stations (four interchange), and 129 route miles, making it the nation's second longest. It blankets downtown Washington with twenty stations and extends into the far-flung suburbs of Shady Grove to the north in Maryland, to Springfield to the south in Virginia, and to Dulles Airport, 25 miles west of the Capitol, and beyond to Loudon County, Virginia. Train controls are fully automated, and Metrorail was an early adopter of magnetic fare cards. I compare that technology to my beloved but decidedly belated hometown system of SEPTA in Philadelphia, which only recently converted from brass tokens—*fungible* tokens, mind you—to fare cards . . . a mere four decades after Washington.

Metrorail is a marvelous way to get around town, as it whisks passengers from the distant suburbs to the very heart of Washington in speedy, quiet comfort, bypassing DC's legendary traffic jams. Whether you are a tourist from Tulsa or a bureaucrat from Bethesda, Metrorail serves most of the key destinations within the District. Getting around Washington would be unthinkable without it. And even though Washingtonians grumble about Metrorail's delays and occasional service outages, it still compares very favorably in terms of frequency, convenience, and comfort to the nation's older "legacy" rapid-transit systems of New York, Boston, Philadelphia, and Chicago. People from all walks of life—and indeed all political persuasions—use it. Even in this highly polarized era, Washingtonians can agree that Metrorail Delays Unite All Parties.

Like the public buildings in the nation's capital, Metrorail's station designs follow a consistent, dignified, and classical architectural style. The stations that were part of the original approved 103-mile plan all were designed by one architectural firm, Harry Weese Associates of Chicago, with substantial input from the federally appointed Commission of Fine Arts. Each station incorporates concrete, granite, bronze, and glass, giving them a uniform look. The underground stations are

WASHINGTON METROPOLITAN AREA TRANSIT AUTHORITY

monumental in scale, but in place of using fluted columns as their signature element, Metrorail used (at least for the earlier stages of the system) a coffered arched ceiling, reminiscent of Union Station's glorious Beaux-Arts central hall and other federal landmarks such as the Capitol dome and Jefferson Memorial.

Left: Union Station foyer

Right: Foggy Bottom Station (Orange, Blue, and Silver Lines)

Metrorail's platforms are long—the length of two football fields—and are largely free of columns, creating a sense of spaciousness in the grand vaulted spaces. The floors are covered in hexagonal brick-colored tiles, and pulsating lights along the platform edge signal the imminent arrival of a train. The downtown interchange stations—Metro Center, Gallery Place, and L'Enfant Plaza—have striking transept vaults, beautifully inspired twentieth-century Cathedrals to Commuting, minus the gargoyles.

WASHINGTON, DC

Metro Center station (Red, Orange, Blue, and Silver Lines)

However, just as the tourist in Washington soon wearies of the endless phalanxes of lifeless, neoclassical government buildings, so too the subway rider in Washington longs for a little more variety—or even just color—in the Metrorail Stations. The preponderance of concrete gives the stations a lifeless and pallid look, like the archetypal Washington bureaucrat (I can say this, having been one for several years!). It hasn't been helped by the ceiling lighting, which, until a recent LED retrofit, was so dim it could pass for mood lighting. Today we would call the massive poured-concrete style "brutalist," originally meant as a term of derision. More recently, it is becoming a term of appreciation—even admiration—much in the way that "impressionism" mellowed from a disparagement to a compliment. But what I wouldn't give for a Boston-style color-coded enameled metal band running along each station wall, just to punch things up a bit!

WASHINGTON METROPOLITAN AREA TRANSIT AUTHORITY

Now it is true that WMATA has an Art in Transit program, with installations in about forty stations. But the artwork is a belated afterthought and often is lost in the surrounding sea of concrete. And much of the art is unmemorable, at best. Compare this with the fabulous station art in Brussels, Naples, and Stockholm to see what "world class" transit design really means (check out those chapters).

The railcars have an unusual lozenge-shaped appearance, maintained consistently over eight series of train car orders spanning five decades and multiple manufacturers from the US, Italy, Spain, France, and Japan.

WASHINGTON, DC

Some of the escalators descend to dizzying depths, such as Wheaton and Woodley Park. Wheaton Station escalator is 230 ft. long—Metro's longest.

Left:
Wheaton Station escalator (Red Line)

Right:
Farragut West Station (Blue, Orange, and Silver Lines)

Distinctive pylons mark station entrances, with color coding for each line. And more recently, the station entrances have been covered by glass canopies, which echo the coffered ceilings of the tunneled Metrorail stations. WMATA has belatedly added these coverings over the escalators, which had been exposed to the elements for decades, with predictable results.

The stations generally are named for places, rather than street addresses, and evoke vivid associations with Washington, such as Dupont Circle, Foggy Bottom, and the Smithsonian. Regrettably, in recent years, Metrorail has been afflicted by an acute case of name inflation. Thus, the once very crisply named "Archives" Station (adjacent to the wonderful National Archives Building) now is cumbersomely labeled "Archives–Navy Memorial–Penn Quarter." "Mt. Vernon Sq" has grown to "Mt. Vernon Sq–7th St–Convention Center." Vienna is now "Vienna–Fairfax–GMU," despite the fact that

WASHINGTON METROPOLITAN AREA TRANSIT AUTHORITY

George Mason University is located *several miles away*. I could go on (as indeed the station names do), but you get the idea. Like one of those congressional pork barrel bills that carries the earmark of each politico who has touched it, WMATA's map has become bloated with hyphenated compromises.

In contrast to the monochromatic station architecture, the Metrorail route map is colorful, lively, and user-friendly. It has arguably become as iconic to Washington as the Tube map is to London. The subway lines are drawn in thick, bold colors, and interchange stations are clearly marked with oversized black bull's-eyes. The Metrorail map shows broad geographic features such as the Potomac River, major parklands, and the city's most notable landmarks: the White House, the Capitol, the Washington Monument, and Lincoln and Jefferson Memorials—just enough to help get one's bearings. The map was designed by Lance Wyman, who also designed the Mexico City Metro graphics (see Mexico City chapter). Wyman originally proposed visual pictograms for each station on WMATA's map, as in Mexico City, but this idea was rejected—perhaps the graphics were deemed too flamboyant for the otherwise conformist architecture.

WMATA's sixth and newest line—the Silver Line—commenced operations on the first half of its route to Loudoun County, Virginia, in 2014.[2] The remaining 11 miles to Dulles Airport and its terminus at Ashburn opened in 2022. Gone will be the $60 cab fares for all but the most spendthrift tassel-loafered lobbyists. Still, it will take twenty stops and fifty-two minutes to get from Metro Center to Dulles. And after fits and starts over the last decade, a 16-mile, $3.4 billion surface light-rail project (the Purple Line, not part of Metrorail) is under construction in the Maryland suburbs, connecting with three subway lines as well as Amtrak and commuter rail.

---

[2] Little-known factoid: The Silver Line could be considered a municipal platypus of a project. It was funded largely by a toll road authority, was financed with bonds issued by an airport authority, and is operated by a transit authority.

WASHINGTON, DC

SUMMARY

The Washington Metrorail system is comprehensive, its service is convenient, and its appearance is dignified. It gets you where you want to go, in and around the district, with great efficiency. In many ways, "America's Subway" is a model for American urban rail transit. But from a transit tourism viewpoint, it is remorselessly dull, like the ubiquitous poured-concrete walls. There is very little to distinguish one station from the next; indeed, that was the explicit objective. In this regard, its blandness may be said to be reflective of a city that lacks an emblematic civic persona. Whether this is due to the transient nature of federal officeholders or the deadening effect of acres of limestone and marble-clad public edifices, it's hard to say. How one wishes for a little variety—or at least color—in the station design. Metrorail: *You can do better!*

SELTZER TOKEN RATINGS (SCALE 1–4)

Category	Rating
CONVENIENCE	4
EASE OF USE	4
QUALITY OF DESIGN	3
PERSONALITY	1

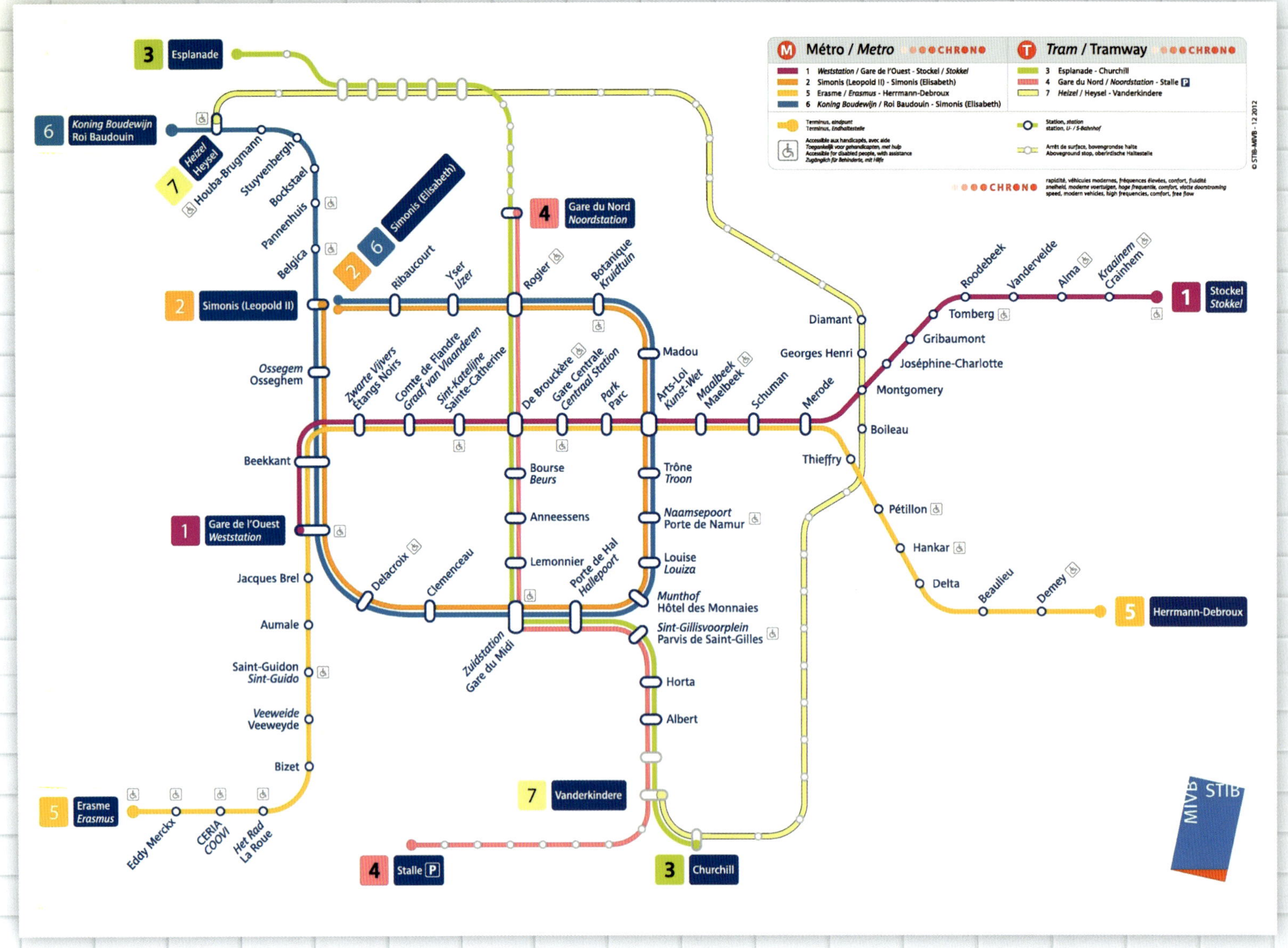

Métro / Metro CHRONO
1 Weststation / Gare de l'Ouest - Stockel / Stokkel
2 Simonis (Leopold II) - Simonis (Elisabeth)
5 Erasme / Erasmus - Herrmann-Debroux
6 Koning Boudewijn / Roi Baudouin - Simonis (Elisabeth)
Tram / Tramway CHRONO
3 Esplanade - Churchill
4 Gare du Nord / Noordstation - Stalle P
7 Heizel / Heysel - Vanderkindere
Terminus, eindpunt
Terminus, Endhaltestelle
Accessible aux handicapés, avec aide
Toegankelijk voor gehandicapten, met hulp
Accessible for disabled people, with assistance
Zugänglich für Behinderte, mit Hilfe
Station, station
station, U- / S-Bahnhof
Arrêt de surface, bovengrondse halte
Aboveground stop, oberirdische Haltestelle
CHRONO
rapidité, véhicules modernes, fréquences élevées, confort, fluidité
snelheid, moderne voertuigen, hoge frequentie, comfort, vlotte doorstroming
speed, modern vehicles, high frequencies, comfort, free flow
© STIB-MIVB - 12 2012
3 Esplanade
6 Koning Boudewijn Roi Baudouin
7 Heizel Heysel
Houba-Brugmann
Stuyvenbergh
Bockstael
Pannenhuis
Belgica
2 6 Simonis (Elisabeth)
2 Simonis (Leopold II)
Ribaucourt
Yser IJzer
Rogier
Botanique Kruidtuin
4 Gare du Nord Noordstation
Madou
Ossegem Osseghem
Zwarte Vijvers Étangs Noirs
Comte de Flandre Graaf van Vlaanderen
Sint-Katelijne Sainte-Catherine
De Brouckère
Gare Centrale Centraal Station
Park Parc
Arts-Loi Kunst-Wet
Maalbeek Maelbeek
Schuman
Merode
Diamant
Georges Henri
Montgomery
Boileau
Thieffry
Pétillon
Hankar
Delta
Beaulieu
Demey
5 Herrmann-Debroux
Roodebeek
Vandervelde
Alma
Kraainem Crainhem
1 Stockel Stokkel
Tomberg
Gribaumont
Joséphine-Charlotte
Beekkant
1 Gare de l'Ouest Weststation
Bourse Beurs
Anneessens
Lemonnier
Trône Troon
Naamsepoort Porte de Namur
Louise Louiza
Munthof Hôtel des Monnaies
Sint-Gillisvoorplein Parvis de Saint-Gilles
Horta
Albert
Jacques Brel
Delacroix
Clemenceau
Zuidstation Gare du Midi
Porte de Hal Hallepoort
Aumale
Saint-Guidon Sint-Guido
Veeweide Veeweyde
Bizet
5 Erasme Erasmus
Eddy Merckx
CERIA COOVI
Het Rad La Roue
7 Vanderkindere
4 Stalle P
3 Churchill
MIVB STIB

BRUSSELS

BRUSSELS
Société des Transports Intercommunaux de Bruxelles (STIB)

System Length	32 route miles
Number of Lines	7 (3 are light rail / pre-Metro)
Number of Stations	78 (15 are pre-Metro underground)
Year Opened	1969
Year of Last Expansion	2009
Annual Ridership	165 million (2019)
Subwayness	86% of stations underground (67 of 78 unique stations in Metro / tunneled pre-Metro)

De Brouckère station entrance (Lines 1, 3, 4, and 5)

In a place known for art and design, from the Renaissance and art nouveau to comic books and beyond, the Brussels Metro offers an unexpected artistic perspective of the city and its local character. The Metro system is a delight, from its charmingly ungainly "M" logo to the major art installations in dozens of stations. The city's regional transportation agency, Société des Transports Intercommunaux de Bruxelles (known as STIB for short), operates an efficient and attractive network that justifiably is a source of tremendous civic pride.

A relatively new system, Brussels presents a fascinating case study of the metamorphosis of a transit network over the course of

TRANSIT TOURISM | 99

SOCIÉTÉ DES TRANSPORTS INTERCOMMUNAUX DE BRUXELLES

its construction. Up until the 1960s, Brussels's public transportation largely consisted of surface streetcars, or trams. To speed passengers' journeys in the crowded, medieval central business district, the city opted in 1969 to inaugurate its underground service in the "pre-Metro" mode—what in the US we would call "light rail." A pre-Metro is an underground segment of surface tram routes that can be upgraded to full metro service at a later date. It is intended to function as an interim phase to meet a city's transportation needs until demand warrants the greater expense of converting the "pre-Metro" to "heavy rail" standard metro service.[1]

Patronage on the initial underground line (now Lines 1 and 5) was so high that STIB converted it into a true metro service seven years later. A second planned underground loop line conceived as pre-Metro was revised middesign to full metro standards, and a third north–south pre-Metro line built largely in the 1970s is now being converted to a full metro. Almost all the tunnels were excavated by digging a trench and then roofing it over—the "cut and cover" method. With these no doubt costly middevelopment conversions from light rail to heavy rail, shouldn't someone have invoked that well-worn Belgian proverb: "Measure twice, cut (-and-cover) once"?

Today, of the seven lines, four are heavy-rail metro and three are pre-Metro, with one in the process of being converted to metro. This system's routes are configured like a four-quadrant square, with branches off several ends, and two bisecting lines crossing in the heart of the city at De Brouckère station. The routes' spindles and nodes call to mind the design of the city's iconic Atomium. Built for Expo 58—the 1958 World's Fair—the Atomium depicts the unit cell structure of an iron crystal, and today it houses a museum about Expo 58. The Atomium consists of nine

---

1 Unlike heavy-rail subways, a pre-Metro typically has lower-capacity one- or two-car train sets powered by overhead wires that serve shorter stations with low-level platforms.

BRUSSELS

spheres linked by interconnecting spokes that radiate outward like the structure of an atom, or branches of Brussels's Metro.

On the Metro map, the number 2 and 6 lines effectively serve as a square "circle" line, bisected by the Metro (Lines 1 and 5) and the underground tram (Lines 3 and 4).

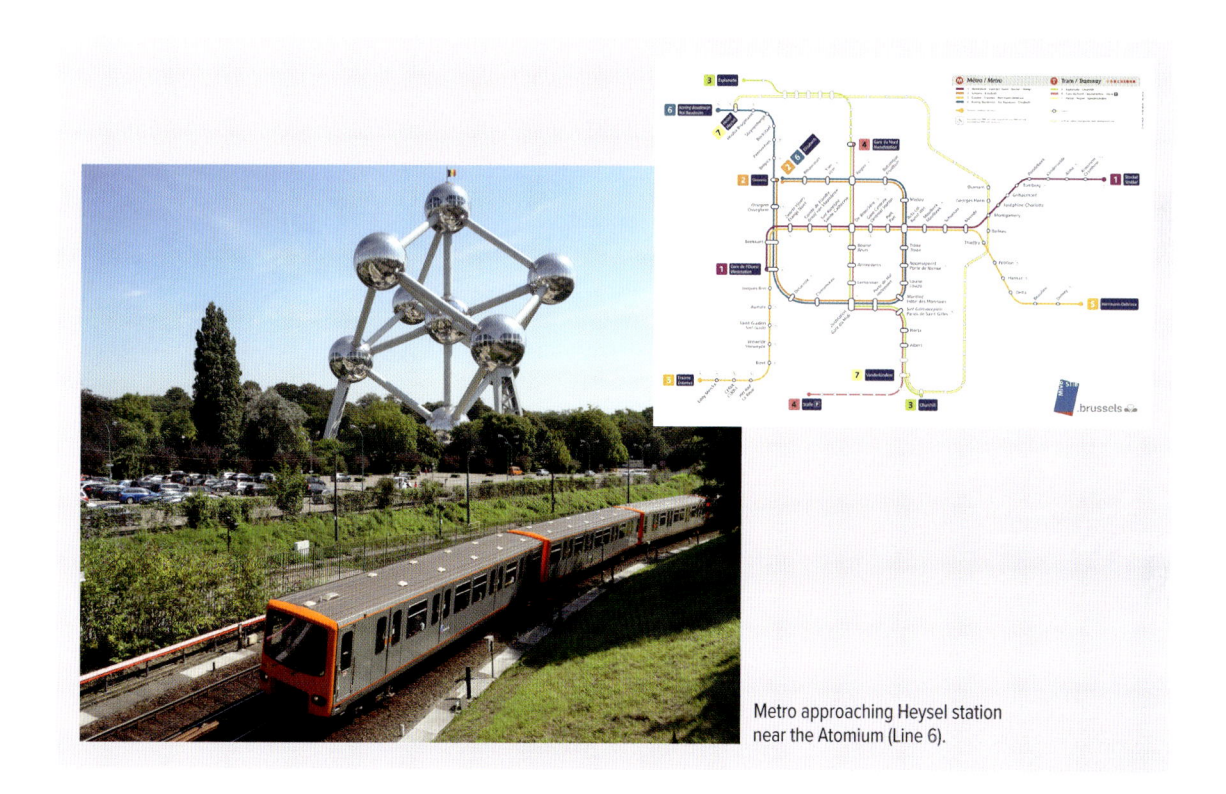

Metro approaching Heysel station near the Atomium (Line 6).

SOCIÉTÉ DES TRANSPORTS INTERCOMMUNAUX DE BRUXELLES

The quirky "M" logo was the result of a competition put to public vote in 1976 and threatens to relieve (if I may use that term) *Manneken Pis* as the most familiar image of Brussels. Given the number of metro systems worldwide that use some variant of the letter M for their logo (over seventy by one count), one can see that Brussels's version clearly broke the mold. Compared to the angular—dare I say masculine—M's of the transit logos for Istanbul, Los Angeles, Mexico City, Milan, Moscow, Paris, and Washington shown below, Brussels's idiosyncratic M appears more informal, more feminine, almost *zaftig*.

| Istanbul | Los Angeles | Mexico City | Milan | Moscow | Paris | Washington |

Citizens of Stockholm proudly describe their subway system as the world's longest art gallery, but Brussels can stake a convincing claim to that title. There are over a hundred installations in sixty-four metro stations throughout the system. Since its inception, STIB has featured contemporary work in the stations by Belgian artists. Why such a strong commitment to fine art? Well, Brussels certainly comes by it honestly, given the great Flemish art tradition ranging from van der Weyden and Brueghel (both Younger and Elder) to Magritte, continuing to today's talented field of artists on display throughout the system. And for those of us who took the Art History 101 course in college and always wondered where the hell the oft-referenced Duchy of Brabant was located, *this is it*.

BRUSSELS

The artwork is not just inserted into stations as an afterthought; rather, each station has been designed around it. And architecturally, each station is different, in sharp contrast to a system such as Washington, DC, where all the stations are standardized. Like a sampler of irresistible Belgian chocolates, each Brussels station contains a surprise! The stations have a variety of different art genres on display, from murals and sculptures to photographs, stained glass, and tile. A sampling of the wide variety of creative artwork is shown below.

Left:
Merode station
(Lines 1 and 2)

Right:
Gare de L'Ouest station
(Lines 1, 2, 5, and 6)

Left:
Etangs Noirs station
(Lines 1 and 5)

Right:
Comte de Flandre station
(Lines 1 and 5)

SOCIÉTÉ DES TRANSPORTS INTERCOMMUNAUX DE BRUXELLES

Just south of the central district at Parvis de Saint-Gilles is an installation by Francoise Schein, whose series of giant tileworks on the universal rights of man are installed in various metros, including Berlin, Lisbon, Paris, São Paulo, and Stockholm.

Left:
Dyade by Francoise Schein at Parvis de Saint-Gille station (Lines 3 and 4)

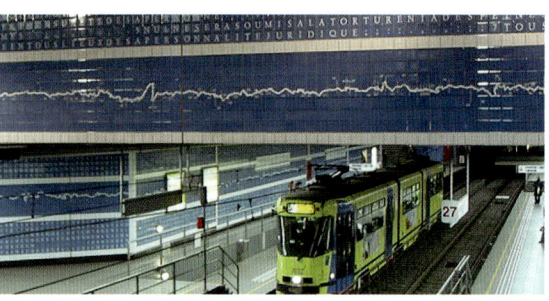

Right:
Herman–Debroux (line 5)

One of the most entertaining stations is Stockel, which shows the cartoon characters made famous by the Belgian comic artist Hergé. Belgium is world renowned for its long history of comic strip art (Tintin, the Smurfs, et al.). In fact, Brussels has an excellent Comics Art Museum housed in an art nouveau building designed by architect Victor Horta.

Left and right:
Tintin in the Metro (Hergé), Stockel station (Line 1)

BRUSSELS

STIB has published a marvelous guidebook (in English!) called *Art in the Metro*, which illustrates the art installations throughout the system and introduces readers to the artists who created them. While there was no guided tour when my wife and I visited, we used the guidebook to pick out selected highlights. And she, normally not even remotely a "subway person," came away captivated.

SUMMARY

The Brussels Metro continues the centuries-old Flemish tradition of showcasing amazing regional artistic talent. Between the variegated architecture and the thoughtfully integrated art, the Brussels Metro, from a design point of view, is the best subway system you've never heard of. And not too shabby a way of getting around town, either. I give it a perfect score.

SELTZER TOKEN RATINGS (SCALE 1–4)

CONVENIENCE	4
EASE OF USE	4
QUALITY OF DESIGN	4
PERSONALITY	4

TRANSIT TOURISM | 105

Budapest metróhálózata / Metro network in Budapest

Látnivalók / Sights

- Országház / Parliament
- Budai Vár / Buda Castle
- Halászbástya / Fisherman's Bastion
- Szabadság híd / Liberty Bridge
- Citadella, Szabadság-szobor / Citadel, Statue of Liberty
- Millenniumi emlékmű / Millennium Monument
- Állatkert / Zoo
- Magyar Nemzeti Múzeum / Hungarian National Museum
- Állami Operaház / Hungarian State Opera
- Központi Vásárcsarnok / Great Market Hall
- Szent István-bazilika / Saint Stephen's Basilica
- Dohány utcai zsinagóga / Dohány street Synagogue
- Gyógyfürdő / Thermal Bath

Vonalak és állomások / Lines and stations

- Metróvonalak / Metro lines: M1, M2, M3, M4
- Átszállóhely / Transfer point
  Metróvonalak közötti átszálláskor nem szükséges új jegyet érvényesíteni.
  On the metro network, single tickets and digital tickets allow transfers between the lines with the first validation on the network.
- Akadálymentes állomás / Accessible station

Átszállási lehetőségek / Transfer options

- HÉV-vonalak / Suburban railway lines (H5, H8, H9)
- Repülőtéri autóbuszok / Airport buses
  - 100E Deák Ferenc tér M ↔ Liszt Ferenc Airport 2 (Külön díjszabás szerint / Special fares apply)
  - 200E Kőbánya-Kispest M ↔ Liszt Ferenc Airport 2
- Vasút / Railway
- Regionális autóbuszok / Regional buses
- Távolsági autóbuszok / Long-distance buses

Járataink közlekedése módosulhat. Kérjük, figyelje kihelyezett tájékoztatóinkat.
The transport services are subject to change. Please check the information boards.

Adatok lezárva: 2023.11.20. / Data current as of 20.11.2023

M1 (yellow) stations
Vörösmarty tér – Deák Ferenc tér – Bajcsy-Zsilinszky út – Opera – Oktogon – Vörösmarty utca – Kodály körönd – Bajza utca – Hősök tere – Széchenyi fürdő – Mexikói út

M2 (red) stations
Déli pályaudvar – Széll Kálmán tér – Batthyány tér – Kossuth Lajos tér – Deák Ferenc tér – Astoria – Blaha Lujza tér – Keleti pályaudvar – Puskás Ferenc Stadion – Pillangó utca – Örs vezér tere

M3 (blue) stations
Újpest-központ – Újpest-városkapu – Gyöngyösi utca – Forgách utca – Göncz Árpád városközpont – Dózsa György út – Lehel tér – Nyugati pályaudvar – Arany János utca – Deák Ferenc tér – Ferenciek tere – Kálvin tér – Corvin-negyed – Semmelweis Klinikák – Nagyvárad tér – Népliget – Ecseri út – Pöttyös utca – Határ út – Kőbánya-Kispest

M4 (green) stations
Kelenföld vasútállomás – Bikás park – Újbuda-központ – Móricz Zsigmond körtér – Szent Gellért tér – Műegyetem – Fővám tér – Kálvin tér – Rákóczi tér – II. János Pál pápa tér – Keleti pályaudvar

BUDA | PEST
Duna | MARGIT-SZIGET | OBUDAI-SZIGET

Utazástervezés valós idejű járatinformációkkal, jegy- és bérletvásárlás
Journey planning based on real-time data and ticketing

BUDAPEST | BKK BUDAPESTI KÖZLEKEDÉSI KÖZPONT

www.bkk.hu | bkk@bkk.hu | +36 1 3 255 255
bkkbudapest | bkkbudapest

BKK Utastájékoztatás

BUDAPEST

BUDAPEST
Budapesti Közlekedési Zrt (Budapest Transit Company)

System Length	24 route miles
Number of Lines	4
Number of Stations	52
Year Opened	1896
Year of Last Expansion	2014
Annual Ridership	354 million (2019)
Subwayness	94% of stations underground

Bajcsy-Zsilinszky út station entrance (Line 1)

Budapest is a city where East meets West—or more specifically, where Buda meets Pest. Buda and Pest were originally two distinct cities. Buda is the older of the two, perched on the hilly western side of the Danube. The first kings of Hungary made Buda their capital in the Middle Ages, and the ancient Royal Palace overlooks a landscape of quaint, winding streets below. Pest lies along the flatter east bank of the Danube and over the years became the commercial and governmental center of the city. The capital city has always been in the crosscurrent of central European events, at various times over the centuries being under Magyar, Turkish, and Teutonic rulers. During

TRANSIT TOURISM | 107

BUDAPESTI KÖZLEKEDÉSI ZRT (BUDAPEST TRANSIT COMPANY)

the Belle Époque, Budapest was co-capital (with Vienna) of the sprawling Austro-Hungarian Empire, and one of Europe's leading cultural centers in music, art, and literature. And in the late nineteenth century, the city became a popular destination because of its salubrious hot-spring mineral baths. With this complex and layered heritage, everything in Budapest has a distinct inflection—not least the language, since Hungarian (to look at it) seems to have cornered the world supply of umlauts, accents, and double acutes.

Budapest has the oldest subway system on the Continent. Opened in 1896, it was built as part of the preparations for the Hungarian National Millennium Exhibition celebrating the thousand-year anniversary of the Magyars settling on the Danube following their migration from the steppes of Russia. A grand new boulevard, Andrássy Avenue, had been built in the 1870s in the Parisian style, connecting the heart of the city to the exhibition grounds in Városliget, a major city park.

The city fathers did not want the thoroughfare's beauty cluttered with streetcars during the six-month festival, so they decided to put the trams underground instead. The initial line was called the Földalatti—literally the "underground"—but today is known as the Millennium Underground or, more prosaically, Metro Line 1. Initially, it was only 3 miles long and built just 10 feet below street level. The line is the world's second-oldest electrified subway after the Northern Line in London, and in 2002 UNESCO placed it on its list of World Heritage Sites both for its architectural beauty and its engineering significance.

The Földalatti's design reflects the proud, confident political environment in which it was built, at the zenith of the Austro-Hungarian Empire's power and prestige. The stations are dignified and formal, resembling nothing so much as a tony Edwardian men's club locker room. Majolica white tiles with cordovan accents line the walls, alongside handsome wooden doorways and wainscoted cabinets. The steel girders are painted hunter green and sport acanthus capitals. And the station signage, with its slim, serifed letterforms, is elegant and old school (in the style of Bodoni

BUDAPEST

Compressed Light). Many of the station entrance stairways are fashioned in delicate wrought iron in the Hungarian Secessionist style (which was a more angular, folksy architectural version of art Nouveau) and are painted yellow, the Line's signature color. The Földalatti was completely restored to pristine condition for the centenary of the subway in 1996. The original cars operated for over seventy-five years before being replaced with modern canary-yellow rolling stock, echoing the entrance railings above.

Hősök Tere station (Line 1): An Edwardian men's locker room?

Of the twenty original train sets manufactured in 1896, one was reserved for the exclusive use of Emperor Franz Josef and his entourage. I had heard about European royal train coaches being manufactured for long-distance rail journeys, but a local subway train reserved exclusively for the monarch? One can imagine a harried commuter of the day seeing the emperor's train speed by his platform and muttering to himself, "What a Royal Pain!"

TRANSIT TOURISM | 109

BUDAPESTI KÖZLEKEDÉSI ZRT (BUDAPEST TRANSIT COMPANY)

Bajcsy-Zsilinszky út station (Line 1)

As with so much else Hungarian, the Földalatti's Bajcsy-Zsilinszky station would make a great Scrabble word; the last syllable alone is worth twenty points, even before counting any double-letter scores.

But you don't need to go all the way to Budapest to see an original Földalatti car. There is one in the collection of the Seaport Trolley Museum, located in charming Kennebunkport, Maine. This working museum has dozens of old transit vehicles on display—mostly trolley cars but some subway cars, motor buses, and the occasional cable car. You can take a 1.5-mile ride on an authentic turn-of-the-century interurban trolley along the old Seacoast route, driven by an operator who appears to be of similar vintage.

Back in Budapest, both Line 2 (east–west) and Line 3 (north–south) are "heavy rail" metros that run in much-deeper underground tunnels. All three lines interchange in the city center at Deák Ferenc, where there is a small museum devoted to the Millennium Underground (Line 1). The second and third lines reflect a distinct shift in style echoing Hungary's more recent history. They were designed with two purposes in mind: first and foremost for underground transport, but also as air-raid shelters during the Cold War. These lines were developed starting in the 1970s with Soviet assistance, while Hungary labored under a Communist regime, and the design hews faithfully to the Russian utilitarian style that dominated the Eastern Bloc.

The stations are boxy, spare, and largely unadorned. In recent years, as BKV (the public operator) has renovated the lines, it has improved the stations' lighting and added some color elements to the walls. While a few of the principal stations have wall photomurals at the platform level, most of the stops are visually bland, save for the bright-yellow and bright-orange modeled plastic chairs fastened to the walls. Still, the stations are clean, commodious, and well lit.

Line 4, completed in 2014, was developed in a more open and robust economic environment. But in contrast to other cities such as Beijing, Istanbul, and Moscow, all of which have rapidly expanded their systems, building subways in Budapest proceeds at a glacial pace. Line 4 was first proposed in the 1970s, and postponed several times for financial and political reasons, finally opening thirty-five years later, in 2014. But it was worth the wait: its stations rival those of any other city in the sophistication of their designs. Line 4 is the only one of Budapest's subway lines where the stations were designed by architects rather than civil engineers, and it offers some of the best contemporary homegrown architecture in the capital.

My two favorite stops are the twin stations on either side of the Danube, designed by Budapest-based Spora Architects: Szent Gellért tér and Föräm tér ("tér" means "square"). To bring light down to the platforms 115 feet below street level, both stations have skylit entry halls with long escalators deftly slotted between the crisscrossing concrete structural beams. Szent Gellért has an almost psychedelic pattern of small, tessellated tiles echoing the exquisite Zsolnay ceramics that decorate the famous thermal baths in the adjacent Hotel Gellért, itself a magnificent pile from the Belle Époque era. I did not notice extensive art installations in Budapest as one sees in Brussels, Naples, and Stockholm. But what makes Line 4 memorable is the architecture, not the artwork.

BUDAPESTI KÖZLEKEDÉSI ZRT (BUDAPEST TRANSIT COMPANY)

Left:
(Line 2), Déli Pályaudvar (South station western terminus)—one of the few with a large art mural

Right:
(Line 4), Föräm tér station. The vertiginous escalators descend eight stories past concrete supports.

Left:
(Line 3), Göncz Árpád Városközpon station. Visual highlight: the bright-orange seating affixed to the walls.

Left and right:
Mörice Zsigmond station separated at birth from Munich's Georg Brauchle-Ring station?

112 | EUROPE—HUNGARY

BUDAPEST

SUMMARY

With its four lines reflecting vastly different styles from the Imperial, midcentury Soviet, and European Community periods, the Budapest metro is a bit of a goulash, entirely appropriate for a city that sits at one of Europe's age-old crossroads between East and West. It is a manageable and friendly system to use. Indeed, on the transit agency's website, BKV proudly states, "We would like Budapest to be the most loveable city in the world." Which naturally invites this question: Have you hugged your subway today?

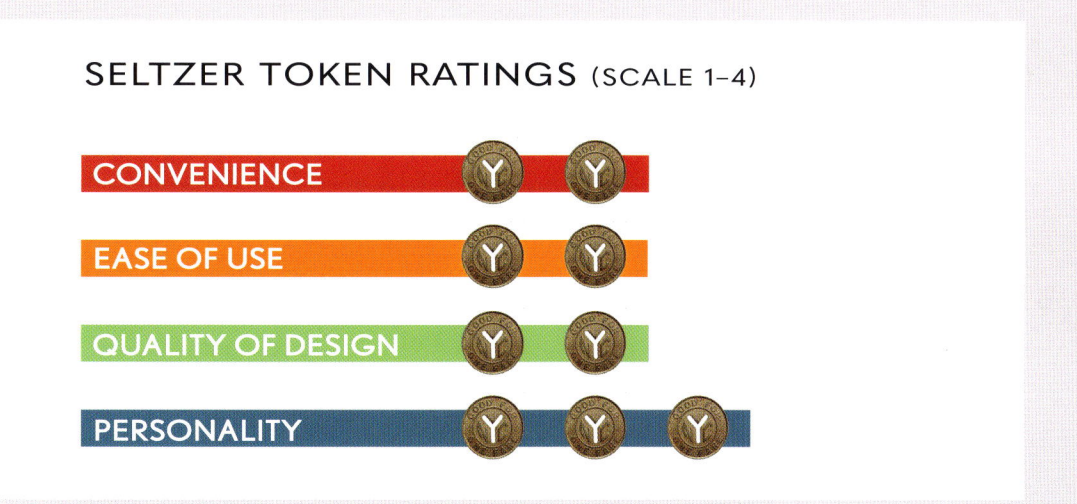

SELTZER TOKEN RATINGS (SCALE 1–4)

CONVENIENCE	2
EASE OF USE	2
QUALITY OF DESIGN	2
PERSONALITY	3

TRANSIT TOURISM | 113

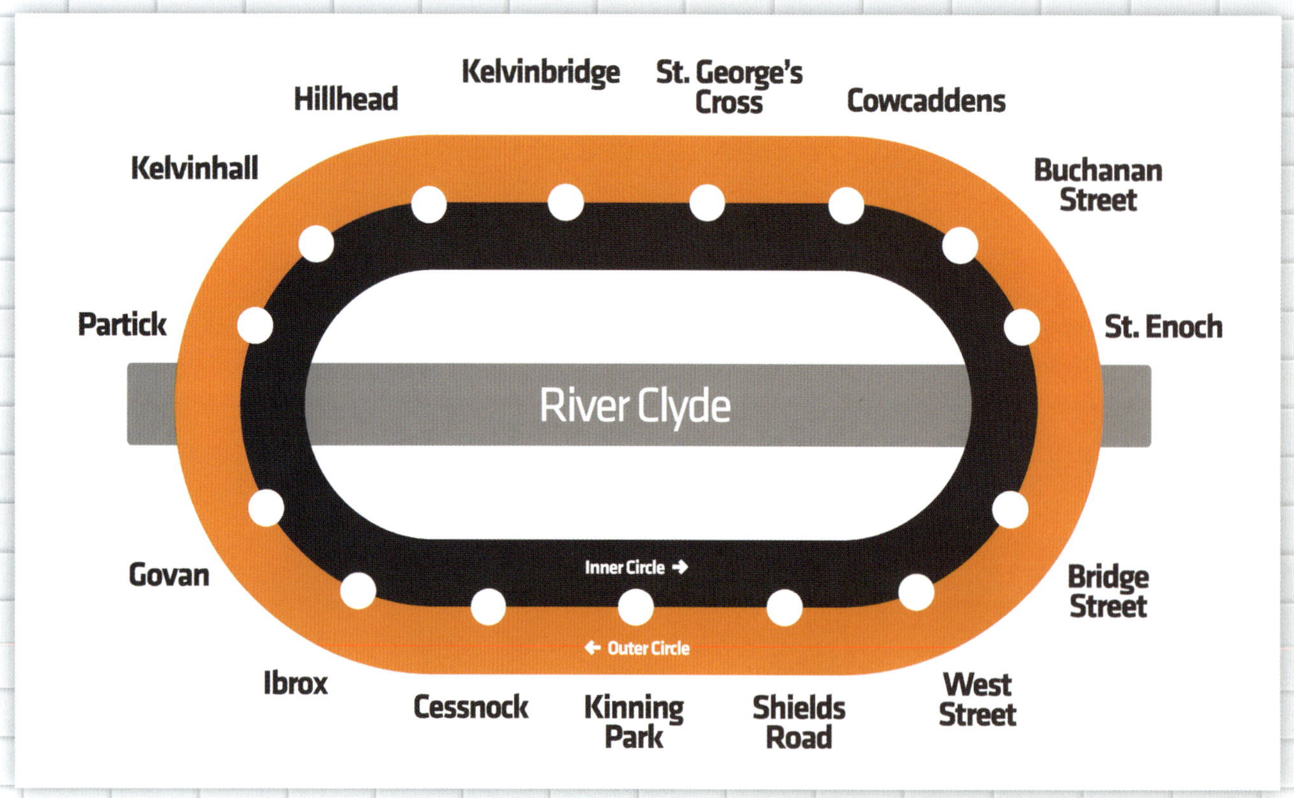
Kelvinbridge
St. George's Cross
Hillhead
Cowcaddens
Kelvinhall
Buchanan Street
Partick
St. Enoch
River Clyde
Govan
Inner Circle →
Bridge Street
← Outer Circle
Ibrox
Cessnock
Kinning Park
Shields Road
West Street

GLASGOW

GLASGOW
Strathclyde Partnership for Transport

System Length	6.5 route miles
Number of Lines	1
Number of Stations	15
Year Opened	1896
Year of Last Expansion	1896 (!)
Annual Ridership	13.1 million (2019)
Subwayness	100% of stations underground

In many ways, Glasgow reminds me of my hometown of Philadelphia: it's a gem with grit. Both cities are known for their quirky local character, self-deprecating humor, and unintelligible accents. And Glasgow, like Philadelphia, was once a huge shipbuilding and industrial center that experienced a painful decline in the second half of the twentieth century but has more recently bounced back as a vibrant, hip, and youthful "small" big city. The two cities also share a fondness for strange delicacies: Glasgow has deep-fried Mars bars, while Philly has scrapple, which is an "everything but the oink" pork product. (Memo to File: The two combined would make an intriguing culinary treat.)

Buchanan Street Entrance

STRATHCLYDE PARTNERSHIP FOR TRANSPORT

Glasgow has a bonnie wee subway that perfectly befits its size and local character. (Locals call it the "subway," and not the "Underground" or the "Tube," as in London.) It consists of but a single circular line 6.5 miles around, and it's entirely underground. The right-side ("Outer Loop") trains run clockwise, and the left-side ("Inner Loop") trains run counterclockwise. Sponsored by the private Glasgow District Subway Company, it opened in 1896, making it the third-oldest system in the world after London and Budapest. In most other cities' subway systems, the radial lines are built first, and if there is a circle line it follows years or even decades later, to allow getting around the city without first having to travel to the center to change lines (cf. Madrid, Moscow, Tokyo, and Beijing).[1] In Glasgow, the circle came first, but despite on-and-off plans over the past century, no radial lines have ever been built.

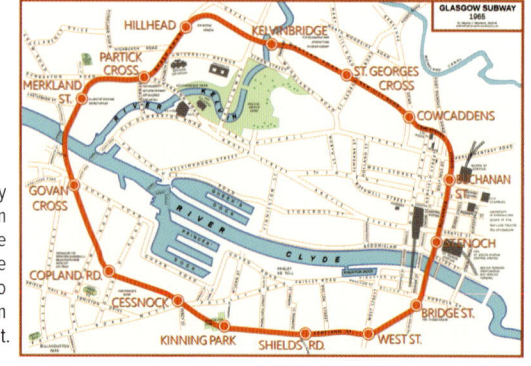

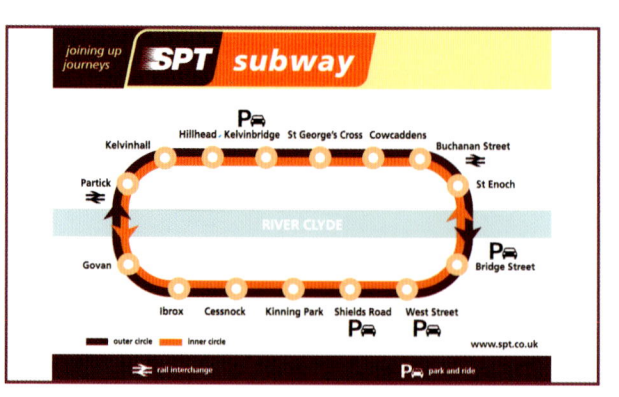

The Glasgow subway map evolved from the 1930s-era style (depicted left) to the 1970s (depicted right) to today, but the system hasn't.

---

[1] The contrast with another city's circle line—Beijing's Line #10—could not be greater. Glasgow's circle line has fifteen stations compared to Beijing's forty-five; it takes fifteen minutes to circumnavigate, compared to 104 minutes in Beijing; and it carries 35,000 daily riders vs. 1.9 million.

GLASGOW

In addition to its small scope, the Glasgow subway is diminutive in scale: it has been characterized as the "world's largest model railway." Everything about it seems tiny: the track gauge is a skinny 4 feet (15 percent narrower than standard gauge), the twin tubes are only 11 feet in diameter, the island platforms are disconcertingly narrow, and the curved car interiors are barely 6 feet high. In circumference, sound, and *shoogle* (the Scots term for the distinctive sway and shake of the cars), riding the Glasgow subway is not unlike sitting in a Whirlpool front-loading dryer, set on low tumble.[2]

The subway serves the heart of the central business district (Buchanan Street and St. Enoch stations) but also some toney neighborhoods to the northwest and some working-class neighborhoods on the south bank of the River Clyde. For example, one of the south-side stations is Ibrox, adjacent to Ibrox Park, home stadium of the vaunted Glasgow Rangers Football Club. On game days it is filled with high-spirited, singing soccer fans, a fair number of whom have had the Breakfast of Champions at the local pub. At such times, passengers are well advised to avoid wearing green and white (the colors of the Rangers' archrival, Celtic Football Club).

When the company decided to develop the subway in the 1890s, electric-powered trains were still a newfangled technology. Instead, they decided on a cable-pulled system, powered from a central steam engine. But it had limited speed (12½ miles per hour), was capacity-constrained, and proved difficult to maintain. Apparently, then (as now) *everybody* complained about cable service! The line was eventually electrified in the mid-1930s after the city acquired it from the private operator, and it was renovated in the late 1970s with replacement cars that were painted a bright orange. Owing to the color of the cars and the configuration of the line, local wags immediately dubbed the subway "A Clockwork Orange," and the name has stuck.

---

[2] With classic Glaswegian humor, the local transit agency (Strathclyde Partnership for Transport) has called its smartphone app the "iShoogle."

STRATHCLYDE PARTNERSHIP FOR TRANSPORT

In preparation for the Commonwealth Games of 2014, the Glasgow firm of Stand Design was hired to create a complete identity rebranding of the old system, with new wayfinding, car livery, maps, and marketing material, much as the MBTA had done for Boston's nearly-as-old system in the mid-1960s. The stations had been a series of drab earth tone ochers, tans, and browns and are now fitted out in a very smart palette of orange, gray, and white.[3] A brand-new fleet of driverless walk-through train sets entered service in 2024, to be followed by midheight platform screens. But despite the cosmetic makeover, it would be prohibitively expensive at this point to try to expand the scale of Glasgow's Victorian-era Lilliputian tunnels and stations.

Kelvinhall before makeover (2006) and after makeover (2014)

[3] Some Glaswegians express nostalgia for the earth tones floors and walls that existed before the makeover; these may be the same sentimentalists who have a predilection for fried Mars Bars...

GLASGOW

Along the station walls, the gray stripes indicate the trains running clockwise, and the orange counterclockwise. Note the size of the passengers relative to the room inside the car.

From street level, most of the station entrances are not stand-alone kiosks, but stairwells embedded in storefronts of commercial buildings or apartment blocks (what in Scotland are nonpejoratively referred to as "tenements"). As a result, the subway entrances are not that conspicuous from the street, and, in some cases, may even be a source of confusion, as in the Kelvinhall Station's entrance shown in the photo to the right.

However, there are several very impressive exceptions. St. Enoch has a delightful turreted Victorian folly by Scots architect James Miller adjacent to the demolished St. Enoch's railway station. It previously served as the headquarters of the Glasgow District Subway Company in the heart of downtown. After being restored and repurposed as a tourist information center, it is now a coffee shop. Immediately adjacent is a graceful and airy contemporary glass pavilion by AHR Architects, reminiscent of Norman Foster's "fosterito" canopied subway entrances in Bilbao:

Cozy interior view of a Glasgow subway car

Subway and subway!

TRANSIT TOURISM | 119

STRATHCLYDE PARTNERSHIP FOR TRANSPORT

Left:
St. Enoch Station entrance and headhouse, Glasgow

Right:
Fosterito entrance to Bilbao Metro Txurdinaga station

Glaswegians seem to take great pride in (and harbor great affection for) their Clockwork Orange; it is almost a mascot for the city. The system has its own official catchphrase, "My Glasgow, My Subway," and Strathclyde Partnership for Transport's website has a section where residents proclaim their devotion to it in video clips. At the new Zaha Hadid–designed Riverside Museum of Transport on the Clyde, one can walk through a full-scale replica of an old station with a vintage car. The subway even has its own music-hall-style anthem, "The Glasgow Underground," with such memorable lyrics as

> The train goes round and round
> You've never lived unless you've been on the Glasgow Underground!

My Glasgow tour guide (through Guiding Architects, an international design-oriented tour service) was Andy Campbell of the aptly named Dress for the Weather Architects. He told me about a hallowed tradition among local college students: a pub crawl called the *Subcrawl*, which involves alighting at each of the fifteen stations and downing a pint at a nearby pub before heading

GLASGOW

on. His firm designed a tour guide pamphlet that maps out not only each station's surrounding architectural and cultural attractions (the Glasgow School of Art and the Kelvingrove Art Museum, for example), but also local pubs with great character, such as the Laurieston, the Lismore, and the Horseshoe Bar. The good news is, if you've been "overserved" and find you've missed your stop, not to worry: it will reappear in due course—like clockwork!

SUMMARY

As idiosyncratic a transit line as any I've ever ridden, Glasgow's subway closely reflects the quirky, friendly, and funny character of the city it has so dutifully served since Queen Victoria's reign. In terms of local character, this small subway runs circles around the much-larger but blander systems serving Tokyo or Beijing. It really needs to be seen to be believed, so, as the locals would say, *"Gaun Yersel!"*[4]

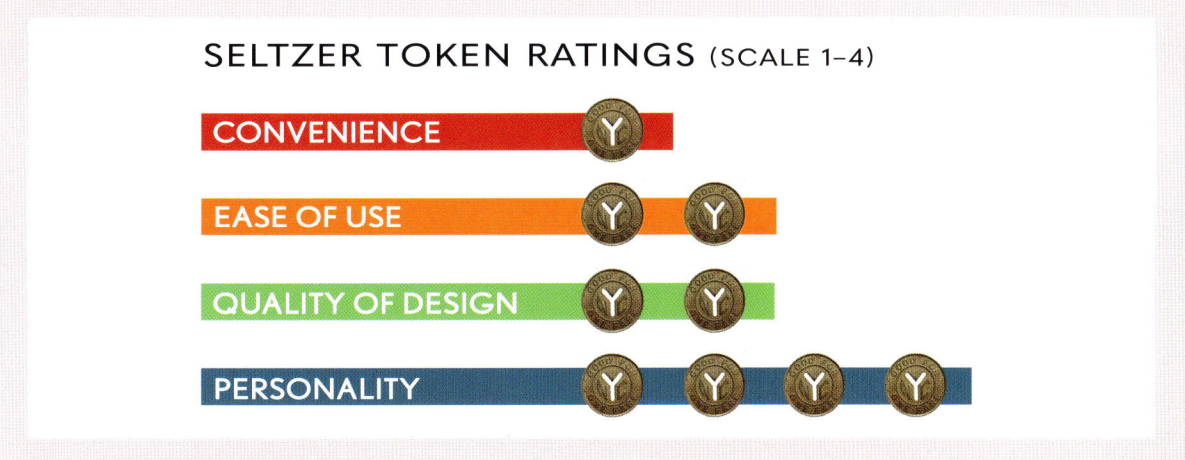

SELTZER TOKEN RATINGS (SCALE 1–4)

CONVENIENCE	1
EASE OF USE	2
QUALITY OF DESIGN	2
PERSONALITY	4

---

4 Glaswegian term meaning "Go for it!"

TRANSIT TOURISM | 121

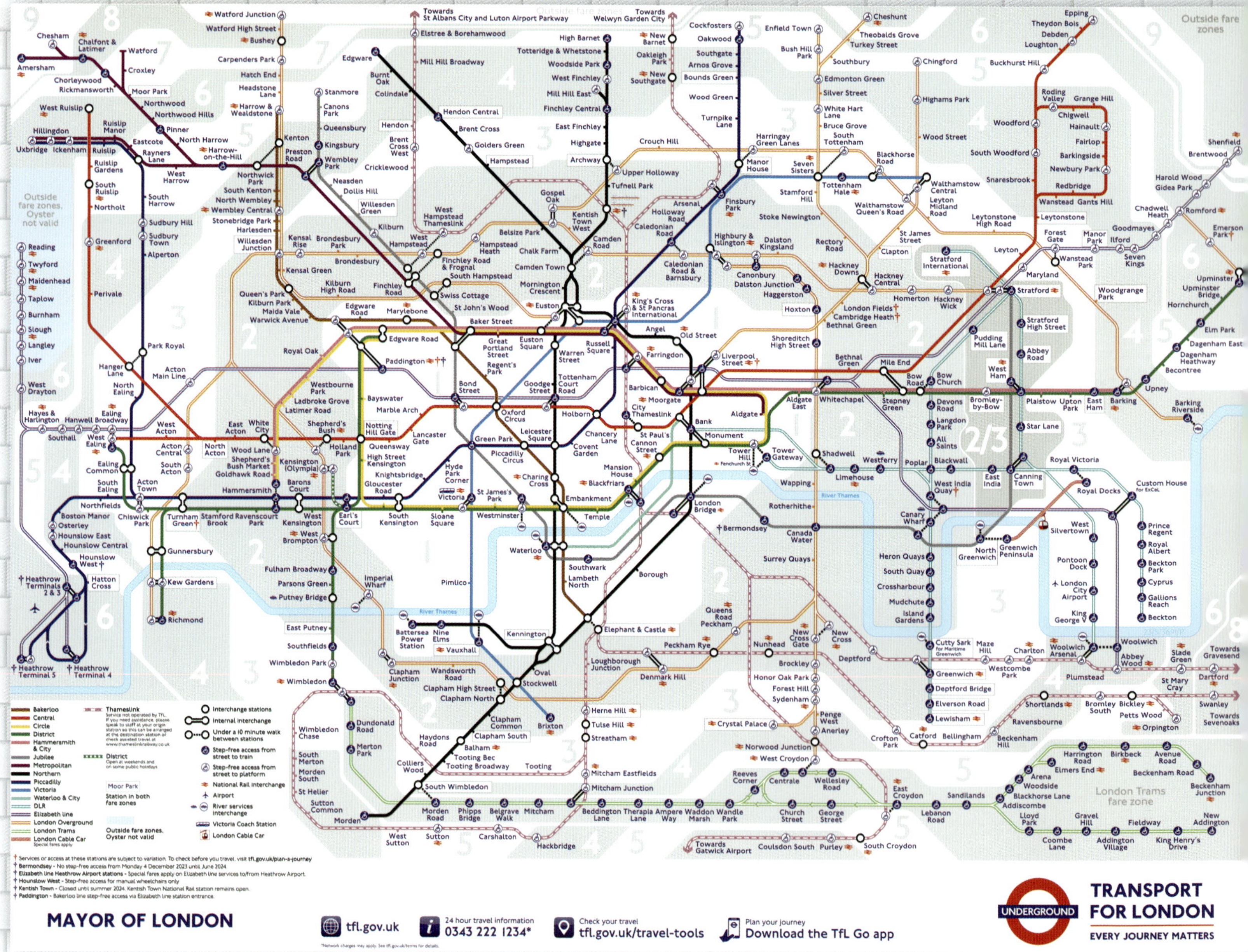

Outside fare zones
Towards St Albans City and Luton Airport Parkway
Towards Welwyn Garden City
London Trams fare zone
Outside fare zones, Oyster not valid
River Thames
Bakerloo
Central
Circle
District
Hammersmith & City
Jubilee
Metropolitan
Northern
Piccadilly
Victoria
Waterloo & City
DLR
Elizabeth line
London Overground
London Trams
London Cable Car
Thameslink
District
Interchange stations
Internal interchange
Under a 10 minute walk between stations
Step-free access from street to train
Step-free access from street to platform
National Rail interchange
Airport
River services interchange
Victoria Coach Station
London Cable Car
Station in both fare zones
Outside fare zones, Oyster not valid
Bermondsey - No step-free access from Monday 4 December 2023 until June 2024.
Hounslow West - Step-free access for manual wheelchairs only
Kentish Town - Closed until summer 2024. Kentish Town National Rail station remains open.
Paddington - Bakerloo line step-free access via Elizabeth line station entrance.
MAYOR OF LONDON
tfl.gov.uk
24 hour travel information
0343 222 1234*
Check your travel
tfl.gov.uk/travel-tools
Plan your journey
Download the TfL Go app
UNDERGROUND
TRANSPORT FOR LONDON
EVERY JOURNEY MATTERS

LONDON
Transport for London (TfL)

System Length	252 route miles[1]
Number of Lines	11[1]
Number of Stations	272[1]
Year Opened	1863
Year of Last Expansion	Northern Line Extension (2021)[1]
Annual Ridership	1.357 billion (2019)
Subwayness	43% of stations underground

I first became acquainted with the Underground when I spent my junior year abroad at the University of Surrey, located in Guildford, about 35 miles southwest of London. Every weekend, I would take British Rail into Waterloo Station and explore the city—not by riding the classic red double-decker buses (whose multiple-destination rolling signboards baffled me), but through the much more comprehensible Tube.

---

[1] The Underground system statistics exclude the Elizabeth Line, which opened in 2022, because it is operated separately by TfL Rail as a commuter rail service with a tunnel through central London.

Notting Hill Gate Station entrance (Central, District, and Circle Lines)

TRANSIT TOURISM

TRANSPORT FOR LONDON

I was so enamored with the Underground and its justly celebrated map that I entered into a wager with two of my classmates that I could memorize the entire system, which at the time (1972) comprised 260 stations and ten lines. I challenged them to look at the system map and pick any two stations, and I would give the most direct route, reciting every station sequentially, including interchanges with other lines.

The stakes for each question were that the winner would be treated to a pint of Double Diamond draught bitter. For the first five rounds, my performance was absolutely flawless: Tooting Bec to Dagenham East, Theydon Bois to Kew Gardens, Knightsbridge to Uxbridge—I *nailed* them all. But then the cumulative effect of the bitters began to take their inevitable toll, impairing my faculties. Try even *saying* "Walthamstow Central" after the fifth pint! Predictably, it ended up being quite an expensive evening for me, and a very rough morning after, struggling to stay awake in statistics class. I had met my Waterloo (change for the Northern Line).

One ancillary benefit of memorizing the Underground map, however, was becoming better acquainted with how English place-names, as expressed in the Tube stops, reveal London's topography and history. Having taken an intro course in Anglo-Saxon—the noble language of *Beowulf* as well as the source of our choicest expletives today—one can begin to recognize the historical context of London: Charing Cross, Elephant & Castle, Marylebone, Southwark—each name reveals a bit of local heritage.[2]

Waterloo Station (Bakerloo Line)

---

[2] A prized possession among my nearly one hundred books about London is Cyril M. Harris's What's in a Name?, explaining the etymology of every Underground station's name.

LONDON

Londoners famously refer to their subway system as the Underground, but this is actually a misnomer, since over half the route mileage is aboveground. Even calling the subterranean portion "the Tube" isn't really accurate, since the system's oldest lines—the District and the Metropolitan, which represent about 20 percent of the tunnels—were excavated using the shallow "cut-and-cover" method rather than through deeper bored cylindrical tunnels.

The Metropolitan—the world's first subway—opened in 1863 as brick tunnels interspersed with open-air trenches. Its purpose was to allow passengers to avoid the enormous surface traffic congestion in central London and provide an easy connection among the capital's major railway termini. The Metropolitan was followed several years later by the District Line, which connected additional railway hubs, and jointly they formed the Circle Line (really a service over preexisting routes rather than a discrete line). But using steam locomotives proved "ill-sooted" to underground travel, to say the least. It was not until electric-traction rail service was introduced in 1890 on the first of several new bored Tube lines that the Underground system dramatically expanded.

Unlike most systems, which identify their lines by color, letter, or number, each Underground line has its own moniker, such as Bakerloo, Piccadilly, Victoria, and Jubilee. For the 150th anniversary of the Underground in 2013, Penguin Books published a twelve-volume set of slim paperback novellas and essays by a dozen authors, each using as a theme one of the Underground Lines.[3] Like the lines themselves, these slender volumes range in length and quality.

---

[3] One of the twelve lines, the East London Line, has since then been reclassified as part of London's "Overground," an inner-city (mostly surface) commuter rail network. And there actually is a thirteenth line, the Mail Rail (London Post Office Railway)—a miniature 6-mile, eight-station line built in the 1920s to transport mail between central London post offices. It no longer is used to carry mail but is now a tourist attraction you can ride on.

TRANSPORT FOR LONDON

From a rider's viewpoint (if not a reader's viewpoint), the most idiosyncratic of the books, and lines, is "The Drain," which is the affectionate (?) nickname given to the Waterloo & City Line. Built in 1898, it shuttles just a mile and a half under the Thames between Waterloo railway terminal and "the City," London's financial district, with no intermediate stops. As I recall from my junior year abroad in the early 1970s, the Drain was used largely by pinstriped gents in curl-brimmed bowlers commuting from their Stockbroker-Tudor villas in Surrey to the City to manipulate the London Interbank Offering Rate, or whatever it is they do there.

Ownership of the various underground lines was consolidated in the first part of the twentieth century, but it was not until Frank Pick, a nondesigner, became publicity director (and ultimately chief executive) of London Transport—the holding company for the tube lines—that a uniform design vocabulary was applied to all elements of the system. Under Pick's leadership, the ubiquitous application of the logo, the lettering, the map, and the poster art together established the Underground's unparalleled reputation among world subway systems for excellence in design. Its logo is, of course, the world-famous roundel (⊖), first introduced in 1908. It was standardized over the following two decades, and the icon is now so strongly identified with getting around London that Transport for London (TfL), the regional transportation authority established in 2000, uses it to designate all manner of transport in the capital region: buses, Overground, trams, taxis, ferries, even bicycles.

LONDON

A similar brand recognition attaches to the Underground's beloved typeface, designed by Edward Johnston in 1913. It is a clean, legible font now known as Johnston Sans-Serif (*sans* coming from the French, "without," and *serifs* being those little framusses at the tops and bottoms of a letterform). I consider myself a man of letters, and in fact my two favorites in this type family are the very distinctive lowercase "l" and "g." The eighteenth-century lexicographer Samuel Johnson famously wrote, "When a man is tired of London, he is tired of life." The obverse of that aphorism could apply equally to this typeface: "When a man is tired of Johnston, he is tired of London." At one hundred years old, Johnston Sans-Serif remains remarkably fresh, and it is so closely associated with the British capital that it has been called "London's handwriting."

ABCDEFGHIJKLMN abcdefghijklmnopq
OPQRSTUVWXYZ rstuvwxyz 123456
7890 (&£.,:;!?-*"")

"London's Handwriting": Johnston's sans-serif font

The original Tube map was designed on a lark by a young London Transport draughtsman named Harry Beck in 1931. It was adopted as the official system map in 1933 and has been a veritable design icon ever since. Inspired by the spare elegance and economy of electrical-engineering diagrams, it was the first transport map to recognize that its goal should be *clarity* rather than *geographic accuracy*. Though its design may seem obvious now to subway riders around the world, it was a major design innovation at the time. Every line on the map was drawn at 45- or 90-degree angles. The dense cobweb of lines in central London was visually expanded, with the outer branches condensed to improve legibility. However, be warned that "objects on the map are

TRANSPORT FOR LONDON

farther than they appear." If you are transferring lines, don't be misled by the single disc marking an interchange station: many transfers require hefty hikes through circular passageways for what seems like furlongs—Bank, Charing Cross, and Paddington are among the worst offenders.

The original edition of Beck's Underground map

With the addition of new services over the last three decades via tube (Jubilee), tram (Croydon), light rail (Docklands), and commuter rail (Overground, and now Elizabeth Line), the system map has gotten increasingly busy, encumbering Mr. Beck's pristine original design. The zebra-shaded fare zones are a particular distraction (see the facing page at beginning of the chapter). The most recent major expansion is the Crossrail project, d/b/a the Elizabeth Line, which commenced operations in 2022. It is a 25-mile-long crosstown commuter rail line, half in tunnel, with nine

LONDON

new underground stations in London, linking Reading and Heathrow in the west to Stratford and Shenfield in the east. Following my taxonomy in this book's introduction, the Elizabeth Line is more properly viewed as a commuter rail line than a true subway line. But having ridden it and seen the handsome new deep-level stations, it is definitely worth experiencing, even if it does clutter Mr. Beck's elegant map.

I still long for the simplicity and elegance of the pocket map from my student days in England in the early 1970s, reproduced below, whose gridlines helped one locate stations listed in the alphabetical order index on the reverse side.

Tube map, 1973

TRANSPORT FOR LONDON

In terms of architecture, most of the Tube stations at platform level share a similar cylindrical design as a result of the shield technique used to excavate the tunnels. Aboveground, the look of the headhouses (entry structures) has evolved over time. In the first two decades of the twentieth century, the architect Leslie Green designed some fifty Tube station entrances for the Piccadilly, Bakerloo, and Northern Lines in an art nouveau style. His signature look was a façade clad in oxblood-glazed terracotta brick (see Covent Garden below). In the 1920s and '30s, over three dozen station headhouses were given a restrained but stylish—and, at the time, modern—look by London architect Charles Holden (see Tooting Bec below). The handsome Portland limestone entries were part of London Transport's strategy to convey a positive image to the riding public.

Left:
Covent Garden Station
(Piccadilly Line), 1907

Right:
Tooting Bec Station
(Northern Line), 1926

130 | EUROPE—ENGLAND

LONDON

London emphatically broke the traditional mold on station architecture with its eleven-station Jubilee Line extension, opened in 1999, which provides access to historically underserved South London. Each station is designed by a different architect, and most of the stations have impressive, muscular forms revealing the dramatic structural engineering of these deep stations. Two of the best in my opinion are Westminster (Michael Hopkins) and Canary Wharf (Norman Foster).

Left: Westminster Station (Jubilee Line)

Right: Canary Wharf Station (Jubilee Line)

Artwork on the system is a different matter. Transport for London's "Art on the Underground" program sponsors temporary installations of artwork in some of the system's stations. But unlike the subways in New York, Stockholm, or Brussels, only a small fraction of London's Underground stations have permanent art installations. Among the best are Tottenham Court Road and Charing Cross. At TCR, bright tile mosaic murals by Sir Eduardo Paolozzi from the 1980s contrast with more-recent, boldly colored geometric murals by French artist Daniel Buren. At Charing Cross, large reproductions of paintings from the nearby National Portrait Gallery are displayed on the Bakerloo Line platforms, along with murals on the Northern Line platforms depicting in the style of

TRANSIT TOURISM | 131

magnified woodcuts medieval scenes of building the Eleanor Cross.[4] The new 1.5-mile Northern Line Extension, which opened in 2021, has very large-scale artwork designed specifically for the two new stations. But major art installations have been more the exception than the rule in London.

Platform wall decorations at Tottenham Court Road Station (Central Line) and Charing Cross Station (Northern Line)

Instead, it is the commissioned wall posters that have established the Underground's global artistic reputation. Starting in the 1920s, these posters have consistently been at the vanguard of graphic design. I am particularly drawn to the offset chromolithography posters from the interwar period, with their bold blocks of color showing places one can visit by the Tube or by bus—often enhanced by captions using Johnston Sans Serif. The same technique was used extensively for British railway travel posters in the interwar years.

---

4 Charing Cross was one of twelve commemorative statues that King Edward I erected following the death of his wife, Eleanor of Castile, with each cross marking where the funeral cortege stopped overnight on its way back from Nottinghamshire to London.

LONDON

A Century of Excellence in London Transport Poster Design

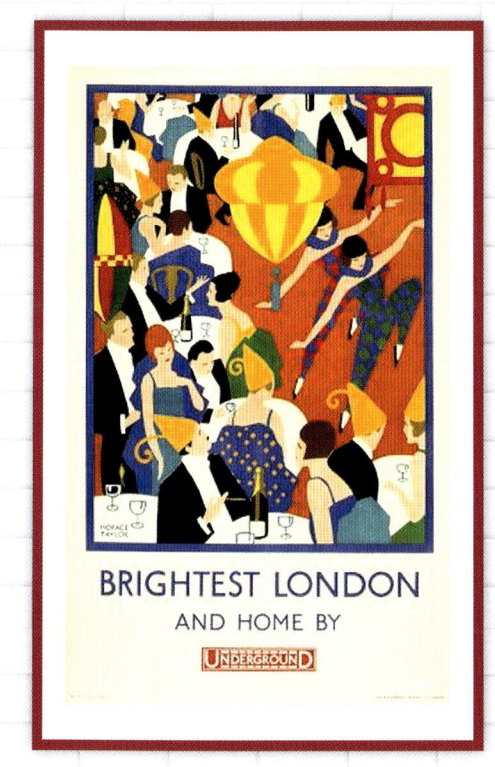

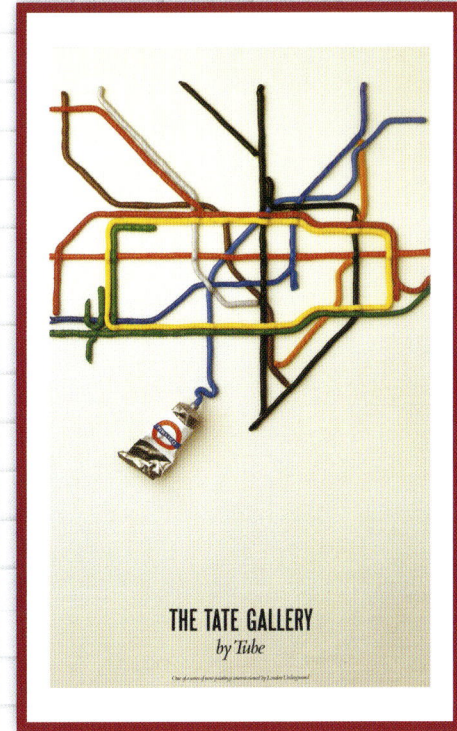

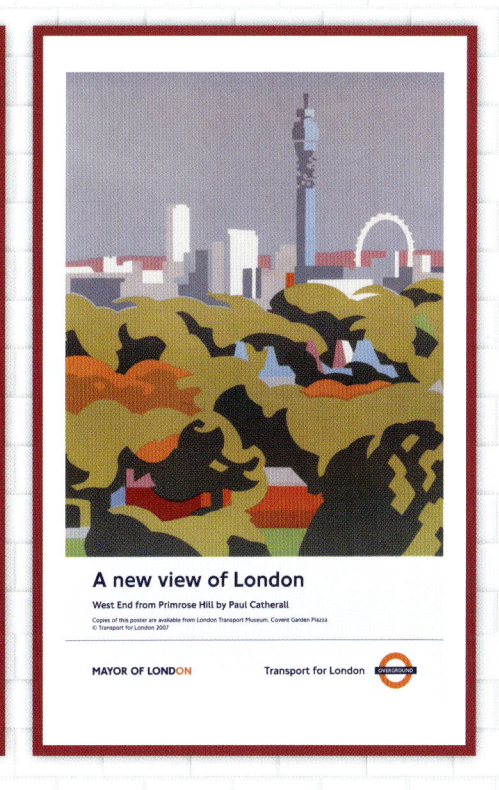

Brightest London and Home by Underground,
Horace Taylor, 1924

The Tate Gallery by Tube,
David Booth, 1987

A new view of London,
Paul Catherall, 2007

TRANSPORT FOR LONDON

Among the London Underground's most emblematic design features are its *moquettes*, the wonderfully varied (and durable) woven fabric patterns covering the seats on trains and buses. May I commend to your attention Andrew Martin's *Seats of London*, which is an encyclopedic and surprisingly entertaining account of Underground seat coverings over the last century.

Vibrant moquette seat covers on a London Underground car

Finally, although not strictly part of the Underground, the London Transport Museum in Covent Garden is a must-see, even for those who are not transit enthusiasts. It is around the corner from the Covent Garden stop on the Piccadilly Line. For an impromptu fitness test, try climbing the 193 vertiginous spiral steps from the platform level to the street exit, rather than taking the lift. The museum has fascinating exhibits, and one that I particularly enjoy is a video display that graphically illustrates the expansion of the Tube over time, almost like watching the unbridled but rectilinear growth of a multicolored kudzu.

LONDON

SUMMARY

Just as one can't admit to having a favorite child, one really shouldn't claim to have a favorite subway system. But if hypothetically one *were* to . . . well, let's just say that London would be a strong contender. There is so much that is distinctive about the Underground, going beyond the tubular shape of many of the stations. There's the universally recognized roundel logo, the century-old typeface, which still looks fresh, the world-renowned schematic map, the moquette seating fabrics with their eye-catching patterns, and the marvelous posters that have set the standard for graphic design over the last century. And, contrary to most Londoners, I don't Mind the Gap; in fact, I rather like it.

In a way, the Underground reflects some of the best features of the English national character: understatement, tidiness, crispness of expression, and a sense of tradition. Taken collectively, the Underground is more closely associated with the city it serves than any other subway system in the world.

SELTZER TOKEN RATINGS (SCALE 1–4)

CONVENIENCE	4
EASE OF USE	4
QUALITY OF DESIGN	4
PERSONALITY	4

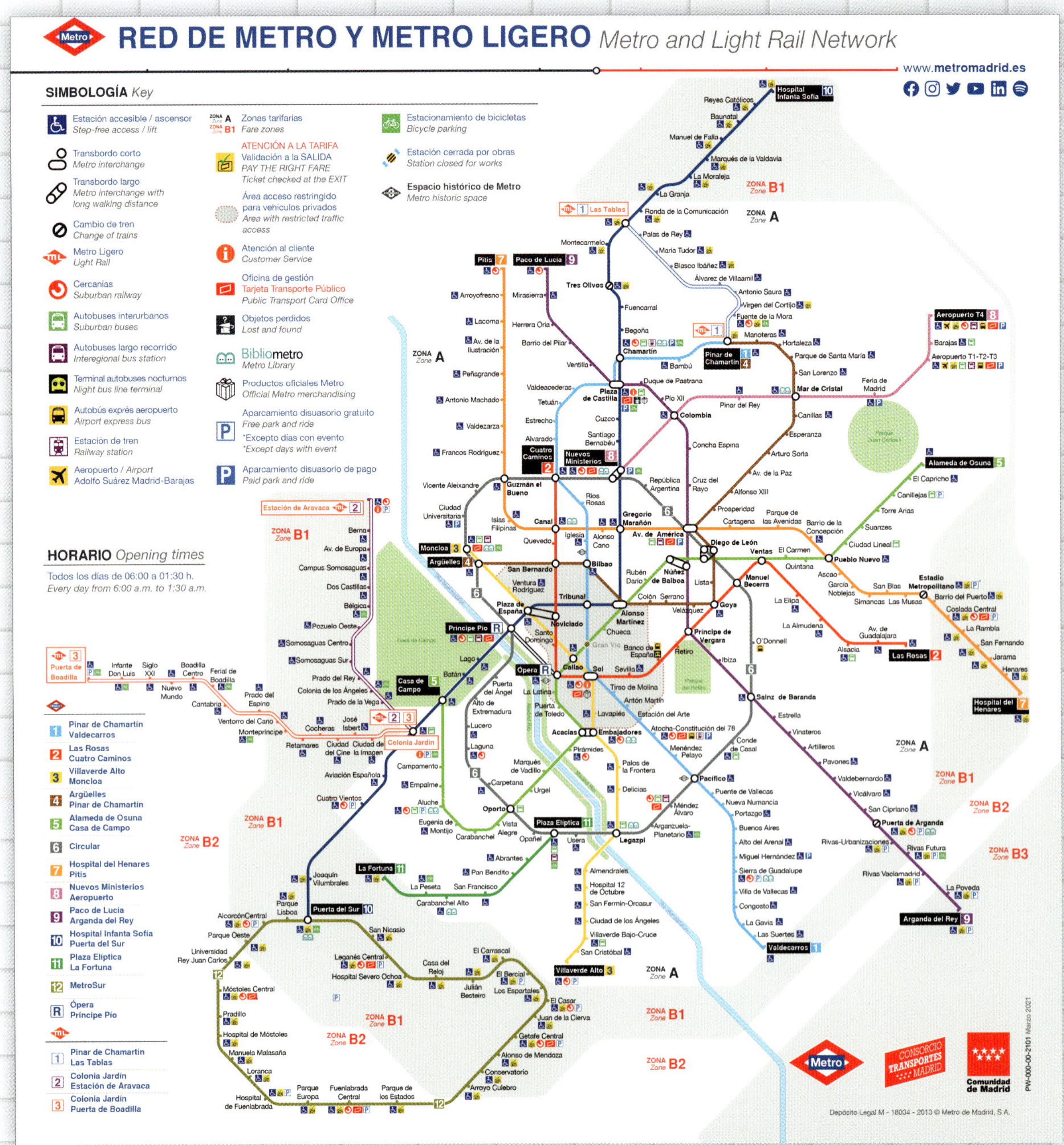

Metro
RED DE METRO Y METRO LIGERO Metro and Light Rail Network
www.metromadrid.es
SIMBOLOGÍA Key
Estación accesible / ascensor
Step-free access / lift
Transbordo corto
Metro interchange
Transbordo largo
Metro interchange with long walking distance
Cambio de tren
Change of trains
Metro Ligero
Light Rail
Cercanías
Suburban railway
Autobuses interurbanos
Suburban buses
Autobuses largo recorrido
Interegional bus station
Terminal autobuses nocturnos
Night bus line terminal
Autobús exprés aeropuerto
Airport express bus
Estación de tren
Railway station
Aeropuerto / Airport
Adolfo Suárez Madrid-Barajas
Zonas tarifarias
Fare zones
ATENCIÓN A LA TARIFA
Validación a la SALIDA
PAY THE RIGHT FARE
Ticket checked at the EXIT
Área acceso restringido para vehículos privados
Area with restricted traffic access
Atención al cliente
Customer Service
Oficina de gestión Tarjeta Transporte Público
Public Transport Card Office
Objetos perdidos
Lost and found
Bibliometro
Metro Library
Productos oficiales Metro
Official Metro merchandising
Aparcamiento disuasorio gratuito
Free park and ride
*Excepto días con evento
*Except days with event
Aparcamiento disuasorio de pago
Paid park and ride
Estacionamiento de bicicletas
Bicycle parking
Estación cerrada por obras
Station closed for works
Espacio histórico de Metro
Metro historic space
HORARIO Opening times
Todos los días de 06:00 a 01:30 h.
Every day from 6:00 a.m. to 1:30 a.m.
1 Pinar de Chamartín – Valdecarros
2 Las Rosas – Cuatro Caminos
3 Villaverde Alto – Moncloa
4 Argüelles – Pinar de Chamartín
5 Alameda de Osuna – Casa de Campo
6 Circular
7 Hospital del Henares – Pitis
8 Nuevos Ministerios – Aeropuerto
9 Paco de Lucía – Arganda del Rey
10 Hospital Infanta Sofía – Puerta del Sur
11 Plaza Elíptica – La Fortuna
12 MetroSur
R Ópera – Príncipe Pío
1 Pinar de Chamartín – Las Tablas
2 Colonia Jardín – Estación de Aravaca
3 Colonia Jardín – Puerta de Boadilla
ZONA A
ZONA B1
ZONA B2
ZONA B3
CONSORCIO TRANSPORTES MADRID
Comunidad de Madrid
PW-000-00-2101 Marzo 2021
Depósito Legal M - 18004 - 2013 © Metro de Madrid, S.A.

MADRID

MADRID
Metro de Madrid, S.A.

System Length	182 route miles
Number of Lines	13 (excludes light rail)
Number of Stations	291
Year Opened	1919
Year of Last Expansion	2015
Annual Ridership	678M (2019)
Subwayness	97% of stations underground

Despite being one of the most extensive systems in the world, with some truly spectacular architecture, the Metro de Madrid is a hidden gem, not often included on tourist itineraries. It may lack the global renown of the Paris Métro or London Underground, but its design suggests influences by both cities' iconic subway systems. Like Paris, Madrid's stations are spaced very close together, the platforms are of shorter length, and the older stations have gracefully vaulted ceilings covered with white ceramic tiles. Like London, Madrid's trains operate on the left-hand side, the agency has a distinctive, iconic logo, and the schematic system map is recognizably "Tubular." Metro

Serrano station entrance (Line 4)

TRANSIT TOURISM | 137

METRO DE MADRID, S.A.

de Madrid's logo was devised in 1919 by noted local architect Antonio Palacios, who also designed the initial stations on Line 1 and many public edifices in Madrid. The logo is a diamond-shaped version of the familiar Underground roundel but also reflects a Parisian look. Palacios had visited Paris to inspect the Métro and surely knew of the Tube; perhaps Madrid's subway is actually the love child of the Paris Métro and the London Underground?

Paris Metro + London Underground = Madrid Metro Logo ?

The Metro celebrated its centenary in 2019 by mounting historical displays along the original Line 1 stations. King Felipe VI replicated the inaugural trip his great-grandfather King Alfonso XIII took embarking from Puerta del Sol, the original terminus. The first 2.5-mile route had eight stations, including one now-decommissioned stop, Chamberí, that today is a Metro museum. The system expanded incrementally over the ensuing decades, growing to five lines with 16 miles and fifty-one stations by 1945. But in contrast to the other more highly developed European subway systems, Madrid's Metro has had a delayed growth spurt, not expanding dramatically after the war until the 1990s and 2000s. For example, just in the four-year period from 2003 to 2007, Madrid added 48 route miles and ninety new stations. Today, with 182 system route miles, it has now surpassed Paris among European systems, behind only London and Moscow, and ranks among the Top 10 systems worldwide in number of stations.

MADRID

The twelve lines (thirteen, if you include the half-mile shuttle line between Ópera and Principe Pio) weave their way through Madrid's urban fabric, connecting at numerous points. In fact, the lines overlap so much that in seven cases they intersect another route twice[1]—and that excludes their fourteen interchange stations with the Line 6 "Circular" route. In addition, Madrid has a second, disconnected circle line, Line 12, called MetroSur, dangling like an expensive bracelet at the southernmost end of the system to serve suburban communities. And a very expensive bracelet it is: at the time of its construction, it was the most costly public works project in Europe.

The system's capital investment continues, most notably with the current work extending Line 11 diagonally across the entire breadth of the city, 20 miles altogether. So ubiquitous is the subway today that Metro de Madrid S.A., the governmental operator, reports that over 75 percent of Madrileños now live within 600 meters of a station.

Left: Ornate tile work at Retiro station, Line 2

Right: Train pulling into Banco de España station, Line 2

---

[1] For those keeping score at home: the double intersections are Lines 1 and 2, Lines 1 and 4, Lines 1 and 10, Lines 2 and 5, Lines 3 and 5, Lines 4 and 5, and Lines 5 and 10.

METRO DE MADRID, S.A.

The very heart of the system is the city's epicenter of Puerta del Sol, a semicircular plaza where three lines interchange. Madrid was established as the nation's capital in the sixteenth century because of its centrality on the Iberian Peninsula, and it is here at Puerta del Sol that one finds the marker for *Kilometre Zero*, a brass pavement plaque from which all road distances from the capital are measured. Originally the medieval city's eastern ("Sun") gate, today it is the site of cafés, shops, and huge gatherings—everything from social protests to annual New Year's Eve celebrations. At the juncture of eight major thoroughfares, Puerta del Sol feels like a neon-lite version of London's Piccadilly Circus aboveground, and a nuisance-lite version of New York's Times Square below. And like Times Square, it too is served by the #1, #2, and #3 trains.

The Metro has many attractions for the keen-eyed traveler. It regularly sponsors musical and theatrical performances in stations and has created themed stations such as the Art station (Atocha), located near three of Madrid's outstanding art museums: the Prado, the Reina Sofía Museum, and the Thyssen-Bornemisza Museum. Chamartin, at a major railway hub, displays meticulously restored classic subway carriages from the first half of the twentieth century. One station, Retiro, has its own art gallery—ExpoMetro—presenting rotating exhibits of contemporary artists.

At Opera, a display of excavated archaeology sites exhibits a fountain and underground aqueduct dating back to the tenth

Puerta del Sol station—Madrid's "Times Square" (Lines 1, 2, and 3)

MADRID

century, when Madrid was under Moorish rule. Goya station on Lines 2 and 4 has reproductions on view of masterpieces by—who else?—Francisco Goya. The park at Plaza de España features statues of Spain's most celebrated author, Miguel de Cervantes, along with characters from his epic tale *Don Quixote*. Metro de Madrid has decorated the station beneath the Plaza with wall graphics displaying the complete 345,000-word text of this masterpiece—a good way to while away the hours in the event your train is running late, exceedingly late. For those seeking more portable reading matter, the subway has its own lending library, Bibliometros, located at a dozen stations.

Below: "Somewhere in La Mancha, in a place whose name I do not care to remember..."; so begins *Don Quixote*—if you can read the fine print on the platform wall...

Plaza de España station (Line 3) featuring the words of Don Quixote

TRANSIT TOURISM | 141

METRO DE MADRID, S.A.

My superb tour guide, Pablo Alvarez de Toledo Müller, director of the Arts Department at Nebrija University in Madrid, took me to the "ghost station" of Chamberí, one of the original stops from 1919 mentioned previously. It closed in the mid-1960s but has reopened as a transit history museum. As trains hurtle by behind protective Plexiglas walls along the platform's edge, you can stroll the platform and see advertisements and directional signs mothballed from a century ago.

Chamberí station museum (Line 1)

Tirso de Molina station (Line 1). Architect Antonio Palacios was inspired by the Paris Metro in his design.

EUROPE—SPAIN

MADRID

While the older stations are beautiful, a number of the stations on the newer lines have dramatic architecture rivaling any other subway system in the world. Nuevos Ministerios shows a mural over the main concourse of Madrid's skyline at twilight—and the columns show disconcertingly large eyes peering at the traveler.

Two views within the Nuevos Ministerios station (Line 10)

METRO DE MADRID, S.A.

Left:
Puerta del Sur station (Line 10)

Right:
Arganzuela-Planetario station, Line 6

Left:
Portazgo station (Line 1), with bold graphics on its walls

Right:
Historic subway trains on display at Chamartín station (Lines 1 and 10)

144 | EUROPE—SPAIN

MADRID

And, boldly, Metro de Madrid has welcomed street art into the subway—but not in the form of unauthorized graffiti. Under the "Line Zero" street art initiative, Metro sponsored an enormous mural by two street artists commemorating the late flamenco guitarist Paco de Lucia, who lived near the station now named for him along the new Line 9 extension.

Between Two Universes by street artists Okuda and Rosch333

METRO DE MADRID, S.A.

In addition to its first-rate art and architecture, Metro's wayfinding graphics are uniformly superb throughout. The current eye-pleasing map, adopted in 2013, replaced after just six years a highly abstract but lowly regarded map by a Spanish graphic designer. In this respect, it parallels New York City's similar unhappy experiment with Massimo Vignelli's overly schematic and largely indecipherable subway map. Between Madrid's new map and refreshed station signage, it is very easy to find one's way through the system's fifty interchange stations. The consistently high-quality "design language" carries over to the company's annual report (thoughtfully translated into English and available online for the truly dedicated), which presents colorful charts showing many of the key performance indicators for the system.

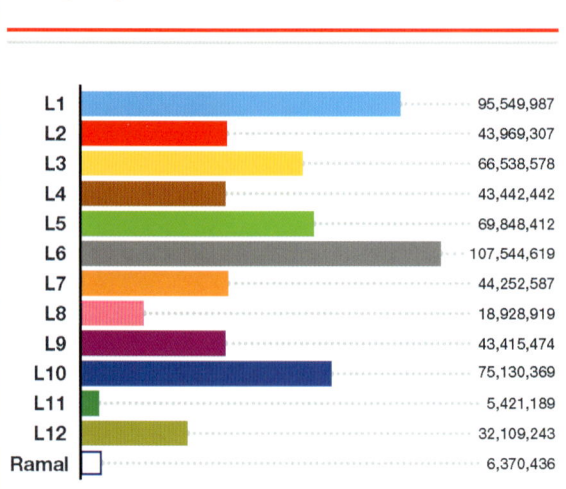

Left: Line 6 route map

Right: Excerpt from Metro de Madrid Annual Report (2018)

Passengers by line

Line	Passengers
L1	95,549,987
L2	43,969,307
L3	66,538,578
L4	43,442,442
L5	69,848,412
L6	107,544,619
L7	44,252,587
L8	18,928,919
L9	43,415,474
L10	75,130,369
L11	5,421,189
L12	32,109,243
Ramal	6,370,436

146 | EUROPE—SPAIN

MADRID

SUMMARY

As one of Europe's largest systems, the Madrid Metro is not only an impressive transportation network; it also has become a cultural icon for Spain's capital city. It serves virtually every neighborhood with fast, convenient service. Its stations range from gracefully vaulted white-tiled stops built a century ago to bold new architectural spaces in the most-recent extensions, unified by smart, clean wayfinding and signage. And the rhomboid-shaped Metro logo has become to Madrid what the Underground roundel is to London: an immediately recognized identifier. I predict that in coming years, the system will be as closely associated with the image of Madrid as the Métro and Underground are to Paris and London. This is easily in the running for one of my favorite metro systems worldwide!

SELTZER TOKEN RATINGS (SCALE 1–4)

CONVENIENCE	4
EASE OF USE	4
QUALITY OF DESIGN	4
PERSONALITY	4

TRANSIT TOURISM | 147

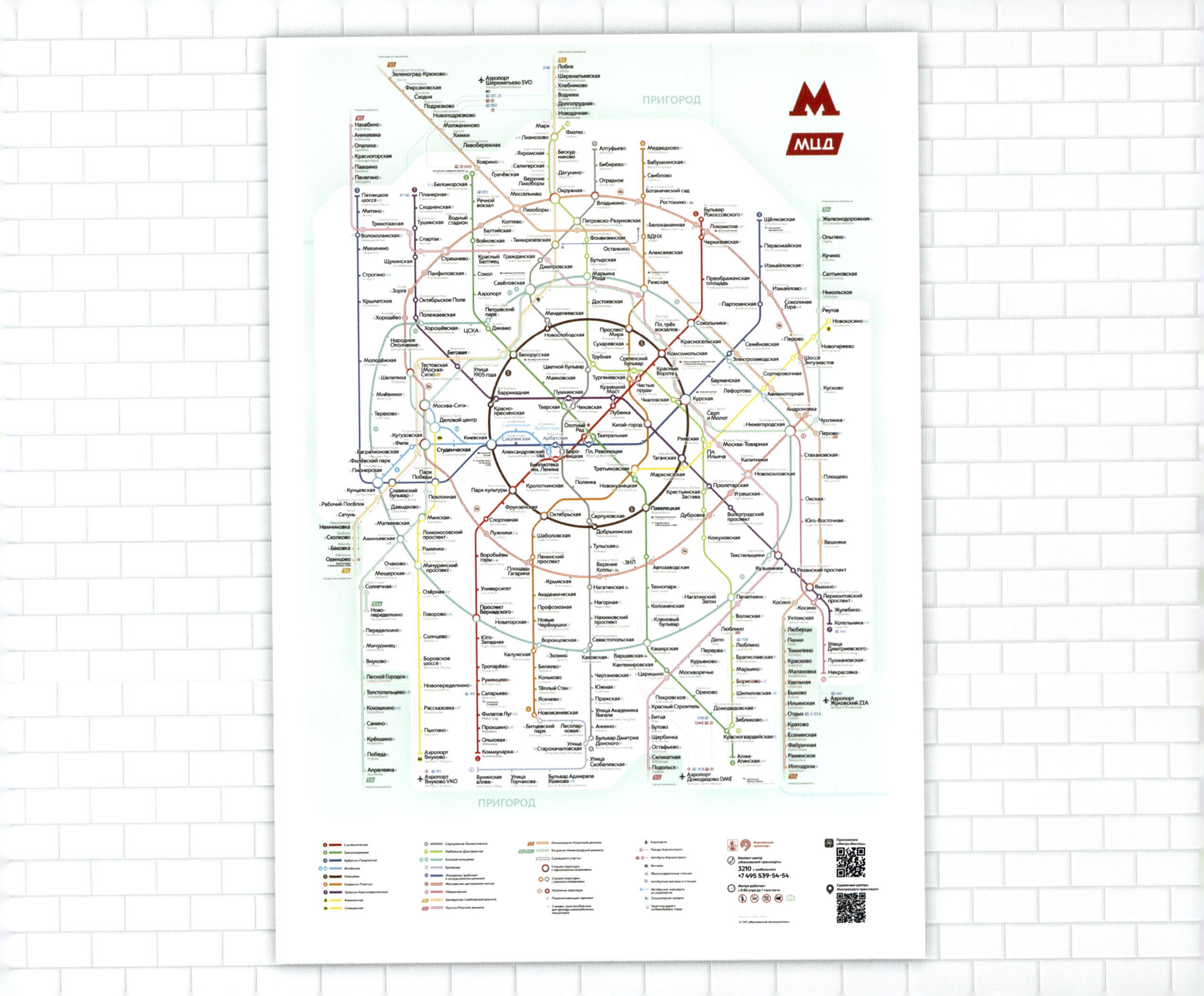

М
МЦД
ПРИГОРОД
Зеленоград-Крюково
Фирсановская
Сходня
Подрезково
Новоподрезково
Молжаниново
Химки
Левобережная
Аэропорт Шереметьево SVO
Лобня
Шереметьевская
Хлебниково
Водники
Долгопрудная
Новодачная
Марк
Лианозово
Физтех
Нахабино
Аникеевка
Опалиха
Красногорская
Павшино
Пенягино
Пятницкое шоссе
Митино
Волоколамская
Мякинино
Строгино
Крылатское
Молодёжная
Кунцевская
Рабочий Посёлок
Сетунь
Немчиновка
Сколково
Баковка
Одинцово
Планерная
Сходненская
Тушинская
Спартак
Щукинская
Речной вокзал
Ховрино
Беломорская
Водный стадион
Войковская
Сокол
Аэропорт
Динамо
Белорусская
Маяковская
Тверская
Пушкинская
Чеховская
Охотный Ряд
Театральная
Площадь Революции
Библиотека им. Ленина
Боровицкая
Александровский сад
Арбатская
Смоленская
Киевская
Кутузовская
Москва-Сити
Деловой центр
Выставочная
Студенческая
Парк Победы
Славянский бульвар
Алтуфьево
Бибирево
Отрадное
Владыкино
Петровско-Разумовская
Медведково
Бабушкинская
Свиблово
Ботанический сад
ВДНХ
Алексеевская
Рижская
Проспект Мира
Сухаревская
Тургеневская
Китай-город
Лубянка
Кузнецкий Мост
Чистые пруды
Красные Ворота
Комсомольская
Курская
Таганская
Павелецкая
Добрынинская
Октябрьская
Парк культуры
Кропоткинская
Фрунзенская
Спортивная
Воробьёвы горы
Университет
Проспект Вернадского
Юго-Западная
Тропарёво
Румянцево
Саларьево
Филатов Луг
Прокшино
Ольховая
Коммунарка
Щёлковская
Первомайская
Измайловская
Партизанская
Семёновская
Электрозаводская
Бауманская
Авиамоторная
Шоссе Энтузиастов
Новогиреево
Новокосино
Перово
Железнодорожная
Ольгино
Кучино
Салтыковская
Никольское
Реутов
Кусково
Чухлинка
Выхино
Жулебино
Котельники
Люберцы
Раменское
Ипподром
Аэропорт Жуковский ZIA
Аэропорт Внуково VKO
Аэропорт Домодедово DME
Бунинская аллея
Улица Горчакова
Бульвар Адмирала Ушакова
Улица Скобелевская
Бульвар Дмитрия Донского
Алма-Атинская
Красногвардейская
Домодедовская
Царицыно
Каширская
Коломенская
Технопарк
Автозаводская
Кожуховская
Печатники
Марьино
Братиславская
Люблино
Подольск
ПРИГОРОД

MOSCOW

MOSCOW*
Moscovsky Metropoliten

System Length[1]	286 route miles
Number of Lines	14
Number of Stations	263
Year Opened	1935
Year of Last Expansion	2023
Annual Ridership	2.5 billion (2019)
Subwayness	93% of stations underground

top: the Moscow subway logo, *bottom*: Lukhmanovskaya station (Line 15)

*Travel essay *readers* rightfully expect that travel essay *writers* actually will have traveled to the places they assay. That generally has been the case for *Transit Tourism*. However, owing to a combination of Acts of God (pandemic's disruption of vacation travel plans) and Acts of Goon (Putin's invasion of Ukraine), my carefully arranged trip to Moscow, where I was to sample its subway, had to be indefinitely postponed. Indeed, the State Department strongly advises US citizens

---

1 The system length, station count, and "subwayness" metrics exclude the Moscow Central Circle Line, which is a surface commuter rail line, and a short monorail segment more akin to a people mover.

TRANSIT TOURISM | 149

MOSCOVSKY METROPOLITEN

no to visit Russia, as of this writing. Still, such is the celebrity of the Moscow Metro that it could hardly be left out of a subway travel book.

Moscow's Metro is impressive in so many respects. With fifteen lines, it is the world's sixth-longest (271 miles) and one of its busiest systems, carrying 2.5 billion annual riders. But what truly sets the Moscow Metro apart is its unique architectural style, shaped by Russian technology, aesthetics, and ideology.

The construction of the Metro itself is an epic story. The initial line of 6 miles and thirteen stations was completed in just two years in 1935, using what has been euphemistically called "volunteer labor" responding to the patriotic call of Comrade Stalin's Second Five-Year Plan. This first subway line (the "Red Line," of course!) was followed by three more lines in the late 1930s and—incredibly—a fourth new line plus an extension to an existing line constructed in the midst of World War II. As one author observed, an avowed purpose of the Moscow Metro was to show the superiority of Communist labor. And with the meager wages, exceptionally long hours, and hazardous conditions, the Soviets demonstrated they far surpassed the capitalist West in their ability to exploit workers.[2]

Today, the system consists of thirteen mostly radial lines, each intersected both by inner and outer circle lines. It is almost entirely underground and is the deepest of the world's major subway systems. The Moscow Metro has over seventy stations located 100 feet or deeper underground, compared to London's Tube, which has only sixteen stations at that depth, or the New York City subway (just a handful). Some of Moscow's stations are considerably deeper, such as Park Pobedy on Line 3, which at 275 feet is the world's third-deepest station—the equivalent

---

[2] Benson Bobrick, *Labyrinths of Iron: A History of World Subways* (Newsweek Books, 1982).

MOSCOW

of a twenty-story building.[3] The depth is attributable to factors more geotechnical in nature (sandy soil, soft gravel, underground streams) than geopolitical (air-raid shelters). The Metro has expanded by an average of two dozen stations each decade since then through a combination of extensions and new routes.

Train at Kuznetsky Most (bridge) station (Line 7)

---

[3] For the curious, officially the world's deepest station is Kyiv's Arsenalna (346 feet), followed by St. Petersburg's Admiralteyskaya (282 feet). Pyongyang's two subway lines are reportedly 360 feet underground but—as with the official North Korean press release that late Dear Leader Kim Il-Sung shot an astounding 38 strokes under par on his *very first* golf outing at the opening of the Pyongyang Golf Club—this claim would benefit from independent verification.

MOSCOVSKY METROPOLITEN

And then there is the intriguing matter of the mysterious "Metro-2"—a separate, supersecret metro line that purportedly was built in the 1960s. Never officially confirmed (or denied) by the Russian government, it is said to connect the Kremlin and other key government installations with an underground "city" built 1,000 feet beneath an outlying neighborhood, and to be capable of housing 10,000 people, presumably keeping them safe from nuclear attack. This is Moscow's version of the "Greenbrier" bunker in West Virginia (the not-so-secret fallout shelter constructed in 1962 to house members of Congress if Washington fell under nuclear attack). But Moscow's secret center is just a quick subway ride away from the halls of power—not the five-hour highway slog from DC in what surely would be less than optimal driving conditions . . .

One of the avowed purposes of the Metro set forth by Stalin and his plucky project manager Nikita Khrushchev was to show the superiority of socialism over capitalism, so the stations were lavishly decorated as "palaces for the people."

Far from the austere constructivist style favored by Russian artists in the 1920s, the stations proudly display an ornate—one might say, bourgeois—style of socialist classicism, in which historical architectural references are placed on monumental public buildings. The stations are absolutely stunning, and the finishes are sumptuous. The aesthetics of the Moscow Metro have been emulated in St. Petersburg and a dozen other Russian and former Soviet cities from Almaty (Kazakhstan) to Yerevan (Armenia), and even as far afield as Pyongyang, North Korea, which surpasses them all for monumentalism. (In sharp contrast to many American subways, the Moscow Metro calls to mind the Louvre, rather than the Loo.)

While the elaborate, arcaded underground stations are justly praised, many of the above-ground entrance halls are major architectural statements in their own right, often designed by other architects than those designing the subterranean spaces. The images that follow show the beauty of the stations, both at platform level and at the street-level entrances.

MOSCOW

Metro stations at concourse and platform levels:

Left:
Elektrozavodskaya station (Line 3), 1944

Center:
Komsomolskaya station (Line 5), 1952

Right:
Arbatskaya station (Line 3), 1953

Left:
Sokol metro station (Line 2), 1938

Right:
Belorusskaya station (Line 5), 1952

TRANSIT TOURISM | 153

MOSCOVSKY METROPOLITEN

Aboveground (street-level entrances):

Left:
Arbatskaya
station entrance (Line 4)

Right:
Krasnye Vorota
station entrance (Line 7)

And the artwork is superb as well, such as the beautiful mosaics on the ceiling of Mayakovskaya station by the Russian artist Aleksandr Deyneka (1899–1969), installed in 1938.

Left and right:
Mayakovskaya station
(Line 2) ceiling mosiacs

154 | EUROPE—RUSSIA

MOSCOW

Mayakovskaya station ceiling, showing placement of mosaics in ceiling coffers

MOSCOVSKY METROPOLITEN

The most lavish and overtly ideological stations are from the late Stalinist era of the early 1950s, depicting the triumphs of the Soviet people. These are sacred spaces, not unlike houses of worship. Following Stalin's eagerly awaited death in 1953 (soon thereafter, his visage was effaced from the murals on the earlier lines), this ostentatious style was replaced by a more restrained, functional look in the mid-1950s and '60s, with less grandiose entranceways. In recent years, Moscow's metro station architecture has trended more modernist and even avant-garde through architectural competitions, including younger designers and the occasional non-Russian architect (such as Zaha Hadid). The most-recent stations include bright colors and are as striking as anything found in Munich, Brussels, or London.

Minskaya station (Line 8A)

MOSCOW

Moscow and Washington may have their differences, yet these two stations look highly compatible.

Left: Krasnogvardeyskaya station in Moscow (Line 2), 1985

Right: Pentagon Station in Washington, DC (Blue and Yellow Lines)

    Station entrances are marked with an illuminated red neon "M" visible from blocks away. Over the years, the design of the "M" logo has varied considerably, in contrast to the constancy of the London Underground's roundel over the last century or the Stockholm tunnelbana "T." Happily, however, several years ago Moscow retained a talented local design firm, Artemy Lebedev Studio, to come up with a standardized but modernized design vocabulary for the Metro that's rooted in the original 1935 design. There is nothing lean, sleek, or remotely Helvetican about it: the logo is a squat, very retro, and exceedingly red "M" with slab serif feet. To me, this expressive "M" is perfectly suited to the Russian persona, and as emblematic of Russia as the turrets of St. Basil's in Red Square.

TRANSIT TOURISM | 157

MOSCOVSKY METROPOLITEN

The Moscow Metro "M"
by Artemy Lebedev Studio

The same design firm also refreshed the Metro map, which has had numerous looks over the years. The current map continues the trend of color coding, with Moscow's circle line being depicted as a perfect circle (unlike other geometrically challenged "circle" lines such as Beijing's beveled-corner rectangle, London's milk bottle, or Tokyo's misshapen blob).

The map also shows two larger interlocking orbital rail lines. The "Central Circle" line is an aboveground commuter rail line operated by Russian Railways, using their own railcars (similar to Tokyo's Yamanote line). On this basis, it, too, deserves an asterisk as a wannabe subway line. However, a new, *true* "Big Circle Line" (Bolshaya Koltsevaya) was completed in 2023 and is 36 miles long with twenty-nine stations. It slightly exceeds in length Beijing's Second Circle Line by 8 miles to become the world's longest underground rail ring route. (Compare that with Glasgow's Lilliputian 6.5-mile subway loop!)

All the other lines in the Moscow Metro are drawn on the map at 45- and 90-degree angles, and station names are shown in both Cyrillic and Roman characters. The only topographical feature shown on the map is a red star at the very center, indicating where the Kremlin is located—a brilliantly simple orientation device. The map gives a very clear depiction of a very complex system. My only quibble is that a dozen of the interchange stations have different names on the different lines, causing unnecessary confusion.

MOSCOW

SUMMARY

Moscow's political system may be appalling, but its subway system is appealing. The Metro is one of the best systems in the world, both operationally and architecturally. It is Europe's largest, now surpassing the London Underground in ridership and route mileage. Its palatial stations from the 1930s are unparalleled for their splendor and opulence, while the most-recent stations are architecturally dazzling as well. Yet, as someone noted, how could a system of government that got it so right *below*ground get it so wrong *above*?[4] A fair question. Nonetheless, Moscow should be at or near the top of everyone's list for memorable metro systems—it certainly is on mine!

SELTZER TOKEN RATINGS (SCALE 1–4)

CONVENIENCE	4
EASE OF USE	3
QUALITY OF DESIGN	4
PERSONALITY	4

---

4 Christopher Herwig and Owen Hatherley, *Soviet Metro Stations*, 2019.

U Bahn München
U4 U-Bahn Linie
U8 Nur zeitweise
U1
U2
U3
U4
U5
U6
U7
U8
Feldmoching
Hasenbergl
Dülferstraße
Harthof
Am Hart
Frankfurter Ring
Milbertshofen
Moosach
Moosacher St.-Martins-Platz
Olympia-Einkaufs-zentrum
Oberwiesenfeld
Olympia-zentrum
Petuelring
Scheidplatz
Bonner Platz
Georg-Brauchle-Ring
Westfriedhof
Gern
Rotkreuzplatz
Maillingerstraße
Stiglmaierplatz
Hohenzollern-platz
Josephs-platz
Theresien-straße
Königs-platz
Karlsplatz (Stachus)
Hauptbahnhof
(Central Station)
Theresienwiese
Schwanthalerhöhe
Garching-Forschungs-zentrum
Garching
Garching-Hochbrück
Fröttmaning
Kieferngarten
Freimann
Studentenstadt
Alte Heide
Nordfriedhof
Dietlindenstraße
Münchner Freiheit
Giselastraße
Universität
Odeonsplatz
Marien-platz
Lehel
Max-Weber-Platz
Arabellapark
Richard-Strauss-Str.
Böhmerwaldplatz
Prinzregentenplatz
Ostbahnhof
Innsbrucker Ring
Messestadt Ost
Messestadt West
Moosfeld
Trudering
Josephs-burg
Kreiller-straße
Sendlinger Tor
Fraunhofer-straße
Kolumbus-platz
Karl-Preis-Platz
Giesing
Silber-horn-straße
Unters-berg-straße
Michaelibad
Quiddestraße
Neuperlach Zentrum
Therese-Giehse-Allee
Neuperlach Süd
Candidplatz
Wettersteinplatz
St.-Quirin-Platz
Mangfallplatz
Goethe-platz
Pocci-straße
Impler-straße
Brudermühlstraße
Thalkirchen (Tierpark)
Laimer Platz
Friedenheimer Straße
Westendstraße
Heimeranplatz
Klinikum Großhadern
Groß-hadern
Haderner Stern
Holz-apfel-kreuth
Westpark
Partnach-platz
Harras
Fürsten-ried West
Basler Straße
Forsten-rieder Allee
Machtl-finger Straße
Aiden-bach-straße
Ober-sendling
Stand: Dezember 2020
CC-BY-SA Zeno Heilmaier

MUNICH

MUNICH
Münchner Verkehrsgesellschaft (MVG)

System Length	64 route miles
Number of Lines	6 (3 "trunk routes")
Number of Stations	100
Year Opened	1971
Year of Last Expansion	2017
Annual Ridership	429 million (2019)
Subwayness	94% of stations underground

Subway entrance Marienthalplatz (Lines U3 & U6)

In September 2016, my wife and I decided we wanted to take a quick getaway trip somewhere overseas we'd never visited. The selection criteria for the destination were that (1) it had to be flyable nonstop from our hometown of Philadelphia, (2) it had to have top-quality modern as well as historic architecture, and (3) it had to have a vibrant urban scene. Oh, and one other requirement (undisclosed at the time to my wife): (4) it had to have a subway. The result? *Wilkommen in München*!

I had no preconceived notions about Munich and hadn't heard much about it from friends either, so I was pleasantly surprised by the charm and walkability of the city and the warmth and friendliness

TRANSIT TOURISM | 161

MÜNCHNER VERKEHRSGESELLSCHAFT

of everyone we met there. I also was puzzled—and delighted—to learn that that the Oktoberfest actually occurs *in September,* happily coinciding with our visit. It would be a real kegger of a trip!

Munich is Germany's third-largest city, with about 1.5 million people—substantially smaller than Berlin and Hamburg, both of which had built their subways in the early years of the twentieth century. Munich's subway system (the Untergrundbahn, or U-Bahn), was built six decades after Berlin and Hamburg and is smart, clean, and efficient. The Münchner Verkehrsgesellschaft (MVG), the public transport operator, makes its stations inviting and attractive through the use of architecture enhanced with bold wall supergraphics and artistic finishes. The system feels very user-friendly, consistent with Munich's overall *gestalt* of openness.

During Germany's economic boom in the 1950s and 1960s, regional car ownership grew five-fold, with a corresponding increase in traffic congestion in downtown Munich's narrow, winding streets. The existing tram system was operating at capacity, so Munich's municipal government decided to go *untergrund*. Construction on the first subway line began in 1965, and shortly afterward the city received notice that it had been awarded the 1972 Olympics. With the prospect of large crowds, the city dramatically accelerated the development timetable, completing in six years what normally would have taken a decade or more. The first leg opened in 1971, serving the heavily traveled north–south corridor. Every several years for the next three decades, a new line or extension was opened. By 2010, the system reached its current configuration of one hundred stations.

Three major trunk lines run through the central business district, and with one exception, each end splits off into two lines serving outlying districts. These six lines are labeled U1–U6. There are two additional routes labeled U7 and U8 that are services rather than separate lines, operating along segments of the six basic routes during peak hours. The system map, while unremarkable, is very readable and visually appealing (see facing page of chapter).

MUNICH

U3 train rolling into Olympia Einkaufszentrum station

Concurrently with the construction of the initial U-Bahn line, a separate 2.5-mile-long rail tunnel through downtown was built for the S-Bahn (Stadtschnellbahn, or urban rapid railway). The S-Bahn network consists of thirteen electrified commuter rail lines serving almost 150 stations throughout the metropolitan region. The commuter train tunnel connects two formerly "stub-end terminals"—the Central station (Hauptbahnhof) and Munich East (Ostbahnhof),[1] and it also serves four intermediate underground rail stations in central Munich. The S-Bahn has interchanges with

---

1 In this respect, the downtown rail tunnel is similar to Philadelphia's Center City Commuter Tunnel, which, when opened in 1984, connected thirteen electrified lines of the former Pennsylvania and Reading railroads that previously terminated at Suburban Station and Reading Terminal. In Munich, however, new railcars, high-level platforms, and more-frequent service all accompanied the opening of the connecting tunnel, in effect transforming the commuter rail network into its own rapid transit system.

MÜNCHNER VERKEHRSGESELLSCHAFT

each of the U-Bahn lines. Munich's regional transit maps show both the S-Bahn and U-Bahn networks as an integrated system, similar to the Paris Métro and RER maps—and with a similarly bewildering "TMI" effect on the overwhelmed tourist.

The dramatic growth in recent years in commuter rail ridership has necessitated a second, parallel commuter rail tunnel with three new downtown stations, now under construction. As for how to depict this new S-Bahn service on the map once the second tunnel is added alongside the existing S-Bahn and U-Bahn routes: *Ach du Lieber*!

All German U-Bahn systems designate station entrances with a common logo of a white "U" on a square blue field rather than the agency's logo, much as the Italian metros all use a white "M" on a square red field. From an architectural perspective, the earliest stations from the 1970s are attractive enough, albeit in a restrained, modernist sort of way. Now four decades old, they require renovations. But as subsequent lines and extensions were added in the 1980s and '90s, the architecture became bolder and more colorful—perhaps attributable to greater civic self-confidence?

More than a dozen Munich architectural firms have contributed designs to this more recent wave of additions, perhaps drawing a page from Montréal's innovation in the early 1960s of using multiple outside architects. Interestingly, a municipal architectural office called the Subway Planning Council is responsible for some of the most dramatic stations throughout the system. The result is a wonderful range of contemporary designs using all sorts of materials and colors. I even discovered a station with multicolored enameled metal panels in Munich (Georg-Brauchle-Ring, shown the facing page) that has a doppelganger in Budapest (Móricz Zsigmond körtér), built a decade later. Georg, say "hallo" to Ziggy (see chapter on Budapest).

MUNICH

George-Brauchle Ring station (Line U1)

MÜNCHNER VERKEHRSGESELLSCHAFT

In cities with older subways such as New York and Chicago, artwork has been added as an afterthought in the decades following the stations' construction. In contrast, for the new extensions in Munich, the artwork has been integrated into the architectural process from the outset. The art installations take the form of murals, wall friezes, mosaics, enamel paintings, and design lighting. Most are very contemporary and abstract designs, as opposed to the more literal, pictorial murals and images one finds in, say, the Beijing subway.

One of my favorite stations is Westfriedhof on the U1, which has magnificent 12-foot-diameter canopy lights designed by the renowned German lighting designer Ingo Maurer. Standing beneath the huge fixtures, one is bathed in colorful light. Another unusual installation can be found at Theresienwiese on the U4/U5, which serves the Oktoberfest fairgrounds. The architect Alexander Freiherr van Branca designed it to look like a brewery vault, getting one in just the mood for that first pint of Märzenbier; he also designed eight other U-Bahn stations in Munich and Bonn.

My superb guide, Christian Denkman, took me via the U3 to the beer halls at the Theresienwiesen fairgrounds. I feel certain he was secretly relieved I'd resisted the temptation to acquire lederhosen and a Bavarian fedora for the occasion. We happened to be seated at one of the long tables at the Fairground beer halls, alongside half a dozen locals in their late twenties, who cordially welcomed me. Everyone conversed in fluent British-inflected English, for my benefit. After the third pint, they felt like family to me: true Münch-kin! And, with beer and pretzels offered as standard fare for breakfast dining, the Bavarian cuisine was well suited to my sophisticated Philly palate.

MUNICH

U1 Westfriedhof station: sitting under the Ingo Maurer lamps that look like the "Cone of Silence" from the TV comedy *Get Smart*

TRANSIT TOURISM

MÜNCHNER VERKEHRSGESELLSCHAFT

U4/U5 Theresienwiese station looks like the inside of a beer barrel

168 | EUROPE—GERMANY

MUNICH

At Marienplatz station, the deep orange of the retrofuturistic pedestrian tunnel continues on the station columns inside this busy, four-level interchange station, which links the U-Bahn U2/U3 Lines with the S-Bahn in the heart of Munich.

TRANSIT TOURISM

MÜNCHNER VERKEHRSGESELLSCHAFT

Superb wall supergraphics at Moosfeld station (U2 Line)

Grosshadern station on the U6 Line has a mural depicting geological strata of the earth's crust, as might have been encountered in excavating the station.

MUNICH

Candidplatz station on the U1 Line—rainbow-colored tiles

All of these handsome photos show the stations with their exposed platforms. It has been reported that platform doors and barriers are coming to Munich's subway platforms by 2028, as a safety measure. While these protective devices undoubtedly will make the system safer, I fear they may diminish the dramatic aesthetics of the stations.

TRANSIT TOURISM | 171

MÜNCHNER VERKEHRSGESELLSCHAFT

Now, there is a subset of transit enthusiasts (if I may let my inner Transit Dweeb come out for a moment) who find studying the track plans of the rail systems fascinating. These track maps show the interconnections, flyover junctions, platforms, and train yards in meticulous detail. In fact, there is an entire website devoted to showing several dozen metro and tram track plans, called cartometro.com.

In looking at Munich's track plan, I came across an unusual mile-long subway tunnel underneath the festival grounds connecting two of the trunk lines, U3 and U4. It does not serve passengers; rather, it is used solely for shuttling out-of-service trains to a nearby maintenance facility. It seems like an extravagance, but I am confident the thrifty Münchners determined it was cheaper excavating this phantom line than building and staffing a second maintenance facility.[2]

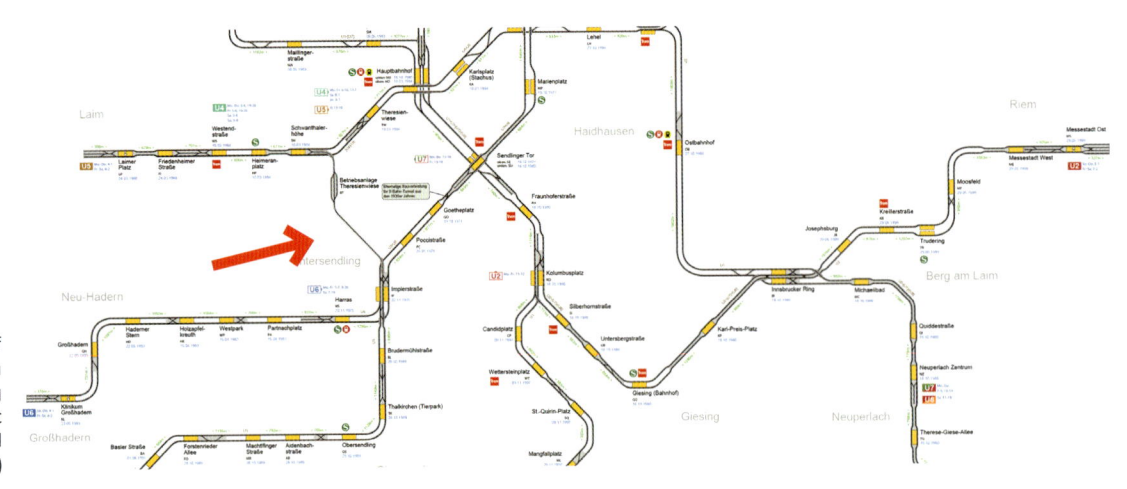

Segment of Munich Track Map from Gleisplanweb.de showing nonpublic rail delivery tunnel (indicated by arrow)

---

2 Curiously, Stockholm has a similar tunnel 1.5 miles long connecting two branches of its Blue Line; it is used only for serving equipment, not passengers.

172 | EUROPE—GERMANY

MUNICH

SUMMARY

Munich's U-Bahn service is prompt, clean, and attractive, with pleasing stations designed by many different architectural firms: arguably the smoothest, sleekest, and—may I say—sexiest subway system I have ever ridden on—the BMW of metros (Bayerische *Metro* Werke?). And yet, the stations are not over-the-top or intimidating architectural statements. Instead, they have a friendly, colorful, and accessible aspect, like the denizens I met. Between the U-Bahn and the transit-like S-Bahn commuter rail system that blanket the city and the region, one can be carless and carefree in Munich. Taking the U-Bahn offers a speedier, greener, and cheaper alternative to taking the U-ber.

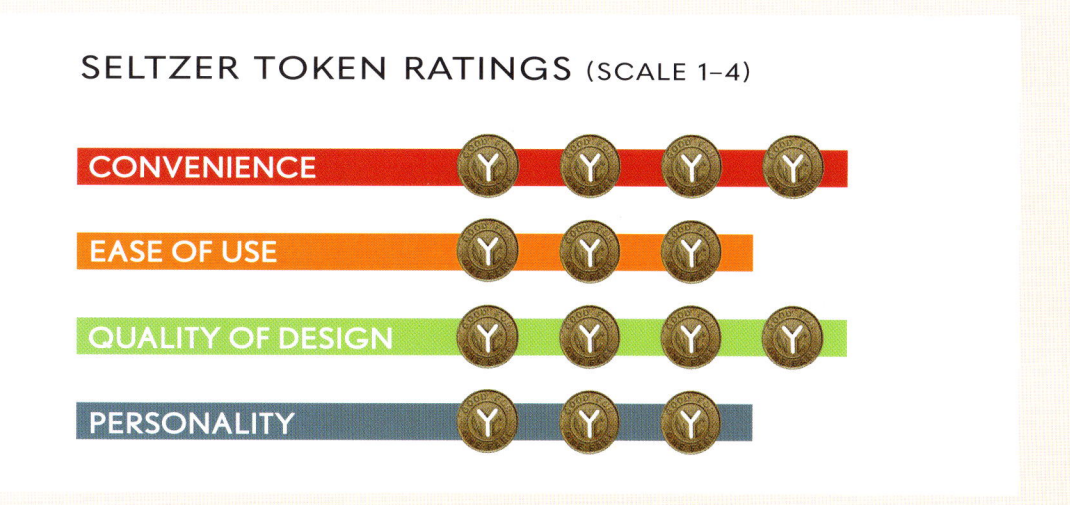

SELTZER TOKEN RATINGS (SCALE 1–4)

CONVENIENCE	4
EASE OF USE	3
QUALITY OF DESIGN	4
PERSONALITY	3

TRANSIT TOURISM | 173

anm
AZIENDA NAPOLETANA MOBILITÀ S.p.A.
Rete integrata su ferro
Integrated rail network
AVERSA CENTRO
MUGNANO
PISCINOLA SCAMPIA
CHIAIANO
FRULLONE
COLLI AMINEI
POLICLINICO
RIONE ALTO
MONTEDONZELLI
MEDAGLIE D'ORO
LINEA 1
MIANO
REGINA MARGHERITA
SECONDIGLIANO
DI VITTORIO
CAPODICHINO AEROPORTO
POGGIOREALE
TRIBUNALE
CENTRO DIREZIONALE
AVERSA CASERTA FORMIA
FRATTAMAGGIORE
CASORIA AFRAGOLA
CASERTA
BENEVENTO
CANCELLO
ACERRA
CASALNUOVO DI NAPOLI
//Alibus>>
STAZIONE CENTRALE
GARIBALDI
GIANTURCO
SALVATOR ROSA
MATERDEI
CAVOUR
MUSEO
MORGHEN
QUATTRO GIORNATE
VANVITELLI
CIMAROSA
FUGA
MONTESANTO
DANTE
DUOMO
UNIVERSITÀ
TOLEDO
C.V. EMANUELE
PORTA NOLANA
CIRCUMVESUVIANA
S. GIOVANNI
BARRA
S. MARIA DEL POZZO
SAN GIORGIO
CAVALLI DI BRONZO
BELLAVISTA
POMPEI CASTELLAMMARE SORRENTO
PIETRARSA
PORTICI ERCOLANO
POMPEI SALERNO
FORMIA
LICOLA TORREGAVETA
QUARTO
QUARTO CENTRO
PISANI
PIANURA
LA TRENCIA
TRAIANO
SOCCAVO
PIAVE
CIRCUMFLEGREA
PETRAIO
PALAZZOLO
MUNICIPIO PORTO
CENTRALE
CHIAIA
PARCO MARGHERITA
AMEDEO
AUGUSTEO
C.V. EMANUELE
FUORIGROTTA
CUMANA
BAGNOLI
CAVALLEGGERI D'AOSTA
POZZUOLI
MOSTRA
AUGUSTO
LALA
ARCO MIRELLI
SAN PASQUALE
MERGELLINA
LINEA 6
LINEA 2
MONTE ECHIA
ASCENSORE
EDENLANDIA
KENNEDY
CAMPI FLEGREI
AGNANO
LEOPARDI
TORREGAVETA
POZZUOLI
GEROLOMINI
CAPPUCCINI
DAZIO
BAGNOLI
MANZONI
S. GIOACCHINO
P.CO ANGELINA
S.ANTONIO
MERGELLINA
Linea 1 / Line 1
Linea 6 / Line 6
Funicolari / Funiculars
Stazione / Station
Stazione dell'arte / Art station
Stazione in costruzione / Station under construction
Scale mobili / Escalators
Nodi di interscambio / Interchanges nodes
Linea 2 Trenitalia / Line 2
Linea Piscinola-Aversa / Piscinola-Aversa line
Circumvesuviana / Circumvesuviana railway
Circumflegrea / Circumflegrea railway
Cumana / Cumana railway
Rete ferroviaria FS-Trenitalia / National and regional railways
Bus Aeroporto Capodichino / Shuttle bus Capodichino Airport
Capolinea bus / Bus terminal
Collegamento marittimo / Boat service
Parcheggio / Parking
Ospedale / Hospital
Museo / Museum
Castello / Castle
Università / University
Ostello / Youth hostel
Stadio / Stadium
Mostra d'Oltremare / Fair district

NAPLES

NAPLES
Azienda Napoletana Mobilità, SpA

System Length	21 route miles[1]
Number of Lines	3[1]
Number of Stations	32[1]
Year Opened	1993
Year of Last Expansion	2024
Annual Ridership	77 million (2019)
Subwayness	91% of stations underground

If any metro system located nearly 100 feet beneath street level could be described as absolutely over the top, it's the Napoli Metropolitana. Pound for pound—or euro for euro—it is architecturally and artistically the most avant-garde subway system anywhere.

Colorful, lively, and gritty, Naples has a history as complicated as its topography. Hemmed in by the Tyrrhenian Sea to the west and mountainous terrain to the east, this crowded city lies in the shadow

---

[1] Includes the Linea Arcobaleno (Rainbow Line), described at the end of the chapter, which is operated by a separate governmental corporation.

Materdei station entrance

TRANSIT TOURISM | 175

AZIENDA NAPOLETANA MOBILITÀ, SPA

of Mt. Vesuvius, just 3 leagues distant. Napoli (as it's called in Italian) derives its name from the Greek "Neapolis," or "new town," and this rather ancient new town has been ruled not only by the Greeks, but also by the Etruscans, Romans, Germans, French, and Spanish. As I struggled to follow the comings and goings over the centuries of Angevin, Aragonese, Habsburg, and Bourbon overlords, it reminded me why I barely attained a Gentleman's C my freshman year in *European History 101, from Plato to NATO* . . .

Naples's public transportation system is similarly complicated. One agency, Azienda Napoletana Mobilità (ANM), manages the buses, trolleys, trams, four funiculars, and two of the metro lines (1 and 6). Metro Line 2, which is actually a commuter rail line that includes a 3-mile downtown tunnel with four stations, is operated by Trenitalia (the "Amtrak" of Italy). Another governmental transport agency, Ente Autonomo Volturno (EAV), operates a short five-station subway line (the "Rainbow Line" because of each station's vivid colors) in the northern suburbs. EAV also operates a narrow-gauge railway circling the base of nearby Mount Vesuvius. Even if you're not a transit aficionado, you may recognize another local funicular that formerly ran to the summit of Vesuvius and inspired the eminently whistleable tune "Funiculì, Funiculà." The line closed in 1944 after the last volcanic eruption, but regrettably the song continues to be sung in elementary schools everywhere.

I had the opportunity to ride the Metropolitana some years ago when touring the Amalfi Coast. Even then, Naples had earned a worldwide reputation for its fantastically creative "Stazioni dell'arte" (Art Stations). However, I was so preoccupied with Naples's *other* world-class reputation—its renowned *borseggiatori*, or pickpockets—that I couldn't properly appreciate the full aesthetic achievement of the stations. As it turns out, I had absolutely no untoward incidents in Naples, but you'll need to read the chapter about Paris for my close encounter of the second kind.

NAPLES

Plans for a subway in Naples got underway in earnest in the 1970s. However, local officials' ability to build it was hampered by the city's hilly topography, financial mismanagement, and the 1980 Iripina earthquake. After several false starts, the initial segment of Naples's first true subway, Line 1, finally opened in 1993. Today, it is an eighteen-station, 11-mile-long, mostly underground line that comprises about two-thirds of what *eventually* will be both a circle *and* a loop. Line 1 (known as "Collinare," or hilly) is unique among world subways in corkscrewing around itself as it makes the steep ascent from the town center by the port up the hillside to the Arenella quarter, 750 feet above sea level. (The corkscrew configuration seems appropriate, since Naples is the capital of the Campania wine region.)

But steep terrain, seismic commotion, and irregular finances have not been the only obstacles in completing Line 1. As with the subway construction in Rome, Istanbul, and Mexico City, excavators working on the project have encountered important archaeological remains, resulting in extensive delays and adding significant cost.

Line 1 train at Pisicnola, one of the three aboveground stations

TRANSIT TOURISM | 177

AZIENDA NAPOLETANA MOBILITÀ, SPA

In Naples, most of the subway line has been excavated with tunnel-boring machines digging 30 yards below street level. This is deep enough to avoid disturbing the soil closer to the surface, where ancient artifacts typically are found. However, the stations themselves do require large surface excavations. The local government corporation developing the metro employs ten full-time archeologists assisted by sixty other staff who sift through the soil dug up at the station sites. For example, the Municipio (City Hall) station is located on landfill adjacent to the port. During excavation, several buried Roman ships were discovered there and had to be carefully exhumed. And the design of the Duomo station incorporates a first-century BCE Roman temple unearthed during construction of the station's lobby.

The distinguishing feature of the Naples metro is its Art Stations, which were part of the second phase of metro construction in 2001. The Neapolitan government views the metro as not just improving mobility but also creating new public spaces, stimulating the regeneration of neighborhoods, and—boldly—*making the metro itself a tourist attraction*. Fifteen different architectural firms were selected on the basis of their capabilities to design stations well suited to their specific environments. And fifteen of ANM's metro stations have highly sophisticated and extensive installations of contemporary art, over two hundred works in all, by one hundred artists from all over the world.

Truth be told, when I visit a city's art museum, I tend to walk rather briskly through the Contemporary Art galleries. I find much of today's art impenetrable, pretentious, or boring—often all three. However, when the artwork is *in a subway station*, it somehow seems more appealing and approachable. One of the Metropolitana's directors described the Art Stations as an "obligatory museum," where people who wouldn't necessarily seek out contemporary art in galleries would enjoy seeing it on their daily commute.

NAPLES

Unlike the benign artwork depicting safe topics on view in the subway stations of, say, Beijing or Moscow, the artwork in Naples tends to be thought provoking and even provocative. And when the art is conceived currently with the architectural design, the results can be spectacular: both CNN and the *London Daily Telegraph* selected Naples's Toledo station as the most impressive metro station of *any European city*. Just for the record, Europe has forty-eight cities with metros, and collectively these systems have a total of 3,285 subway stations. So, for little Napoli with its thirty-two-station system to win first prize, well, Holy Toledo!

Several of my favorite stations are shown on this and the next few pages, starting with Toledo. The elliptical skylight at Toledo extends almost ten stories up from the station level to the plaza above. Called the "Cone of Light," it suggests what the view might look like gazing upward from the inside of Mt. Vesuvius.

"Cone of Light," Toledo station (Line 1)

TRANSIT TOURISM | 179

AZIENDA NAPOLETANA MOBILITÀ, SPA

Another marvelous installation is at Universita station, fashioned by the internationally renowned industrial designer Karim Rashid, who incorporates sculpture, lighting, floor images, and 3-D moving lenticular prints.

Aluminum sculptures and lenticular moving-picture light boxes. Karim Rashid, Universita station.

NAPLES

At the Garibaldi station, the famous Italian artist Michelangelo Pistoletto has installed two of his "Mirror Paintings," which he creates by adhering life-size photo images of people onto reflective steel. In walking by them, the observer becomes part of the composition:

Garibaldi station: Stazione-2 by Michelangelo Pistoletto, photographs on steel-mirrored panels

AZIENDA NAPOLETANA MOBILITÀ, SPA

Materdei has beautiful wall murals throughout the station.

NAPLES

And Salvator Rosa station presents something unusual I hadn't seen before. Artwork is displayed not only in the station itself but also *outside* on the walls of the buildings surrounding it. Up the hill from the port, this neighborhood center has playful decorations on the surrounding apartment blocks, as well as fanciful outdoor sculptures in the park by the station entrances. This unorthodox exterior artwork seems highly appropriate for a station named after a seventeenth-century Neapolitan painter who specialized in fanciful, romanticized landscapes.

AZIENDA NAPOLETANA MOBILITÀ, SPA

The stations' entrances are readily visible from the street. In Italy, the subways of Rome, Milan, Genoa, and Naples all use the same marker at station entrances: a white "M" on a fire-engine-red square background (M). In Naples, the governmental–system operator of Lines 1 and 6, Azienda Napoletana Mobilità, has its own specific logo on the cars, which bears a curious resemblance to Amtrak's logo. Since both were introduced in 2000, they may have been separated at birth, except that Naples's logo shows that pesky volcano lurking in the background.

And then there is the curious *Linea Arcobaleno* (Rainbow Line) in the northern suburbs, where each of the six stations is themed in a different color. This 6-mile segment, which opened in 2005, is operated by a separate agency, EAV, and eventually will be connected to the rest of the system when the Line 1 circle is completed.

Views of Giugliano station, Metro EAV's Rainbow Line

EUROPE—ITALY

NAPLES

SUMMARY

Although it's a smaller system, not making the top 100 worldwide subway systems in terms of route miles, Naples's metro, like its civic persona, is highly theatrical and idiosyncratic and makes an outsized impression. The city's dramatic topography, the system's strange corkscrew configuration, and the remarkable Art Stations all combine to give the Metropolitana a unique flavor and make it an unexpected find. In fact, the city is promoting the subway itself as one of Naples's principal tourist attractions. And there is more to come, since Line 1's three-quarter circle edges toward completion a mere half century after work first began. Perhaps the only element lacking is a rousing Neapolitan tune to serve as the metro's official anthem, similar to its Campanian companion, the Vesuvius funicular. But somehow, I don't think a song titled *"Metropolitani, Metropolitana"* rolls off the tongue as easily.

SELTZER TOKEN RATINGS (SCALE 1–4)

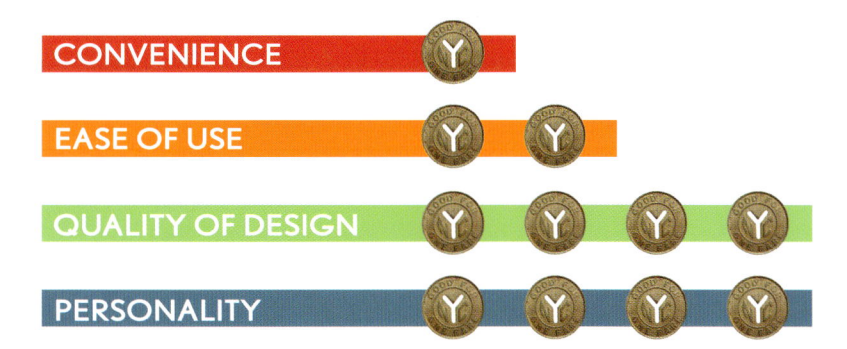

CONVENIENCE	1
EASE OF USE	2
QUALITY OF DESIGN	4
PERSONALITY	4

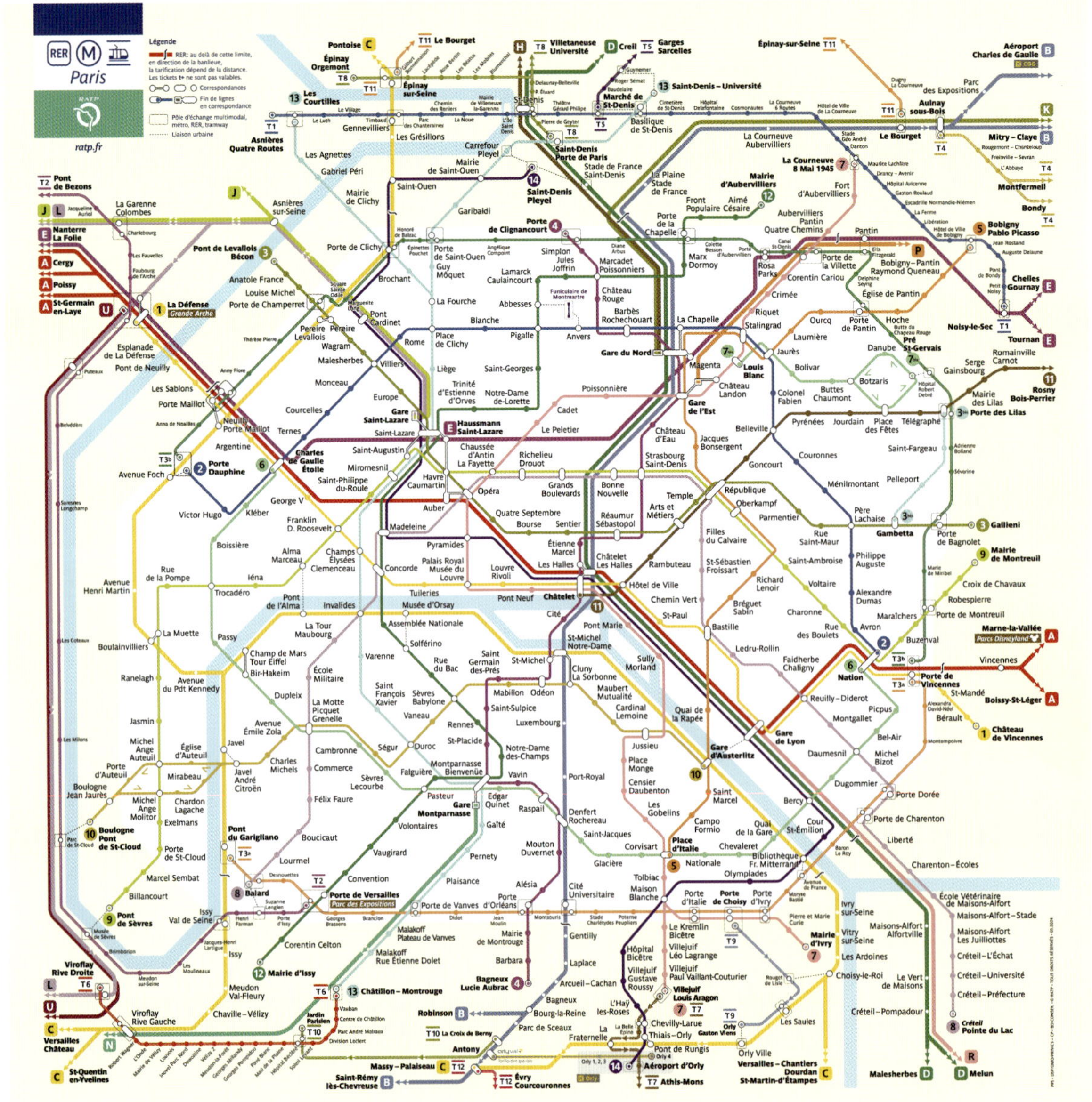

RER
M
Paris
RATP
ratp.fr
Légende
RER: au delà de cette limite, en direction de la banlieue, la tarification dépend de la distance. Les tickets t+ ne sont pas valables.
Correspondances
Fin de lignes en correspondance
Pôle d'échange multimodal, métro, RER, tramway
Liaison urbaine
Pontoise
Épinay Orgemont
Le Bourget
Villetaneuse Université
Creil
Garges Sarcelles
Épinay-sur-Seine
Aéroport Charles de Gaulle
Épinay sur-Seine
Les Courtilles
Saint-Denis – Université
Marché de St-Denis
Basilique de St-Denis
St-Denis
Gennevilliers
Les Grésillons
Asnières Quatre Routes
Aulnay sous-Bois
Le Bourget
Mitry – Claye
Parc des Expositions
Montfermeil
Bondy
La Courneuve Aubervilliers
La Courneuve 8 Mai 1945
Saint-Denis Porte de Paris
Stade de France Saint-Denis
La Plaine Stade de France
Carrefour Pleyel
Mairie de Saint-Ouen
Saint-Denis Pleyel
Les Agnettes
Gabriel Péri
Mairie de Clichy
Saint-Ouen
Garibaldi
Mairie d'Aubervilliers
Front Populaire
Aimé Césaire
Fort d'Aubervilliers
Aubervilliers Pantin Quatre Chemins
Bobigny Pablo Picasso
Pont de Bezons
La Garenne Colombes
Asnières sur-Seine
Nanterre La Folie
Cergy
Poissy
St-Germain en-Laye
Pont de Levallois Bécon
Porte de Clichy
Porte de Clignancourt
Simplon
Jules Joffrin
Marcadet Poissonniers
Porte de la Chapelle
Marx Dormoy
Pantin
Bobigny – Pantin Raymond Queneau
Chelles Gournay
Anatole France
Louise Michel
Porte de Champerret
Brochant
Porte de Saint-Ouen
Guy Môquet
Lamarck Caulaincourt
Château Rouge
Barbès Rochechouart
Rosa Parks
Corentin Cariou
Porte de la Villette
Église de Pantin
Crimée
La Défense Grande Arche
La Fourche
Abbesses
Funiculaire de Montmartre
Riquet
Stalingrad
Ourcq
Porte de Pantin
Hoche
Pré St-Gervais
Noisy-le-Sec
Tournan
Esplanade de La Défense
Pont de Neuilly
Pereire Levallois
Pereire
Wagram
Pont Cardinet
Rome
Place de Clichy
Blanche
Pigalle
Anvers
La Chapelle
Gare du Nord
Jaurès
Laumière
Danube
Serge Gainsbourg
Romainville Carnot
Rosny Bois-Perrier
Les Sablons
Porte Maillot
Malesherbes
Villiers
Liège
Saint-Georges
Magenta
Louis Blanc
Bolivar
Botzaris
Mairie des Lilas
Porte des Lilas
Monceau
Europe
Trinité d'Estienne d'Orves
Notre-Dame de-Lorette
Poissonnière
Château Landon
Colonel Fabien
Buttes Chaumont
Neuilly Porte Maillot
Courcelles
Gare Saint-Lazare
Cadet
Gare de l'Est
Pyrénées
Jourdain
Place des Fêtes
Télégraphe
Argentine
Ternes
Haussmann Saint-Lazare
Saint-Lazare
Le Peletier
Château d'Eau
Jacques Bonsergent
Belleville
Saint-Fargeau
Porte Dauphine
Charles de Gaulle Étoile
Saint-Augustin
Chaussée d'Antin La Fayette
Richelieu Drouot
Strasbourg Saint-Denis
Goncourt
Couronnes
Avenue Foch
Miromesnil
Saint-Philippe du-Roule
Havre Caumartin
Opéra
Grands Boulevards
Bonne Nouvelle
Temple
République
Ménilmontant
Pelleport
George V
Auber
Quatre Septembre
Arts et Métiers
Oberkampf
Victor Hugo
Kléber
Franklin D. Roosevelt
Madeleine
Bourse
Sentier
Réaumur Sébastopol
Parmentier
Père Lachaise
Gambetta
Gallieni
Pyramides
Filles du Calvaire
Rue Saint-Maur
Porte de Bagnolet
Boissière
Alma Marceau
Champs Élysées Clemenceau
Concorde
Palais Royal Musée du Louvre
Louvre Rivoli
Étienne Marcel
Les Halles
Châtelet Les Halles
Rambuteau
Saint-Sébastien Froissart
Saint-Ambroise
Philippe Auguste
Mairie de Montreuil
Rue de la Pompe
Iéna
Avenue Henri Martin
Trocadéro
Pont de l'Alma
Invalides
Tuileries
Musée d'Orsay
Pont Neuf
Châtelet
Hôtel de Ville
Chemin Vert
Richard Lenoir
Voltaire
Alexandre Dumas
Croix de Chavaux
Robespierre
Porte de Montreuil
Cité
Saint-Paul
Bréguet Sabin
Charonne
Maraîchers
La Muette
Passy
La Tour Maubourg
Assemblée Nationale
Pont Marie
Bastille
Rue des Boulets
Avron
Buzenval
Marne-la-Vallée
Parcs Disneyland
Boulainvilliers
Champ de Mars Tour Eiffel
Bir-Hakeim
Solférino
Saint Germain des-Prés
St-Michel
St-Michel Notre-Dame
Sully Morland
Ledru-Rollin
Faidherbe Chaligny
Nation
Porte de Vincennes
Vincennes
Boissy-St-Léger
Ranelagh
Avenue du Pdt Kennedy
École Militaire
Varenne
Rue du Bac
Cluny La Sorbonne
Saint-Mandé
Bérault
Château de Vincennes
Dupleix
Saint François Xavier
Sèvres Babylone
Mabillon
Odéon
Maubert Mutualité
Cardinal Lemoine
Quai de la Rapée
Reuilly – Diderot
Picpus
Jasmin
La Motte Picquet Grenelle
Vaneau
Saint-Sulpice
Luxembourg
Gare de Lyon
Montgallet
Bel-Air
Avenue Émile Zola
Rennes
Michel Ange Auteuil
Église d'Auteuil
Javel
Ségur
Duroc
St-Placide
Notre-Dame des-Champs
Jussieu
Gare d'Austerlitz
Daumesnil
Michel Bizot
Charles Michels
Cambronne
Montparnasse Bienvenüe
Place Monge
Porte d'Auteuil
Mirabeau
Javel André Citroën
Commerce
Sèvres Lecourbe
Falguière
Vavin
Port-Royal
Censier Daubenton
Saint Marcel
Dugommier
Boulogne Jean Jaurès
Michel Ange Molitor
Chardon Lagache
Félix Faure
Pasteur
Gare Montparnasse
Edgar Quinet
Raspail
Denfert Rochereau
Les Gobelins
Porte Dorée
Exelmans
Volontaires
Gaîté
Saint-Jacques
Campo Formio
Quai de la Gare
Bercy
Cour St-Émilion
Porte de Charenton
Boulogne Pont de St-Cloud
Porte de St-Cloud
Pont du Garigliano
Boucicaut
Mouton Duvernet
Corvisart
Place d'Italie
Chevaleret
Bibliothèque Fr. Mitterrand
Liberté
Vaugirard
Pernety
Glacière
Nationale
Olympiades
Charenton – Écoles
Marcel Sembat
Lourmel
Convention
Plaisance
Alésia
Tolbiac
Billancourt
Balard
Porte de Versailles
Parc des Expositions
Porte de Vanves
Porte d'Orléans
Cité Universitaire
Maison Blanche
Porte d'Italie
Porte de Choisy
Porte d'Ivry
École Vétérinaire de Maisons-Alfort
Maisons-Alfort – Stade
Pont de Sèvres
Val de Seine
Issy
Corentin Celton
Malakoff Plateau de Vanves
Mairie de Montrouge
Gentilly
Le Kremlin Bicêtre
Mairie d'Ivry
Ivry sur-Seine
Vitry sur-Seine
Maisons-Alfort Alfortville
Maisons-Alfort Les Juilliottes
Créteil – L'Échat
Malakoff Rue Étienne Dolet
Barbara
Laplace
Hôpital Bicêtre
Villejuif Léo Lagrange
Villejuif Paul Vaillant-Couturier
Les Ardoines
Créteil – Université
Viroflay Rive Droite
Mairie d'Issy
Meudon Val-Fleury
Bagneux Lucie Aubrac
Arcueil – Cachan
Villejuif Gustave Roussy
Villejuif Louis Aragon
Choisy-le-Roi
Le Vert de Maisons
Créteil – Préfecture
Châtillon – Montrouge
Bagneux
Bourg-la-Reine
L'Haÿ les-Roses
Chevilly-Larue
Créteil – Pompadour
Viroflay Rive Gauche
Chaville – Vélizy
Robinson
Parc de Sceaux
Les Saules
Créteil Pointe du Lac
Versailles Château
Jardin Parisien
La Croix de Berny
Antony
La Fraternelle
Thiais – Orly
Pont de Rungis
Orly Ville
Versailles – Chantiers
Dourdan
St-Martin-d'Étampes
Massy – Palaiseau
Aéroport d'Orly
Malesherbes
Melun
St-Quentin en-Yvelines
Saint-Rémy lès-Chevreuse
Évry Courcouronnes
Athis-Mons

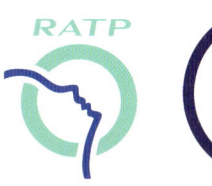

PARIS

PARIS
Régie Autonome des Transports Parisiens (RATP)

System Length	141 route miles
Number of Lines	14 (plus two short branches)
Number of Stations	405
Year Opened	1900
Year of Last Expansion	2024
Annual Ridership	1.56 billion (2019)
Subwayness	94% of stations underground

We have Paris to thank for inventing the universal transit term "metro." It's the sobriquet for La Compagnie du Chemin de Fer Métropolitain de Paris, S.A.—the Paris Metropolitan Railway Company—one of the two companies responsible for constructing the original system at the turn of the twentieth century. Ten lines were built and opened in rapid succession between 1900 and 1913, resulting in an extensive citywide network in record time and giving the Métro its homogeneous and undeniably Gallic style. One would have to look to Beijing or Shanghai a century later to find a similar scope of subway construction activity in such a short period.

Rome station entrance (Line 2)

TRANSIT TOURISM | 187

RÉGIE AUTONOME DES TRANSPORTS PARISIENS

Today, the Métro consists of fourteen separate lines (along with two small branch lines) and four hundred stations. The Métro routes crisscross Paris, resulting in multiple interchanges on each of the lines—some intersecting the same line twice. As a result, it doesn't much matter which station you choose to start your journey, since there are multiple alternatives to reach your destination. Most of the system is underground, but generally just below street level. One of the exceptions is in the hilly Montmartre section, where the deepest station—Abbesses—is nearly 120 feet down and fittingly is pronounced "abyss."

The Métro stations are spaced closely together—on average just 600 yards apart—half the typical distance of most subway systems. While a few lines follow more or less straight paths, most take twists and turns as they pirouette through Paris under the diagonal boulevards, especially Lines 7 and 8. And while Paris has no "Circle Line" today, it does currently have two *semi*circle lines (2 and 6), largely following the path of the old city walls. Thus, one can circumnavigate central Paris in a mere fifty-two stops, albeit with a line changeover at Étoile or Nation.

Five of the fourteen lines use the Parisian innovation of rubber-tired vehicles, a technology that provides a quieter and smoother ride, with faster acceleration and the ability to climb steeper grades. This pneumatic technology, introduced in 1956 on Line 11, has been exported with great success to newer systems in Montréal and Mexico City. Today, about twenty other subway systems worldwide have at least one rubber-tire line. And two of the Métro's lines—the recently revamped Line 1 (the oldest) and Line 14 (the newest, opened in 1998)—are fully automated. Line 4, which has a stop on Île de la Cité by Notre Dame, is to be automated next.

More is yet to come. The Grand Paris Express is a major expansion project currently under construction, and represents Europe's largest urban transportation initiative. It consists of four completely new Métro lines and two extensions that will add 122 miles and eighty-two stations by 2030. A major feature is Line 15, a 47-mile orbital with thirty-six stations that will exceed even Moscow's recently completed Big Circle Line as the longest underground route in the world.

PARIS

Rubber-tired train leaving Passy station (Line 6)

However, it is the *style* and not the statistics about the Métro that make it so indelibly associated with Paris. The original stations have gently cambered ceilings clad in beveled white tiles (*carrelage métro*), with blue-enamel station wall plaques and wide, dark platforms. *Très Parisien!* It is as unselfconsciously stylish as the French curve template that the engineers undoubtedly used to design the gracefully vaulted stations.

RÉGIE AUTONOME DES TRANSPORTS PARISIENS

Left:
Tiled, vaulted ceiling of Solferino station (Line 12)

Right:
Abbesses station entrance (Line 12)

Pleasing, elliptical curves are also found in the station entrances, designed in flamboyant art nouveau fashion by Hector Guimard. A total of 86 of the original 141 sinuous, organic station entrances made of forged iron still are in use, along with a couple of Guimard's spectacular fan-shaped glass-and-iron "dragonfly" édicules (covering kiosks), one of which was relocated to the aforementioned Abbesses station. Guimard's entryways have greatly influenced our design sense of Paris. They are such exquisite works of art that New York's Museum of Modern Art has installed one of them in its sculpture garden. Two others have been exported to Montréal and Mexico City, put to more workaday use as station portals, not just museum pieces.

PARIS

In more-recent times, architects have taken contemporary riffs on Guimard. The entrance to the Palais Royal-Louvre station (*below, left*) looks like a pop art version of one of his Belle Époque portals, while the Saint-Lazare canopy entrance by noted architect Jean-Marie Charpentier (*below, right*) could be a twenty-first-century interpretation of his glass edicules.

Left:
Palais Royal—
Musée du Louvre station entrance (Line 1)

Right:
Métro entrance in front of Gare St-Lazare (Lines 3, 12, 13, and 14)

Many of the stations have been modernized over the last century in phases, starting in earnest during the 1960s with paneling installed over the familiar white tiles in about seventy-five stations. In the 1970s, twenty stations were remodeled with then-trendy (but now-dated) orange-and-red earth-tone tiles. Most recently, there has been a return to the original turn-of-the-century aesthetic, providing improved lighting and original or restored white tilework, with the modernist addition of brightly colored plastic shell seating (*coques*) along the platforms.

RÉGIE AUTONOME DES TRANSPORTS PARISIENS

Surprisingly for a city that's world renowned for its art, the Métro's artworks program isn't nearly as extensive as that of other major cities, such as Brussels, Stockholm, or New York. Maybe it's because the elegantly tiled stations are deemed artistic enough as they are. Still, there are perhaps a dozen stations with unique architecture or design features. Among the highlights:

1. **Louvre-Rivoli** station (Line 1) was rebuilt in 1968 to show replicas of statuary and other artifacts in the Louvre Museum, adjacent to the station—one of the first "artistic" makeovers of a subway station anywhere.

2. **Arts et Métiers** station (Line 11) is a Jules Verne steampunk makeover completed in 1994 of an older station to commemorate the two hundredth anniversary of the Conservatoire National des Arts et Métiers, a science and industry museum adjacent to the station. Lots of brass fittings and pipes.

PARIS

3. Concorde station (Line 12) has a marvelous installation by the Belgian artist Françoise Schein replicating the Declaration of Rights of Man and the Citizen. Installed in 1991 to commemorate the two hundredth anniversary of the Declaration's adoption, her piece consists of 44,000 white tiles with blue lettering spelling out the Declaration, but without spacing or punctuation, so it works as both an informational display and an abstract tile design. She has also done installations on the same theme in subway stations in Berlin, Brussels, Lisbon, São Paulo, and Stockholm.

RÉGIE AUTONOME DES TRANSPORTS PARISIENS

Current Métro logo

In terms of its "brand identity," the Métro has never used one consistent logo like the London Underground roundel. Rather, its marker has varied over the years, from stenciled letters on a red background to a red M and then a yellow M, until they finally settled on a simple blue M inside a circle to mark the station entrances. Surprisingly restrained.

Complementing the Métro is a separate underground express commuter rail network called the Réseau Express Régional (RER), which has been superimposed on—or more accurately, infra-imposed *under*—the Métro system.[1] Built between the 1970s and 1990s, RER's 365-mile suburban rail network includes five routes running through central Paris in 47 miles of deep tunnels.

The RER interconnects with the Métro at ten underground stations, some of which are massive subterranean spaces such as Châtelet-Les Halles, reputedly the world's largest subway station—and certainly one of the busiest. Prior to the RER's expansion, Les Halles was the "belly of Paris," a massive historic wholesale market that each day supplied the city with food. Nowadays, Les Halles feeds the city with half a million daily commuters. Many Parisians of a certain age still feel great regret about the demolition fifty years ago of the mid-nineteenth-century glass-and-iron market pavilions that had been such an integral part of the city's character. Les Halles' market sheds easily could have become to Paris what repurposed Covent Garden market has become to London. Its replacement, a huge, impersonal entrance to a bland underground shopping mall, is a poor substitute. But the destruction of Les Halles spurred a historical-preservation movement that mobilized public and political support for converting the abandoned Gare d'Orsay railway terminal across the Seine into a superb museum of French impressionist and postimpressionist art.

---

[1] Strangely, French railways travel on the left-side track, whereas the Métro (and autos) travel on the right. Blame it on the bloody Brits, who provided France with the initial rail technology back in the early nineteenth century.

PARIS

In this way, Les Halles' sacrifice had a silver lining, much as the destruction of the old Pennsylvania Station in New York spawned America's historical-preservation movement in the US and helped save the threatened Grand Central Terminal.

Régie Autonome des Transports Parisiens (RATP), the regional transportation agency responsible for both RER and Métro, has its own *highly unusual* logo. RATP explains it as a stylized map showing the River Seine bounded by the Boulevard Périphérique, but the agency also notes that the image "can be viewed as a human face symbolizing progress and humanism." However, as one wag on a transit blog recently observed, "It looks more like the profile of a woman enjoying herself immensely . . . " "*Chacun à son goût*," as they say.

"Chacun à son goût": to each his own taste

In addition to having an evolving logo, the Paris Métro, unlike London's Underground, has used different typefaces for signage over time. More recently, they have settled on a bespoke lettering style—*Parisine*—which is a subtle sans serif mix of upper- and lowercase letters. While not nearly as memorable as Guimard's art nouveau typeface, it is highly sensible rather than highly sensual, suggesting it will age well.

In terms of cartography, the latest system map shown on the facing page of this chapter is very hard to read, since it squeezes in the five RER lines and thirteen tram lines as well as the sixteen Métro lines. And with its regimented 45- and 90-degree angles, the map seems soulless, or worse—from a Gallic viewpoint—lacking *panache*.

I find the midcentury Métro maps such as the reproduction of one shown on the next page much more visually appealing and easier to read, even though—or perhaps, precisely because—they are charmingly irregular, as with certain French verbs. It clearly shows, for example, Lines 4 and 7 winding through the city in an organic sinewy fashion, not unlike the iron filigree on a Guimard station entrance.

TRANSIT TOURISM | 195

RÉGIE AUTONOME DES TRANSPORTS PARISIENS

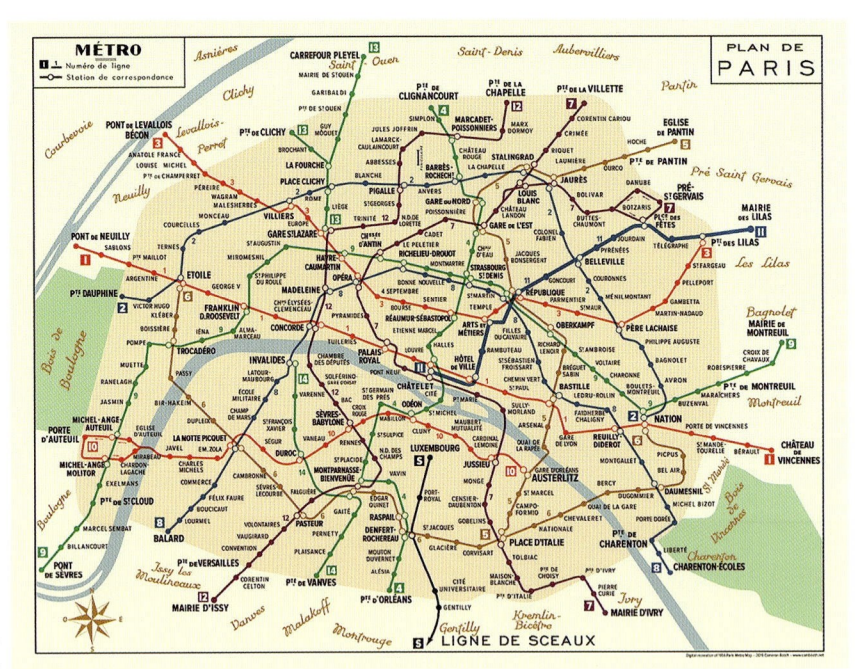

Reproduction of Paris Métro map, ca. 1956

Strangely, for all the times I have ridden subways over the decades in forty-plus cities on four continents, the only instance–when anyone tried to pickpocket me was in Paris, going through the turnstile at Charles De Gaulle–Étoile station, underneath the Arc de Triomphe. Not having adequate command of my high school French, I was limited to shouting out a few choice Anglo-Saxon expletives. Apparently, even in Paris—well known for its disdain of foreigners who won't *parle en français*—my message was acknowledged, since the highwayman (or should I say, subwayman) quickly turned heel, leaving me and my euros in tact. *Zut alors!*

PARIS

SUMMARY

Paris has one of the world's classic and classiest subway systems. It is a wonderful combination of *Belle Époque* styling and twenty-first-century efficiency, and it is hard to walk three blocks in Paris without happening upon one of its four hundred stations. The Métro is inseparable, functionally and culturally, from the city it serves, and has given its name to dozens of systems around the world. It is curious that there isn't more contemporary artwork displayed in the stations, but the white-tile vaulted stops are works of art in their own right. In short, the Métro is as emblematic of the City of Light as berets, baguettes, and Beaujolais.

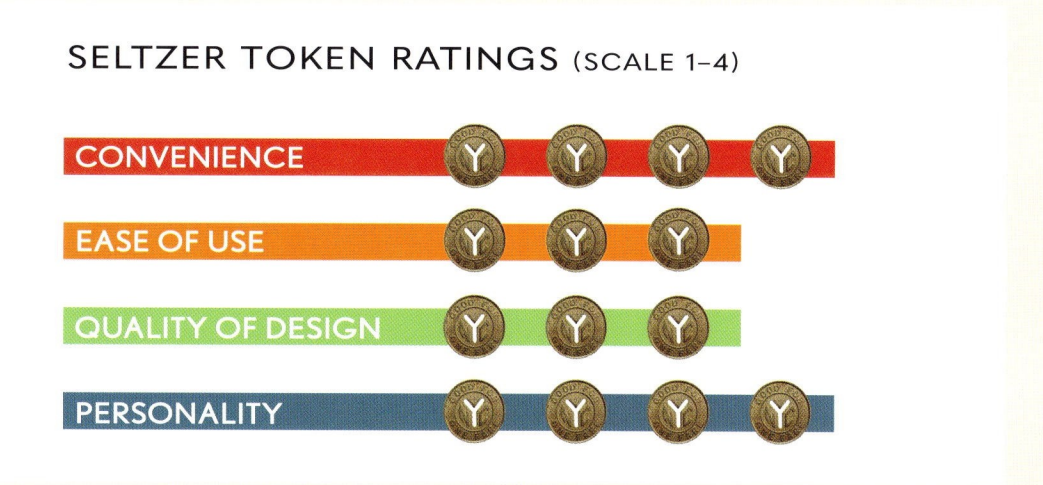

SELTZER TOKEN RATINGS (SCALE 1–4)

CONVENIENCE	4
EASE OF USE	3
QUALITY OF DESIGN	3
PERSONALITY	4

AVGÅNSTIDER I REALTID PÅ TUNNELBANAKARTA.SE
T10 Hjulsta
Tensta
Rinkeby
Rissne
Duvbo
Sundbybergs centrum
Solna strand
Huvudsta
T11 Akalla
Husby
Kista
Hallonbergen
Näckrosen
Solna centrum
Västra Skogen
Stadshagen
Fridhemsplan
S:t Eriksplan
Odenplan
Rådmansgatan
Hötorget
Rådhuset
T
T11 Kungsträdgården
T10
T14 Mörby centrum
Danderyds sjukhus
Bergshamra
Universitetet
Tekniska högsk.
Stadion
Östermalmstorg
T13 Ropsten
Gärdet
Karlaplan
Hässelby strand
T19
Åkeshov
T17
Alvik
T18
Hässelby gård
Johannelund
Vällingby
Råcksta
Blackeberg
Islandstorget
Ängbyplan
Åkeshov
Brommaplan
Abrahamsberg
Stora mossen
Alvik
Kristineberg
Thorildsplan
Gamla stan
Slussen
Axelsberg
Örnsberg
Aspudden
Liljeholmen
Hornstull
Zinkensdamm
Mariatorget
Mälarhöjden
Bredäng
Sätra
Skärholmen
Vårberg
Vårby gård
Masmo
Fittja
Alby
Hallunda
T13 Norsborg
Midsommarkransen
Telefonplan
Hägerstensåsen
Västertorp
T14 Fruängen
Medborgarplatsen
Skanstull
Gullmarsplan
Skärmarbrink
Globen
Enskede gård
Sockenplan
Svedmyra
Stureby
Bandhagen
Högdalen
Rågsved
T19 Hagsätra
Blåsut
Sandsborg
Skogskyrkogården
Tallkrogen
Gubbängen
Hökarängen
Farsta
T18 Farsta strand
Hammarbyhöjden
Björkhagen
Kärrtorp
Bagarmossen
T17 Skarpnäck

STOCKHOLM

STOCKHOLM
Storstockholms Lokaltrafik

System Length	67 route miles
Number of Lines	7
Number of Stations	100
Year Opened	1950
Year of Last Expansion	1994
Annual Ridership	462 million (2019)
Subwayness	47% of stations underground

With a metropolitan population of 2.4 million, Stockholm is situated on fourteen islands where Lake Mälaren flows into the Baltic Sea. Spared by Sweden's neutrality from any war damage over the last century, Stockholm surely ranks as one of Europe's most picturesque capitals. The central business district's low skyline is punctuated by church spires, monumental palaces, and stately civic buildings and is eminently walkable (or skateable, depending on the season). While Sweden can no longer boast of being the world naval power it was for much of the seventeenth century, it has earned a global reputation for being an influential innovator in such fields as engineering, cinematography, sexual mores, and—*even more excitingly*—subway stations!

Entrance to Stadion station (Red Line)

TRANSIT TOURISM | 199

STORSTOCKHOLMS LOKALTRAFIK

Stockholm's metro system is—quite literally—a rock star: twenty of the system's one hundred[1] stations are carved out of the city's granite and gneiss bedrock and painted with bold graphics and images. They are unlike the stations of any other system anywhere and undoubtedly are one of the highlights of a visit to Stockholm, along with savoring pickled herring washed down with aquavit.[2]

Kungsträdgården station (Blue Line)

Despite its relatively modest size, Stockholm has a highly developed transit system, fanning out in ten branches from where the three trunk lines meet at T-Centralen. This is the busiest station of the "T" (the Tunnelbana or underground railway) and is located underneath the Stockholm Central railway station, which serves regional and long-distance rail travelers. In 2017, Stockholm

---

1 There is actually a 101st station—an abandoned, half-finished "ghost" stop (evocatively called in Swedish a spökstation), which is located on the Blue Line beneath a forest preserve.
2 For the uninitiated, aquavit ("water of life") is the Swedish national drink, a strong (45 percent alcohol) distilled grain-and-potato mash infused with herbs. Judging from its astringent flavor, it must also make a highly effective graffiti remover, since the subway stations I visited were spotless!

STOCKHOLM

opened a new underground commuter rail station that was actually built *below* the metro lines to accommodate expanded service on the Pendeltåg (suburban commuter lines), as part of a 4.5-mile crosstown rail tunnel linking the northern and southern suburbs. There has been a flurry of similar crosstown commuter rail tunnels opened in recent years or under construction, including in Beijing, Istanbul, London, Munich, and Paris.

Each metro branch is color-coded by its associated trunk line—Gröna, Röda, and Blå, if you're working on your svenska. The first phases of the metro (the Green Line), opened in the 1950s by taking a tram line tunnel built in the early 1930s, upgrading it to metro standards, and extending it largely aboveground to serve the rapidly growing surrounding suburban communities and new towns. The Red Line followed in 1964, and the Blue Line a decade later. These second two lines are mostly underground, and all the lines have been extended several times in subsequent years.

The trains operate on the left-hand track, which was consistent with how road traffic in Sweden operated, up until a massive nationwide switchover to the right side of the road on March 9, 1967. As I understand it, the government of Sweden initially considered phasing in the driving-side change gradually, starting with cars bearing odd-numbered license plates, but this approach ultimately was deemed problematic. . .

Since 2009, the Stockholm Metro has been operated by a private company that is a subsidiary of the Hong Kong Mass Transit Railway Corporation, a shareholder-owned corporation. Stockholm thus is one of the few cities whose subway system is operated by the private sector. Other cities include two MTR-managed transit systems in Australia, several in China, and Buenos Aires's "Subte." With a very few exceptions, most subways systems are not self-supporting from fares and commercial revenues and rely upon governmental subsidies to operate. Still, a handful of systems have elected to contract out operations to private companies, with the objective of achieving superior service at a lower required subsidy level.

STORSTOCKHOLMS LOKALTRAFIK

Sweden has long enjoyed a reputation for excellence in contemporary design, from Orrefors crystal to IKEA furniture: The adoption of the now-emblematic "T" symbol for Tunnelbana as the system logo evidenced the city's commitment to embrace smart-looking graphic design. The symbol is conspicuously posted on unusual lozenge-shaped, three-sided signposts at each station, with the T suggesting transit, train, and travel as well as tunnel. This logo inspired the designers responsible for the Massachusetts Bay Transportation Authority's graphic makeover in 1965 to adapt the same T symbol for Boston.

Left: Metro entrance marker

Right: Metro train near Gamla Stan (Old Town) station

One often hears the Swedish national character described as *lagom*—taking everything in moderation—but insofar as the subway goes (and, for the record, it goes all the way to Hjulsta on the Blå Line), Stockholm went "full bore," starting with the underground extensions in the early 1970s. Nowhere in all of subwaydom is there a more successful integration of architecture, engineering, artwork, and urban planning.

STOCKHOLM

The functionalist design style of the first generation of stations built in the 1950s has been called "Late Lavatorial" because of their boxlike structure and extensive reliance on plain ceramic tiling. An early adopter of the concept of "Art for the People," the Stockholm metro began setting the standard for sophisticated design in the mid-1960s. In 1971, the Stockholm Transport Art Advisory Council established a policy that the stations should have artwork themed to the local surroundings above and around them.[3] For the stations built since the 1970s, the artists worked jointly with architects as the station designs were conceived. And Stockholm has subsequently remodeled sixty of its earlier stations to incorporate major art installations, in some cases thirty or even forty years after they had initially opened. Today, almost every station on the Tunnelbana hosts major artwork, and Stockholm proudly claims that the "T"—with its 67 route miles—is the world's longest art gallery. This civic commitment to incorporating artwork has since been added to several of the commuter rail (Pendeltåg) and tram line stations as well.

The initial Green Line was built largely aboveground, except for the downtown section, which was excavated using a shallow trench "cut-and-cover" method. Subsequent lines and extensions were built by tunneling much deeper, drilling or blasting through the hard bedrock, to minimize disruption at street level. This provided the opportunity to create "cave stations"—large underground caverns with dramatic, uneven surfaces. To save money on wall finishes, the authorities in the early 1970s began coating the raw rock surface with 3 inches of sprayed concrete. The resulting surface provides a beautiful contrast between the rough walls, revealing the natural contours of the rock, and the smooth, modern finishes of the platforms and fixtures. The walls serve as giant canvases for Swedish artists to paint their inventive compositions.

---

[3] Other cities have since adopted this policy, nowhere more so than Beijing, with many of its 399 stations containing murals and other artwork reflecting their historical environs.

STORSTOCKHOLMS LOKALTRAFIK

The Progress of Art over 17,000 Years, from Cave Dwellings to Cave Stations:

Upper: Lascaux Caves, France

Lower: Tensta station (Blue Line)

204 | EUROPE—SWEDEN

STOCKHOLM

Successive stations constructed in the 1970s and '80s grew more elaborate, and there are now twenty cave stations throughout the system. My personal favorite is Kungsträdgården (King's Garden) station, Stockholm's deepest at 120 feet, constructed in 1987. Excavated near the remnants of the historic seventeenth-century Makalös Palace (once one of Stockholm's grandest homes, but demolished nearly two hundred years ago), the station includes casts of statuary and other finds from the site. The artist added statuary and architectural features so that it appears as if one had stumbled upon an archaeological site. This line is being extended from K'gården in two branches running beneath the harbor to the south and east, to be completed by 2030.

Left:
Kungsträdgården station
(Blue Line)

Right:
Solna centrum station
(Blue Line)

Many of the station designs are based on local landmarks on the streets above. Each platform has a compass showing which way north is, for orientation.

TRANSIT TOURISM | 205

STORSTOCKHOLMS LOKALTRAFIK

When the Red Line was extended in 1973, the local authority commissioned murals and sculptures for the Tekniska Högskolan (Technological College) station, depicting the history of engineering and technology, and outfitted the nearby Stadion station to commemorate Stockholm's hosting of the 1912 Olympic Games. The Universitetet station has a tile work installation by Francoise Schein with the Declaration of Human Rights spelled out in Swedish, similar to the works she has created in French for stations in Paris and Brussels, among other cities.

Francoise Schein, *Declaration of Human Rights* mural at Universitetet station (Red Line)

STOCKHOLM

The photos on this page and the next page show the superb range of artistry on display in the Stockholm metro.

Top:
T-Centralen station
(Red, Green, Blue Lines)

Bottom:
Rådmansgatan station (Green Line), with image of famed Swedish dramatist August Strindberg

TRANSIT TOURISM | 207

STORSTOCKHOLMS LOKALTRAFIK

Top: Rådhuset station (Blue Line)

Bottom: Stadion station (Red Line), serving the stadium where the 1912 Stockholm Olympics were held.

STOCKHOLM

SUMMARY

Spelunking through Stockholm's cave (and other) subway stations is a great way to see underground art while getting around this beautiful city. The art installations are spectacular, fully immersive experiences that have had a worldwide impact in changing public perceptions regarding what subways could—and should—look like. Several extensions with a dozen additional stations are currently under construction, and the architects' renderings demonstrate that Stockholm is maintaining its commitment to superb artistic installations at the new stops. Even half a century on, the Stockholm metro stations look smart and hip—just like the city itself. I award the system a perfect four-token rating—tied with Brussels, London, Madrid, and Montréal for pride of place!

SELTZER TOKEN RATINGS (SCALE 1–4)

CONVENIENCE	Y Y Y Y
EASE OF USE	Y Y Y Y
QUALITY OF DESIGN	Y Y Y Y
PERSONALITY	Y Y Y Y

TRANSIT TOURISM | 209

北京城市轨道交通线网图
Beijing Rail Transit Lines
图例：
Legend
地铁一号线 地铁八通线
地铁二号线
地铁四号线 地铁大兴线
地铁五号线
地铁六号线
地铁七号线
地铁八号线
地铁九号线
地铁十号线
地铁十一号线
地铁十三号线
地铁十四号线
地铁十五号线
地铁十六号线
地铁十七号线
地铁十九号线
地铁房山线
地铁昌平线
地铁亦庄线
地铁燕房线
S1线
西郊线
亦庄T1线
首都机场线
大兴机场线
换乘站
站内换乘 暂缓开通
北
NORTH
扫码使用北京地铁服务小程序
Scan the QR Code to Use the Beijing Subway Mini Program
请扫码获取更多信息
Please Scan QR Code for More Information
交通运输服务监督电话 Transportation Service Supervision Hotline 12328
北京轨道交通路网乘客服务热线 Beijing Rail Transit Passenger Service Hotline 96123
北京地铁服务热线 Beijing Subway Service Hotline 96165
北京地铁官方网站 Beijing Subway Official Website https://www.bjsubway.com

BEIJING

北京地铁
BEIJING SUBWAY
Beijing Subway Group Company Ltd.

System Length	505 route miles
Number of Lines	23 lines (20 subway, two airport, one maglev)
Number of Stations	470 stations
Year Opened	1971
Year of Last Expansion	2023
Annual Ridership	2.3 billion (2019)
Subwayness	81% of stations underground

Entrance to Hujialou station (Lines 6 and 11)

Lao-Tzu, the fifth-century BCE Chinese philosopher, famously wrote that "a journey of a thousand miles begins with a single step." For me and my wife, Lisa, however, our 1,000-mile, three-week tour of China in 2017 ended abruptly with a single *mis*step. On our first full day of sightseeing—an overcast morning—we were shuttled to a rather wild, rural section of the Great Wall an hour or so north of Beijing. Neither of us had the right footwear for the overgrowth and rough terrain leading to the wall. Following a magnificent walk along an almost empty section of the wall, we picked our way down a steep slope just as the heavens opened. Under treacherously

TRANSIT TOURISM | 211

BEIJING SUBWAY GROUP COMPANY LTD.

muddy conditions, Lisa lost her footing and ended up breaking several vertebrae. Although not a life-threatening accident, it did require her to remain in bed for several days at our hotel in Beijing until she recuperated sufficiently for us to fly back to the States. Her confinement, while unfortunate, did afford me the unexpected opportunity of repurposing our personal guide to give me an extensive tour of Beijing's burgeoning subway network over the next few days, with an occasional historical or cultural site thrown in.

When one thinks of China, one thinks of growth. But as spectacular as the growth of the Chinese economy has been over the past forty years (400-fold increase), the expansion of China's subway systems is even more astonishing (800-fold). Beijing opened the nation's very first subway line in 1971. Fast-forward to today, and there are forty-five cities across China with subway systems, thirty-three of which have opened just since 2010, and six more cities have new systems under construction.

Beijing's subway system expanded dramatically to accommodate the city's explosive population growth. When the first ten-station line opened in 1971, Beijing had 4.5 million inhabitants. As recently as the year 2000, Beijing had only two transit lines, but its population had grown to 10.3 million. Since 2002, Beijing's subway construction has continued at breakneck pace: at least one new line or extension has opened every year over the last decade, and in the last two decades the city's population has doubled. There are now twenty-three separate lines, of which fifteen are operated by a municipal corporation, four by a public-private entity that includes Hong Kong's very successful Mass Transit Railway Corporation, and four by two other operators.

System-wide, Beijing's subways currently run on 505 route miles, and an additional 132 miles with two new lines and seven extensions are scheduled to open by 2029. To put this in perspective, since opening in 1971, Beijing has built more miles of subway than the combined size of America's four large American "legacy" systems (New York, Chicago, Boston, and

BEIJING

Philadelphia). Beijing and Shanghai jockey back and forth for the title of "world's largest system," as each city's subway continues expanding, leaving other cities far behind (as of this writing, Beijing leads by a whisker).

It is not just the extent of capital investment that's so breathtaking, but the *speed* with which the lines have been built. Each subway line on average is about 18 miles long and typically is completed in under five years. For most new subways in the United States, it takes twice that time or longer, covering considerably shorter distances.[1]

And yet, despite its size, Beijing's complex system is actually quite easy to understand. Unlike the Tokyo system, where the lines are jumbled and squooshed together against Tokyo Bay like an overcrowded rush-hour train, Beijing's system—mostly intersecting horizontals, verticals, and diagonals—follows the very orderly street plan for the city. The urban grid was laid out in the fourteenth century during the early Ming dynasty. It was organized according to *fengshui* principles and numerology in order to promote harmonious social order, with the Emperor's Palace situated in the Forbidden City at the very center. And for a visitor, the Beijing system map reflects this sense of order across a vast scale. The network map of subway lines could almost be one of those well-proportioned and elegant Chinese ideograms, writ large, like the initial Mandarin character for "railroad" (鐵).

Line 1, running east–west, was the city's only route for a dozen years, until the Inner Loop (Line 2) opened in 1984. Less a loop than a beveled rectangle, Line 2 follows the path of the former inner city walls, built in the fifteenth century under the Ming dynasty. These walls, which were

---

[1] Concurrently, while all this subway construction has been going on, Beijing also has built a 6-mile rail tunnel for suburban commuter trains underneath the city, which connects two of its major railway stations—Beijing and Beijing West. It is a kind of Chinese "Crossrail" or "RER"—yet, it hardly merits a Wikipedia entry compared to the much more extensive subway construction activity.

BEIJING SUBWAY GROUP COMPANY LTD.

50 feet tall and once extended for 15 miles, survived numerous invasions and natural disasters for half a millennium but alas could not survive the Great Leap Forward in the mid-1960s. The ancient fortifications were demolished by Mao Zedong's decree to accommodate Line 2 and Ring Road 2 above it. All that remains of the wall today is a 1-mile segment where the subway line jogs over to serve Beijing's main railway station.

In fact, Beijing's stations express a strong sense of place through their names, many of which are derived from neighboring historical or geographic landmarks rather than street names. Some of the station names are real tongue twisters. Line 15 is not only the deepest and one of the longest of Beijing's subways, but it also can boast the longest station name: Qinghuadongluxikou. (By the time you're able to ask if this is your stop, the train has left the station.)

Yet, even for someone whose knowledge of Mandarin is limited to transliterating menus, one begins to recognize patterns in the place-names. Applying transit toponymy to deconstruct the station names, one sees recurring elements giving a sense of place, such as "qiao" (bridge), "xiao" (little), and "-men" (gate). So, for example, on the Line 2 Inner Loop, eleven of the eighteen station names reflect the ancient wall portals: Xizhimen (Western Gate), Hepingmen (Gate of Peace), Funchengmen (Gate of Abundant Success), and Fuxingmen (Gate of Revival).

Beijing has an Outer Loop subway as well (Line 10), which runs underneath the third Ring Road. At 35 miles, it had been the longest circular subway route in the world until being edged out by less than half a mile by Moscow's Big Circle Line in 2024. By way of comparison, the more celebrated Chunnel is 31 miles long.

Beijing's subway stations are generally presentable enough but, from a design perspective, run no risk of winning the Pritzker Prize. Most are low-ceilinged rectangular spaces with very little architectural drama. But they are all very civil spaces: well lit, spotless, and most offer clean

BEIJING

toilets—although not as handsomely appointed as Tokyo's. All the signage is very helpfully transliterated Pinyin style into Roman characters, with key travel directional signs in English. Since the 2008 Summer Olympics, every station entrance has had baggage-screening equipment for security purposes—remarkable for a system that carries on average six million passengers daily.

A typical Beijing subway station: Huoying (Line 8)

Beijing's two oldest lines are very plain looking indeed. But once Beijing was designated as the host city for the 2008 games, the city launched an ambitious program to make its subway system appear as close to world class as possible, by incorporating architectural flourishes and commissioning major art installations at many of the new stops. Since then, the architectural styling has improved, as shown by the station views on the next page.

TRANSIT TOURISM | 215

BEIJING SUBWAY GROUP COMPANY LTD.

Left: South Gate of Forest Park station (Line 8)

Center: Concourse of Jin'anqiao station (Line 6)

Right: Beitucheng station (Line 8)

The most prevalent form of artwork is murals made from mosaic tiles, depicting scenes of historical or neighborhood cultural significance. But there are also plenty of frescos, reliefs, sculptures, decorated cylindrical columns, and contemporary lighting based on Chinese lanterns. Beijing now ranks as one of the world's leading cities for "underground art," but not in the sense of counterculture imagery—quite the opposite. Rather than being edgy or even mildly challenging, the artwork tends toward the "safe" and "harmonious." In that way, it's not unlike the sanitized reportage found in the easy-to-hold/painful-to-read official Communist Party English-language tabloid, *China Daily*. Shown above on the right is Beituchung station (Lines 8 and 10) adjacent to the Olympic Sports Center, containing supergraphics of Ming-dynasty porcelain patterns—one of the more unusual art installations.

Of the dozens of notable pieces of artwork in the stations, my favorite might be in Line 8's Nanluoguxiang station, titled *Memories of Beijing*. It's a series of glass tile wall murals showing historical characters and settings, composed of some four thousand amber blocks, each of which contains some memento contributed by local residents (coins, badges, old photos). It is possible to scan a QR code next to each object to see a write-up and video about the item and its provenance.

BEIJING

Nanluoguxiang station (Line 8)

A close-up of the amber blocks with the objects within:

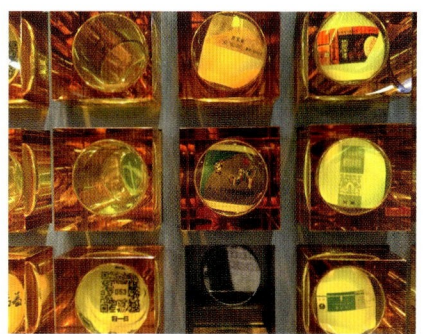

TRANSIT TOURISM | 217

BEIJING SUBWAY GROUP COMPANY LTD.

Brian Salter, a British expat living in Beijing, has published a terrific Kindle book called *Underground Art in the Beijing Subway*, documenting art installations in nearly two hundred stations on eighteen lines. It is one of the few books (in English) I have found about the Beijing subway. Below are views of some of the attractive murals found in the system:

Left:
Xisi station
(Line 4)

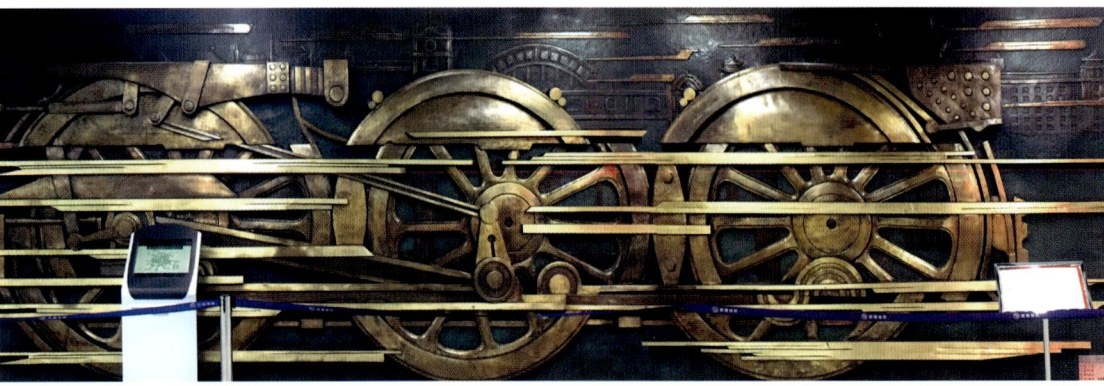

Right:
Xidan station
(Line 4)

Huangcun Railway Station
subway concourse
(Daxing Line)

BEIJING

SUMMARY

It is an amazing feat for Beijing to start from Nowheresville in 1970 and rise to become one of the world's largest subway systems today—and there is no sign that it's slowing down. Worldwide, it currently ranks in the top three in number of subway lines, number of stations, system route length, and ridership. The stations, while largely functional in appearance, efficiently handle the daily ebb and flow of one of the world's most populous cities. As the quantity of stations has increased, so has the quality of design, with greater emphasis on architecture and art installations since the 2008 Olympics. Because the system is expanding so rapidly, it definitely warrants a return visit to see whether the transit architecture belowground becomes as daring and inventive as Beijing's new commercial and civic architecture aboveground.

SELTZER TOKEN RATINGS (SCALE 1–4)

CONVENIENCE	4
EASE OF USE	4
QUALITY OF DESIGN	2
PERSONALITY	2

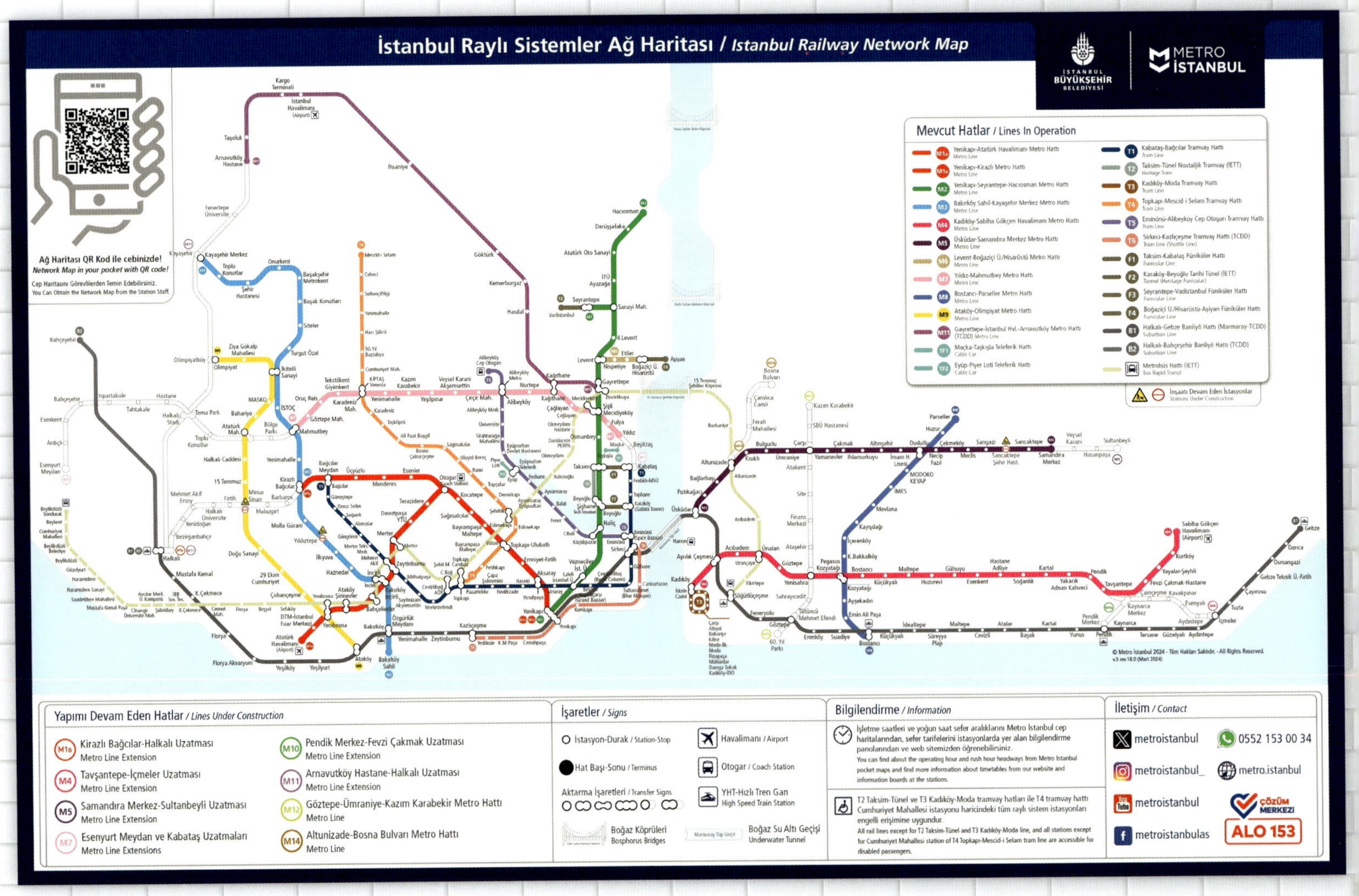

İstanbul Raylı Sistemler Ağ Haritası / Istanbul Railway Network Map
İSTANBUL BÜYÜKŞEHİR BELEDİYESİ
METRO İSTANBUL
Ağ Haritası QR Kod ile cebinizde!
Network Map in your pocket with QR code!
Cep Haritasını Görevlilerden Temin Edebilirsiniz.
You Can Obtain the Network Map from the Station Staff.
Mevcut Hatlar / Lines In Operation
M1A Yenikapı-Atatürk Havalimanı Metro Hattı Metro Line
M1B Yenikapı-Kirazlı Metro Hattı Metro Line
M2 Yenikapı-Seyrantepe-Hacıosman Metro Hattı Metro Line
M3 Bakırköy Sahil-Kayaşehir Merkez Metro Hattı Metro Line
M4 Kadıköy-Sabiha Gökçen Havalimanı Metro Hattı Metro Line
M5 Üsküdar-Samandıra Merkez Metro Hattı Metro Line
M6 Levent-Boğaziçi Ü./Hisarüstü Metro Hattı Metro Line
M7 Yıldız-Mahmutbey Metro Hattı Metro Line
M8 Bostancı-Parseller Metro Hattı Metro Line
M9 Ataköy-Olimpiyat Metro Hattı Metro Line
M11 Gayrettepe-İstanbul Hvl.-Arnavutköy Metro Hattı (TCDD) Metro Line
TF1 Maçka-Taşkışla Teleferik Hattı Cable Car
TF2 Eyüp-Piyer Loti Teleferik Hattı Cable Car
T1 Kabataş-Bağcılar Tramvay Hattı Tram Line
T2 Taksim-Tünel Nostaljik Tramvay (İETT) Heritage Tram
T3 Kadıköy-Moda Tramvay Hattı Tram Line
T4 Topkapı-Mescid-i Selam Tramvay Hattı Tram Line
T5 Eminönü-Alibeyköy Cep Otogarı Tramvay Hattı Tram Line
T6 Sirkeci-Kazlıçeşme Tramvay Hattı (TCDD) Tram Line (Shuttle Line)
F1 Taksim-Kabataş Füniküler Hattı Funicular Line
F2 Karaköy-Beyoğlu Tarihi Tünel (İETT) Tunnel (Heritage Funicular)
F3 Seyrantepe-Vadistanbul Füniküler Hattı Funicular Line
F4 Boğaziçi Ü./Hisarüstü-Aşiyan Füniküler Hattı Funicular Line
B1 Halkalı-Gebze Banliyö Hattı (Marmaray-TCDD) Suburban Line
B2 Halkalı-Bahçeşehir Banliyö Hattı (TCDD) Suburban Line
Metrobüs Hattı (İETT) Bus Rapid Transit
İnşaatı Devam Eden İstasyonlar Stations Under Construction
© Metro İstanbul 2024 - Tüm Hakları Saklıdır. - All Rights Reserved.
v.3 rev.18.0 (Mart 2024)
Yapımı Devam Eden Hatlar / Lines Under Construction
M1B Kirazlı Bağcılar-Halkalı Uzatması Metro Line Extension
M4 Tavşantepe-İçmeler Uzatması Metro Line Extension
M5 Samandıra Merkez-Sultanbeyli Uzatması Metro Line Extension
M7 Esenyurt Meydan ve Kabataş Uzatmaları Metro Line Extensions
M10 Pendik Merkez-Fevzi Çakmak Uzatması Metro Line Extension
M11 Arnavutköy Hastane-Halkalı Uzatması Metro Line Extension
M12 Göztepe-Ümraniye-Kazım Karabekir Metro Hattı Metro Line
M14 Altunizade-Bosna Bulvarı Metro Hattı Metro Line
İşaretler / Signs
İstasyon-Durak / Station-Stop
Hat Başı-Sonu / Terminus
Aktarma İşaretleri / Transfer Signs
Havalimanı / Airport
Otogar / Coach Station
YHT-Hızlı Tren Garı High Speed Train Station
Boğaz Köprüleri Bosphorus Bridges
Marmaray Tüp Geçit
Boğaz Su Altı Geçişi Underwater Tunnel
Bilgilendirme / Information
İşletme saatleri ve yoğun saat sefer aralıklarını Metro İstanbul cep haritalarından, sefer tarifelerini istasyonlarda yer alan bilgilendirme panolarından ve web sitemizden öğrenebilirsiniz.
You can find about the operating hour and rush hour headways from Metro Istanbul pocket maps and find more information about timetables from our website and information boards at the stations.
T2 Taksim-Tünel ve T3 Kadıköy-Moda tramvay hatları ile T4 tramvay hattı Cumhuriyet Mahallesi istasyonu haricindeki tüm raylı sistem istasyonları engelli erişimine uygundur.
All rail lines except for T2 Taksim-Tünel and T3 Kadıköy-Moda line, and all stations except for Cumhuriyet Mahallesi station of T4 Topkapı-Mescid-i Selam tram line are accessible for disabled passengers.
İletişim / Contact
metroistanbul
metroistanbul_
metroistanbul
metroistanbulas
0552 153 00 34
metro.istanbul
ÇÖZÜM MERKEZİ
ALO 153

ISTANBUL

ISTANBUL
İstanbul Büyükşehir Belediyesi
(Istanbul Metropolitan Municipality)

System Length	151 route miles
Number of Lines	11
Number of Stations	158
Year Opened	1989
Year of Last Expansion	2024
Annual Ridership	542 million (2019)
Subwayness	91% of stations underground

Şişhane station (Line M2)

For historical significance, architectural splendor, and sheer natural beauty, the city of Istanbul is unsurpassed. Situated on the Sea of Marmara, Istanbul is perched on either side of the Bosporus Strait, connecting the Black Sea to the Mediterranean—a position that has given the city key advantages in trade and defense since antiquity. It's a city that straddles both cultures and continents—Europe and Asia, included here with Asia because of Türkiye.

Originally founded by the ancient Greeks as Byzantium, it was renamed Constantinople after the death of the Roman emperor Constantine. The city served as the capital of the eastern Roman and

TRANSIT TOURISM | 221

İSTANBUL BÜYÜKŞEHIR BELEDIYESI (ISTANBUL METROPOLITAN MUNICIPALITY)

Byzantine Empires until the mid-fifteenth century. With the Ottoman conquest and for nearly five centuries thereafter under the sultans, it was the heart of the Ottoman Empire. The colloquial term "Istanbul" (from the Greek phrase meaning "in the city") was formally adopted as the city's name in 1930.

Its stunning array of mosques, palaces, and lively covered markets all combine to make Istanbul a unique and beguiling place. But for me, as a lapsed muni finance banker, it is Istanbul's ancient infrastructure that holds special appeal—particularly the fifth-century wall along the western edge of the old city. Theodosius II, emperor of the Eastern Roman Empire from 408 to 450 CE, built these fortifications stretching 4 miles from the Golden Horn Bay to the Sea of Marmara. The Byzantine walls held attackers literally at bay for nearly a thousand years while Constantinople reigned as arguably the world's most important city. It took 50,000 Turkish troops and seventy cannons dragged over 100 miles from Adrianople to the Bosporus for Mehmed the Conqueror to breach the city walls in 1453. Accompanied by my terrific young guide, Ugur Ildiz, we transited the Theodosian Wall with considerably less effort for just the price of a metro ticket (3.50 Turkish lira) by alighting at the Topkapi ("Cannon Gate")–Ulubatli station on the M1 Line.

Istanbul lays claim to having the world's second-oldest underground railway, after London's Metropolitan Line. The Tünel, opened in 1875, is an underground cable-hauled funicular running one-third of a mile from the Galata port area to the Beyoğlu commercial district, up a 200-foot hill. Originally powered by two steam engines, it was converted to electricity in the 1940s. Fully restored to its original splendor in 2007, it is a handsome piece of nineteenth-century engineering, and well worth the ninety-second trip. It also has some beautiful contemporary tile illustrations from the famed Iznik workshops, but more on that later. Notwithstanding its name, however, the Tünel and Istanbul's other more recent underground funicular do not really qualify in my book as "true" subways—I think of them as being more akin to underground ski gondolas.

ISTANBUL

View of the Tünel

The city would need to wait over a century for its first bona fide metro to begin service. Istanbul's population in 1950 was one million, but by 1989 it had swelled to six million. That was the year the first actual subway line (M1) opened. Since then, both the city's population and its subway system have grown dramatically: as of 2024, Istanbul had over sixteen million inhabitants and the city had opened up ten more subway lines, most of them since 2012.

The system's expansion has been positively dizzying (like the Whirling Dervishes one sees at the Mevlevi Lodge near the Tünel's summit station). Ten more new lines or major extensions are under construction and expected to open by. When the twelve new lines and extensions are completed (shown as gray outlines on the map), it is safe to say that Istanbul's public transport system will be truly Byzantine in its complexity. As Istanbul's metro expands, it will surpass Madrid as Europe's fourth-largest system, and London, Paris, and Moscow soon may be "hearing footsteps."

İSTANBUL BÜYÜKŞEHIR BELEDIYESI (ISTANBUL METROPOLITAN MUNICIPALITY)

And this does not take into account another huge underground rail investment: the Marmaray. This $4.5 billion commuter rail project opened in 2013, linking and upgrading two existing suburban rail lines on the European and Anatolian (Asian) sides of the Bosporus. The two continents are now connected by a new underwater rail tunnel—the deepest submerged tunnel in the world—which runs 200 feet below the water's surface. The principal underground station is Yenikapı at the ancient port wall, connecting to two metro lines. Excavating Yenikapı station itself was a mammoth undertaking. Although they didn't in fact discover any remains of mammoths, they *did* uncover lots of other important finds, including an eight-thousand-year-old Neolithic village and remains of two dozen ships that had sunk to the harbor floor seven centuries ago.

The delays caused by having to redesign Yenikapı station and carefully sift through the soil for objects and structures reportedly added four years and half a billion dollars to the construction cost. The station complex and a planned museum and "archaeopark" adjacent to the station will exhibit some of the most important artifacts from the site.

Yenikapi station, (Line M2)

ISTANBUL

Like a Seljuk tile mosaic, the segments of Istanbul's metro are being assembled into an integrated pattern, but at the rapid pace more commonly associated with new subways in major Chinese cities rather than, say, Naples's painstakingly slow process of gingerly excavating around archaeological sites.

Boğaziçi Üniversitesi station (Line M6)

From an architectural viewpoint, Istanbul's metro stations are not nearly as dramatic as those found in newer lines elsewhere described in this book (Budapest, London, Moscow, Munich, and Naples). But what sets the system apart from all others is the widespread use of magnificent tile murals depicting historical events and local landmarks, as well as intricate, abstract patterns.

In the sixteenth and seventeenth centuries, the town of Iznik, located about 50 miles southwest of Istanbul, was famous internationally as a center of decorative Turkish tiles and pottery. Fashioned principally from quartz rather than clay, these tiles are both durable and colorful, with vivid coral reds, azure turquoises, and cobalt blues. The sultans decorated many of their most prominent religious and civil buildings (such as Topkapi Palace and the Blue Mosque) with Iznik tiles, in addition to exporting them to Europe.

İSTANBUL BÜYÜKŞEHIR BELEDIYESI (ISTANBUL METROPOLITAN MUNICIPALITY)

With the decline in influence of the Ottoman Empire, the Iznik workshops also declined in quality and had ceased operations by the end of the seventeenth century. After a gap of over three centuries, the Iznik tile works were revived by a nonprofit foundation in the 1990s and began producing quartz tiles again. The combination of the Iznik tile murals at many of the stations and the stenciled tile pattern motifs in the railcars gives the metro system a distinct Levantine inflection.

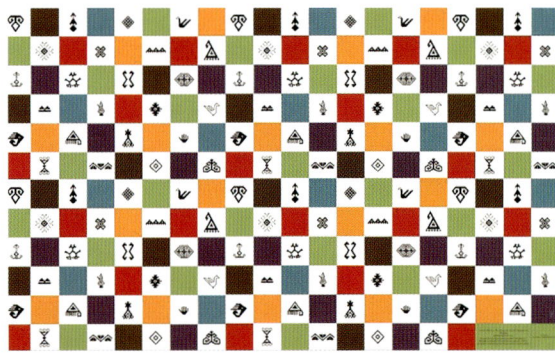

Top left: M4 Küçükyali station. Iznik tile decorations incorporating Hittite, Seljuk and Ottoman patterns.

Top right: Taksim station (Line M2), Istanbul metro's busiest station

Right: Beautiful Iznik tiles depicting galleons at Taksim

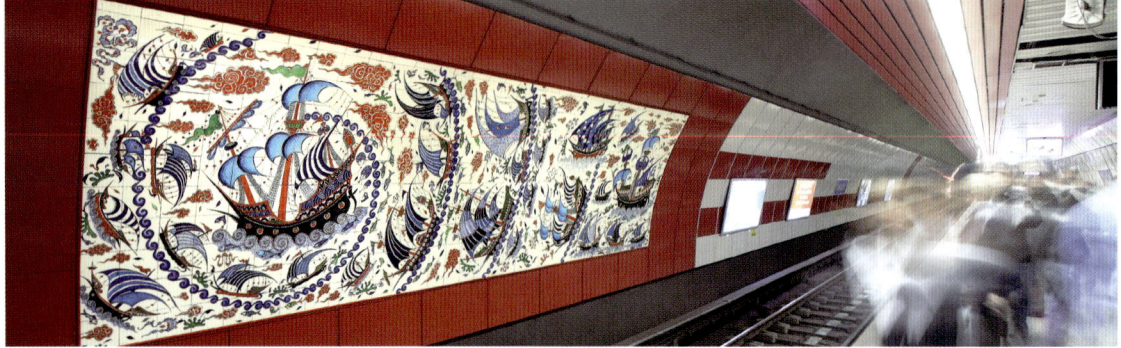

ASIA—TÜRKIYE

ISTANBUL

Although the system is predominantly underground, the M2 line, in a rare aboveground appearance, runs over the Golden Horn Harbor on a cable-stayed bridge. Haliç station is located smack-dab in the middle, allowing passengers to walk to harborside destinations at either end.

Line M2
crossing the Golden Horn
(station in the middle)

İSTANBUL BÜYÜKŞEHIR BELEDIYESI (ISTANBUL METROPOLITAN MUNICIPALITY)

Istanbul's metro employs two attractive logos: the corporate logo consists of a blue M with a red chevron beneath it, while at street level the station entrances are marked by a teardrop-shaped red-and-blue symbol with a white M above a red arrow pointing down. Each subway car carries the municipal logo, which is one of the most emblematic city marks I have ever seen: it depicts a mosque with minarets atop seven triangles for the seven hills of Istanbul. The castellated semi-circle at the bottom represents the European and Asian sides of the city, separated by a gap signifying the Bosporus. Very cool, indeed!

Corporate Logo   Station Entrance Logo   Municipal Logo

ISTANBUL

SUMMARY

Istanbul's rapidly expanding metro system represents a remarkable public investment in improving mobility and access in this major, amazing metropolis. The stations are not architecturally flashy, but the station wall tile decorations do a wonderful job evoking the city's rich Levantine character and customs. Be advised, however, that there are limits on the extent to which Istanbulite traditions carry over into the metro: I discovered that haggling over prices, which is so readily expected in the Grand Bazaar, is not as keenly welcomed by the metro-station cashiers. A return visit is definitely warranted in several years' time to see the build-out of other key segments of this impressive system.

SELTZER TOKEN RATINGS (SCALE 1–4)

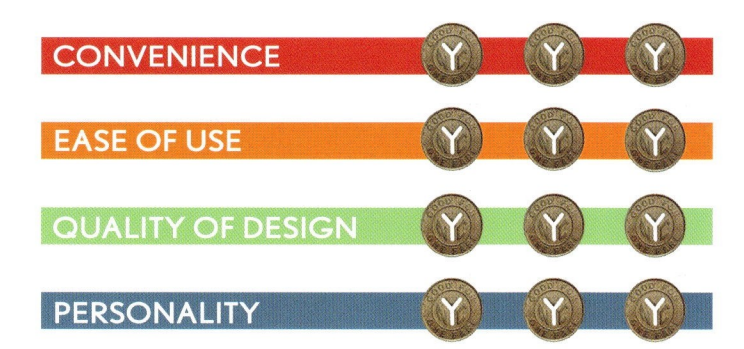

CONVENIENCE	3
EASE OF USE	3
QUALITY OF DESIGN	3
PERSONALITY	3

TRANSIT TOURISM

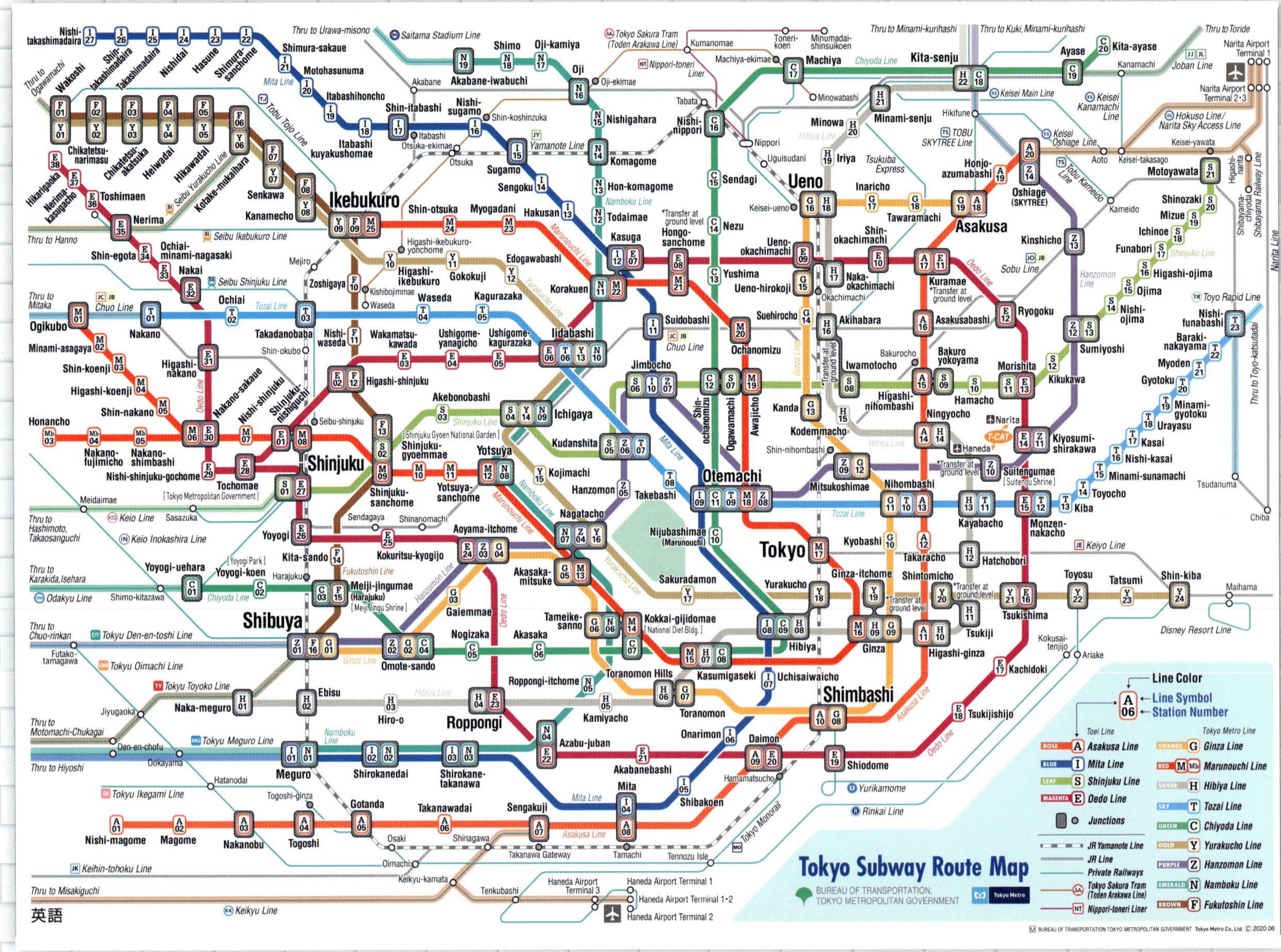

TOKYO

TOKYO
Tokyo Metro Co., Ltd., and Toei Subway
(Tokyo Metropolitan Bureau of Transportation)

System Length	189 route miles
Number of Lines	13
Number of Stations	286
Year Opened	1927
Year of Last Expansion	2020 (new station)
Annual Ridership	3.9 billion (2019)
Subwayness	89% of stations underground

Higashi-ginza station entrance, serving both Tokyo Metro's Hibiya Line and Toei's Akasura Line

For a transit enthusiast like myself, Tokyo, home of the world's most extensive urban railway network, feels like Seventh Heaven. (It can also feel like the Eighth Circle of Hell during the rush-hour crush.) Tokyo in recent years has been the world's busiest subway system, with 3.9 billion riders per year, even though it's ranked just eighteenth in overall system size, attesting to its busyness.

Its map is surely the busiest as well: It depicts not only the city's thirteen subway lines, but also a profusion of commuter rail, monorail, tram, and automated guideway lines serving this city of fourteen million (thirty-eight million if one counts the Greater Tokyo-Yokohama

TRANSIT TOURISM | 231

TOKYO METRO CO., LTD., AND TOEI SUBWAY

metropolitan region). Like the flashing pachinko machines of the Shinjuku District's game parlors, the transit map displays a mazelike array of potential pathways one can follow.

The subway system is not just visually complex but operationally complex as well. It has two different operating companies; three different track gauges; a combination of conventional steel-on-steel wheel, rubber-tired, and monorail vehicles; and power supplied through third-rail, overhead catenary and linear induction. Nine of the lines are operated by Tokyo Metro Co., Ltd. (Tokyo Metro), marked by a stylized "M" logo. It is a public enterprise whose shares are currently held by the government of Japan and the Tokyo metropolitan government. In sharp contrast to American transit systems, the Tokyo Metro actually has been profitable (at least, up until the pandemic). In fact, the government successfully launched an IPO of Tokyo Metro shares in October, 2024 in a rare case of a public transportation agency actually "going public." The flotation generated $2.3 billion of proceeds that reduced government ownership of the enterprise by 50 percent, and the shares soared 45 percent in value following the offering. The smaller Tokyo Metropolitan Bureau of Transportation (TOEI), is a municipally owned system operating four lines as well as an automated guideway. It is branded with a stylized ginkgo leaf logo—the emblem for the Tokyo Metropolis—also said to represent the letter "T" for Tokyo...

Akihabara station (Hibiya Line)

232 | ASIA—JAPAN

TOKYO

But the plot thickens! As if a system consisting of thirteen subway lines weren't complicated enough, ten of those lines also have one or more *commuter rail* companies running trains in the two subway companies' tunnels through central Tokyo. For example, the Asakusa subway line (operated by TOEI) also accommodates three private rail companies operating suburban commuter trains through its downtown tunnels. This commuting "cohabitation" was introduced in the 1960s in an effort to relieve the pressure on the major railway terminals and the circular Yamanote commuter rail line. Further complicating matters, several of the commuter rail companies operate trains through their *own* subway tunnels and underground stations serving downtown Tokyo. As a result, the bright-line distinction I had been attempting to draw in this book differentiating subways from commuter rail lines becomes hopelessly blurred in Tokyo. That being said, this chapter is focused on the thirteen "bona fide" subway lines.

A private company built Tokyo's initial subway, the Ginza Line, in 1927. It was the very first subway line in East Asia, inspired by a Japanese businessman's trip to London in the early 1920s, where he saw the benefit of the Underground firsthand. Because of the Second World War and the widespread destruction that resulted, a second subway line didn't open in Tokyo until the early 1950s. But as the Japanese economy boomed and the city's population burgeoned during the "miracle decades" that followed, there was a flurry of subway construction activity. Ten additional lines opened in the 1960s through the 1980s—a growth spurt that would be replicated by Chinese cities thirty years later when they, too, experienced an economic boom. But nary a track mile has been added to Tokyo's subway system in the last fifteen years…

Each of Tokyo's subway lines is numbered and color-coded, but the lines commonly are referred to by the first initial of their names, rather than their numbers. For example, Chiyoda Line is labeled "C," Ginza Line "G," Hibiya Line "H," and so on. The station stops generally are named after neighborhoods or places rather than streets, which makes sense given Japan's idiosyncratic

TOKYO METRO CO., LTD., AND TOEI SUBWAY

way of assigning addresses. (Explaining Tokyo's address format would require a chapter in its own right, since it avoids any reference to the street on which the building is located.) Helpfully, every station on the subway has its own unique identifying letter and number, making navigating the system manageable for visitors from abroad.

So, even if you are worried about deciphering the *romaji* (Roman character phonetic spelling) of the station names, just follow the station numbers. For example, Kyōbashi and Kayabachō stations can avoid being confused because the former is labeled G-10, as the tenth stop on the Ginza Line, while the latter is an interchange for both the Hibiya and Tozai Lines and is labeled H-13 and T-11. Got it? (Fair warning: this *will* be covered on the final exam.) This numbering protocol, augmented by directional arrows on the floor, color-coded wall graphics, and bilingual signs in Japanese and English, make it surprisingly easy to navigate Tokyo's enormous subway system.

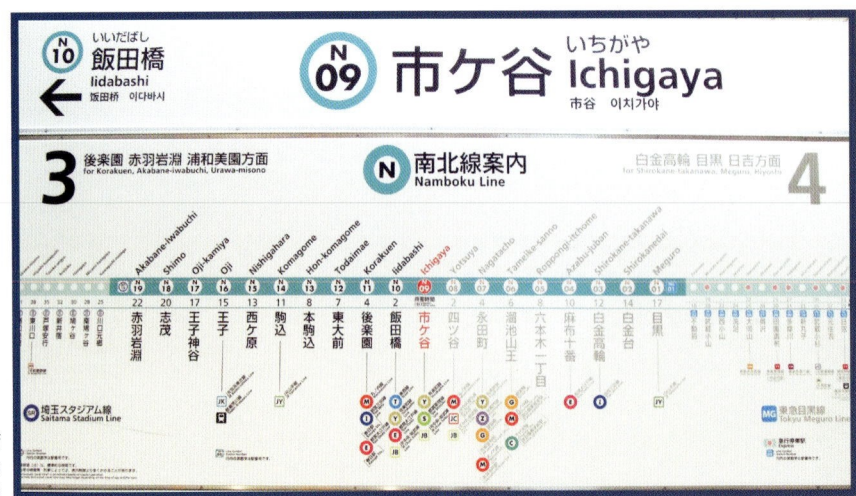

Easy-to-read listing of Nambuko Line stations at Ichigaya

234 | ASIA—JAPAN

TOKYO

For the better part of a day on my visit to Tokyo, I commandeered our delightful tour guide, Keiko Kamei, to give me a native's insights on the city's extensive subway system. No doubt relying on sophisticated operations research analysis, she choreographed an elaborate twelve-step tour crisscrossing central Tokyo, involving seven different subway lines plus the Yamanote surface "circle line"—and still left time for the obligatory visit to a pachinko parlor in Shinjuku.

The design of Tokyo's older stations is clean and bright but on the whole bland, with low ceilings, plain tiled walls, and broad cylindrical columns. Typical-looking stations for both Tokyo Metro (Omote-sandō on the Hanzōmon Line) and TOEI (Ichigaya on the Shinjuku Line) are shown below:

Left: Omote-sandō station (Chiyoda, Ginza, and Hanzōmon Lines)

Right: Ichigaya station (Namboku, Shinjuku, and Yūrakuchō Lines)

A majority of the lines have been converted to platform edge gates for safety, and many of the stations have public restrooms, which I would rate with three Michelin stars (meaning they warrant a "special journey" even if you don't have a "special need"). As is the case in Japan generally, one rarely sees any litter in the subway—even though public trash cans can be hard to find. Remember to bring your small plastic disposal bag with you!

TOKYO METRO CO., LTD., AND TOEI SUBWAY

And then there are the platform attendants impeccably dressed like customs officers with caps and gloves (the *oshiya*, or pushers), who "assist" passengers in boarding crowded trains during rush hour. To discourage inappropriate behavior, some of the lines offer women-only cars during rush hour, similar to those in Mexico City.

Tokyo's newer lines have been more adventurous in their architectural design. The Ōedo Line, completed in 2000, is a circle line intersecting eleven of the twelve other subway lines. Entirely underground in deep-bored tunnels for the full length of its 26-mile, thirty-eight-station circuit, it is the longest subway line in Japan, as well as the most expensive ($12 billion). The Ōedo Line has been referred to as Tokyo's "Jubilee Line," in that both lines were built around the turn of the millennium with an emphasis on high-quality architectural design (see London chapter).

And like the Jubilee Line, but in contrast to other Tokyo subway lines, the Ōedo line used a different architect for each of its stations, resulting in more-distinctive spaces. Artwork at each station was funded by private companies, in many cases incorporating as themes the history of the local neighborhoods they serve, similar to Beijing.

Left: Nakano-sakaue (Oedo Line)

Right: Tocho-mae (Oedo Line)

TOKYO

And on the Fukutoshin Line 13 (the newest, started in 1983–94; latest extension, 2008), each station has an individual design concept. Shibuya, one of the busiest in the entire system, was designed by internationally renowned architect Tadao Ando, who has called it an "underground spaceship" because of its saucerlike aperture, allowing light to reach the train platforms three levels down. (An *underground* spaceship—wait until Elon Musk hears about this!) More recently, some of the older lines have been getting design makeovers, such as the Ginza Line—now almost a century old—where five stations have recently seen large art installations added.

Shibuya station (Fukutoshin Line)

TOKYO METRO CO., LTD., AND TOEI SUBWAY

Many of the stations have extensive retail shopping and underground links to nearby train stations, department stores, and office buildings. Montréal has underground shopping as well, but Tokyo is much more intensely developed, in part because of the huge number of passengers passing through on a daily basis. Most of the stores serve everyday needs (convenience shops, shoe repair, a quick bite), but their dining is not limited to fast food: Sukiyabashi Jiro, reputedly Tokyo's best sushi restaurant (and among its most expensive, at $450 per person), is tucked away in the warren of passageways within Ginza station. There is room for only ten guests at its counter for the 7:30 p.m. seating, where a nineteen-course meal is served.[1] Exact change is not required.

With nearly 90 percent of Tokyo's subway system underground, the opportunities it affords for sightseeing while in transit are limited. Perhaps the most scenic line (but technically not part of the Tokyo subway system) is the Yurikamome automated people mover. It is a 9-mile-long, rubber-tired aerial line that winds around from the Shimbashi train station to an island in Tokyo Harbor, where the International Exhibition Center is located. The harbor crossing over the Rainbow Bridge affords spectacular views of downtown Tokyo.

---

[1] If you're a foodie, a cheaper alternative is to rent on Netflix David Gelb's critically acclaimed 2011 documentary about the restaurant and its top chef, called *Jiro Dreams of Sushi*. The Ginza subway station makes a cameo appearance.

TOKYO

SUMMARY

Tokyo's subway system is extensive, quick, punctual, clean, thrifty, and courteous (that's half of the Boy Scouts' oath, right there). It is also the world's busiest system and, no doubt, offers the most diverse range of rail services. Tokyo clearly ranks as one of the world's great subway systems in terms of scope, complexity, and ridership but is somewhat of a disappointment architecturally and artistically. Still, it gets the job done efficiently for nearly nine million daily commuters, and it's an indispensable facet of city life. On the list of quintessential things to do when visiting Tokyo, riding the subway is right up there along with checking out the Tsukiji Fish Market and attending a sumo wrestling match at the Kokugikan National Arena.

SELTZER TOKEN RATINGS (SCALE 1–4)

CONVENIENCE	4
EASE OF USE	4
QUALITY OF DESIGN	1
PERSONALITY	2

The map is unusual for transit agencies in showing major streets as well as subways lines and stations.

BUENOS AIRES
Subterráneo de Buenos Aires S.E.

System Length	38 route miles
Number of Lines	6
Number of Stations	90
Year Opened	1913
Year of Last Expansion	2019
Annual Ridership	338 million (2019)
Subwayness	100% of stations underground

The Obelisk in the Plaza de la República, the iconic symbol of Buenos Aires, stands above the interchange station for the B, C, and D lines

Buenos Aires anchors a huge metropolitan area of some fourteen million residents, with an outsized style and self-esteem to match. In the downtown area, stately Second Empire edifices line its broad, tree-lined boulevards, and Porteños—as its sophisticated residents are known—animate its lively café scene. All of this explains why, with characteristic Argentinian modesty, locals consider Paris to be "the Buenos Aires of the North"... But B.A. is also a city of idiosyncrasies. Not only is the city home to the elaborate ritual of the tango, but it also boasts the planet's largest concentration of psychotherapists. There are some 60,000 of them, perhaps busy counseling Porteños

TRANSIT TOURISM | 241

SUBTERRÁNEO DE BUENOS AIRES S.E.

despairing of learning the tango. And of course there is the unspeakable, barely potable, national drink of *mate*, a bitter brew tasting like a combination of dried ragweed and 3-in-1 oil. At the café, I recommend opting for the latte rather than the mate…

Subway car showing the livery of the Metrovías, the private operator

Style and idiosyncrasy also characterize the city's subway, popularly known as the "Subte"—short for *subterráneo*—a name as uniquely associated with Buenos Aires as the "Tube" is with London, or the "L" with Chicago. Opened in 1913, the Subte was the first subway in Latin America, and indeed the entire Southern Hemisphere. And for bragging rights in the Spanish-speaking world, it predates even Madrid's Metropolitano by six years. Four of its six lines were already operating by the Second World War, in contrast to other Latin American cities' subways, all of which were built since the late 1960s. Although the system is owned by the City of Buenos Aires, it has been operated since 1994 through a concession agreement with a for-profit corporation, Metrovías, and more recently, EMOVA. Having a subway run by a private company is definitely the exception rather than the rule, since almost all systems worldwide are operated by governmental authorities.

BUENOS AIRES

The system consists of six lines and ninety stops linked by ten interchange stations, making it relatively complex for a smaller system (the Subte ranks ninety-second worldwide in subway route miles). The lines generally run under the broad thoroughfares carved through the dense city in the first part of the twentieth century, much in the manner of Baron Haussmann's Parisian boulevards. The first subway line was also built in this period, inspired by the then-new Paris Métro.

The heart of the system, where three of the lines converge, is Plaza de Mayo, the political, commercial, and spiritual center of B.A. since the city's founding in 1580. This public square is surrounded by national landmarks, including the Metropolitan Cathedral, Argentina's central bank, and the Casa Rosada Presidential Palace, from whose balcony Eva Perón (Evita) addressed thousands of ardent followers. Nearby, three lines intersect at the Obelisk, a smaller Southern Hemisphere version of the Washington Monument that serves as the symbol of the city.

But, in contrast to most other cities, the Subte's interchange stations bear different names depending on the line, requiring added diligence by the rider. For example, the connecting stations at the Obelisk are 9 de Julio (Line B), Diagonal Norte (Line C), and Carlos Pellegrini (Line D)—it's a locus without a focus! Thus, the Subte's subtle complexity made it an ideal setting for a 1990s science fiction film called *Möbius*, named after the single-sided, ring-shaped form beloved by topologists. In the film, a new peripheral line interconnecting with the existing lines creates (in mathematical terms) a "topological singularity," resulting in a subway train getting caught in another dimension.[1] And you thought changing trains at Times Square for the Shuttle was disorienting…

Buenos Aires's first line (A) is a veritable museum piece. With its tidy white tile walls, color-accented borders, and painted steel girders, it reminded me of the 1896 Földalatti Line in Budapest

---

[1] The movie is based on an entertaining science fiction short story from 1950 called "A Subway Named Möbius," written by A. J. Deutsch about what happened to similar effect in Boston's subway when the "Boylston Shuttle" was opened.

TRANSIT TOURISM | 243

SUBTERRÁNEO DE BUENOS AIRES S.E.

(compare two photos below). The stations are largely unchanged from over a century ago, and the original subway cars remained in use for nearly a century until replaced in 2013, much to the consternation of many Porteños. Their issue was *not* the advanced age of the rolling stock, but the opposite: they missed the familiarity of the quaint but ancient, creaking cars.

Left: Peru station (Line A) in Buenos Aires

Right: Vörösmarty utca station (Line 1) in Budapest

But the more recent lines have their aesthetic appeal as well. Two dozen of the stations on Lines C, D, and E were built in the 1930s and are decorated with impressive tile murals depicting the history of Argentina, the landscape of Spain, local folklore, and scenes of life in Buenos Aires during that era. In fact, Line C is known as "the Spanish Line" because many of the murals depict the Spanish countryside. Thirty stations on four of the lines have been entered into Argentina's National Registry of Historic and Artistic Monuments as culturally significant artifacts. Several other so-called Art Stations on the D Line (Tucuman, Olleros, and Juramento) show rotating displays of art objects from the City Museum.

BUENOS AIRES

Left:
Mural on Lavalle station
(Line C), 1934

Right:
Moreno station
(Line C)

   In 1995, shortly after Metrovías became the system operator, it hired a talented Porteño graphic designer named Ronald Shakespear to do a complete makeover of the system's graphics. Tasked with making the Subte easier to navigate and with rejuvenating the overall look of the system, Shakespear selected a contemporary typeface (Frutiger), introduced simplified wayfinding signs, designed a new color-coded map, and made station entrances more visible. His graphics for modernizing the aging stations allowed a complete rebranding, similar to what the Cambridge Seven design firm did for Boston in the mid-1960s. The result is a "house style" that is not just informational but also an expression of the Subte's—and indeed B.A.'s—civic identity. The redesign centers the brand on the unique local character by showcasing the "Subte" nickname and respects the proud history reflected in the stations' tile murals, while putting forward a fresh and stylish set of graphics that was affordable within the city's (indeed, the nation's) reduced circumstances.

SUBTERRÁNEO DE BUENOS AIRES S.E.

The photos below of Plaza Italia (Line D) show how the stations are enlivened by bright graphics and art installations. The newer stops have some eye-catching art installations, such as Medalla Milgrosa station (Line E), Venezuela station (line H), and San Jose de Flores station (Line A).

Left:
Plaza Italia station (Line D)

Right:
General San Martin station (Line C)

Left:
Venezuela station (Line H)

Right:
San Jose de Flores station (Line A)

BUENOS AIRES

One of my personal favorites is the José Hernández station on Line D, remodeled in 2015 with large images celebrating Lionel Messi, Argentina's magical midfielder. Indeed, seasoned Subte commuters seem able to navigate quickly through rush-hour crowds with the same skill and dexterity as "La Pulga" does in zipping past defensive backs on the soccer pitch.

José Hernández station (Line D)

SUBTERRÁNEO DE BUENOS AIRES S.E.

Echeverría station
(Line B)

248 | SOUTH AMERICA—ARGENTINA

BUENOS AIRES

SUMMARY

The Buenos Aires Subte, like the city itself, has a sophisticated and attractive style—or more accurately, three styles, reflecting its three periods of development. The quaint, spruced-up industrial look of the original line dating from the 1910s, the wonderful station tile-work murals from the three lines built in the 1930s and 1940s, and finally—after a half-century gap in subway construction—a very contemporary look for the new Line H and several extensions of existing lines opened since the millennium. Fortuitously, the Subte and its passengers were spared much of the tediously functional architecture of the 1950s through the 1970s. A 2015 plan approved by the federal legislature would add at least two more subway lines F and G, filling in the missing alphabet letters and interconnecting the six existing lines at multiple locations. If fully built out, however, the more complex system may run the risk of creating a real Möbius strip—with "Carlos del Subte" suffering the same fate as his Boston cousin of song and legend, Charlie of the MTA.

SELTZER TOKEN RATINGS (SCALE 1–4)

CONVENIENCE	3
EASE OF USE	2
QUALITY OF DESIGN	3
PERSONALITY	3

TRANSIT TOURISM | 249

7
Jundiaí
Várzea Paulista
Campo Limpo Paulista
Botujuru
Francisco Morato
Baltazar Fidélis
Franco da Rocha
Caieiras
Perus
Vila Aurora
Jaraguá
Vila Clarice
Pirituba
Piqueri
Lapa
Água Branca
Palmeiras-Barra Funda
Luz
Brás
1
Tucuruvi
Parada Inglesa
Jardim São Paulo-Ayrton Senna
Santana
Carandiru
Portuguesa-Tietê
Armênia
Tiradentes
São Bento
Sé
700m
Japão-Liberdade
São Joaquim
Vergueiro
Paraíso
Ana Rosa
Vila Mariana
Santa Cruz
Praça da Árvore
Saúde
Ultrafarma
São Judas
Conceição
Jabaquara
A
Vila Galvão
Cecap
B
Taboão
13
Aeroporto-Guarulhos
Parada Rodoviária
Guarulhos-Cecap
Engº Goulart
USP Leste
Comendador Ermelino
São Miguel Paulista
Jardim Helena-Vila Mara
Itaim Paulista
Jardim Romano
Engº Manoel Feio
Itaquaquecetuba
Aracaré
Calmon Viana
12
11
Estudantes
Mogi das Cruzes
Braz Cubas
Jundiapeba
Suzano
Poá
Ferraz de Vasconcelos
Antonio Gianetti Neto
Guaianases
José Bonifácio
Dom Bosco
Corinthians-Itaquera
3
Artur Alvim
Patriarca-Vila Ré
Guilhermina Esperança
Vila Matilde
Penha
Carrão
Tatuapé
Belém
Bresser-Mooca
Pedro II
República
Santa Cecília
Mal. Deodoro
Júlio Prestes
8
Amador Bueno
Santa Rita
Itapevi
Engº Cardoso
Sagrado Coração
Jandira
Jardim Silveira
Jardim Belval
Barueri
Antonio João
Santa Terezinha
Carapicuíba
Gen. Miguel Costa
Quitaúna
Com. Sampaio
Osasco
Pres. Altino
Imperatriz Leopoldina
Domingos de Moraes
C
Luiz Bortolosso
km 21
Ceasa
Amador Aguiar
Vila Yara
Villa-Lobos-Jaguaré
Cidade Universitária
Pinheiros
Hebraica-Rebouças
Cidade Jardim
Vila Olímpia
Berrini
400m
Morumbi
750m
Granja Julieta
João Dias
Socorro
Jurubatuba
Autódromo
Primavera-Interlagos
Grajaú
Bruno Covas
Mendes-Vila Natal
9
4
Taboão da Serra
Vila Sônia
Profª Elisabeth Tenreiro
São Paulo-Morumbi
Butantã
Faria Lima
Fradique Coutinho
Oscar Freire
Paulista
Pernambucanas
Consolação
Higienópolis-Mackenzie
Anhangabaú
2
Vila Madalena
Santuário N. Sa. de Fátima
Sumaré
Clínicas
Trianon-Masp
Brigadeiro
Chácara Klabin
Santos-Imigrantes
Alto do Ipiranga
Sacomã
Tamanduateí
5
Capão Redondo
Campo Limpo
Vila das Belezas
Giovanni Gronchi
Santo Amaro
Largo Treze
Adolfo Pinheiro
Alto da Boa Vista
Borba Gato
Brooklin
Campo Belo
Eucaliptos
Moema
AACD-Servidor
Hospital São Paulo
Diadema
Piraporinha
São Bernardo
Ferrazópolis
Juventus-Mooca
Ipiranga
São Caetano do Sul
Prefeito Walter Braido
Utinga
Prefeito Saladino
Prefeito Celso Daniel
Santo André
Capuava
Mauá
Guapituba
Ribeirão Pires
Antônio Bespalec
Rio Grande da Serra
10
Vila Prudente
Oratório
São Lucas
Camilo Haddad
Vila Tolstói
Vila União
Jd. Planalto
Sapopemba
Fazenda da Juta
São Mateus
Jardim Colonial
15
Sônia Maria
GRU
N

SÃO PAULO

SÃO PAULO
Companhia do Metropolitano de São Paulo

System Length	55 route miles
Number of Lines	5
Number of Stations	83
Year Opened	1974
Year of Last Expansion	2021
Annual Ridership	1.49 billion (2019)
Subwayness	69% of stations underground

Brigadeiro station entrance in Avenida Paulista, in the heart of São Paulo's business district

São Paulo, Brazil's principal city, is brimming with people, vitality, and style, all three of which are evident in its bustling, efficient, smart-looking subway system, the São Paulo Metro.

Latin America's largest metropolis (twelve million in the city proper, twenty-three million in the metropolitan area), São Paulo is Brazil's commercial, financial and cultural center. Visually, it resembles a landlocked version of Los Angeles—a sprawlingly large, surprisingly green economic juggernaut. Its rapid growth has spawned multiple subcenters of commercial development, similar to Los Angeles, and endless phalanxes of high-rise apartments march to the horizon. The

TRANSIT TOURISM | 251

COMPANHIA DO METROPOLITANO DE SÃO PAULO

city's demographics are also surprisingly diverse. While it is by far the world's largest Portuguese-speaking city, six million of its residents are of Italian descent, a million claim Arab ancestry, and 650,000 are ethnically Japanese, all the result of great migrations in the early twentieth century.

The city's public transport is similarly variegated, consisting of the "heavy rail" metro, a commuter rail network, a monorail line, two independent trolley bus systems, several bus rapid-transit lines, and an enormous regular bus system operated almost entirely by private companies.

The first segment of the Metro opened only in 1974. Subsequent lines and incremental extensions have opened almost every year since then, with more under construction. The Metro today consists of five mostly underground rail lines and one aboveground monorail. It is now the busiest, if not the biggest, transit system in Latin America, narrowly edging out Mexico City in ridership, with a system about half its size. All the infrastructure was built by the state agency Companhia do Metropolitano de São Paulo, branded as MetroSP. Three of the five subway lines are operated by MetroSP, and two of the lines are operated by private companies—ViaQuatro (Yellow Line) and ViaMobilidade (Lilac Line). Several new Metro and monorail lines are being developed under private long-term concessions, which is atypical in the world of public transport.

Train approaching Armenia station

SÃO PAULO

The Metro carries some 3.5 million passengers daily. Yet, despite the system's expansion in recent years, it is still undersized for the city it serves. In terms of route mileage, it barely makes the "Top 60" of subways worldwide. Istanbul, Tokyo, and Moscow—all cities of similar population—have subway systems that are two to three times larger. However, MetroSP is currently building two new lines (a metro and a monorail) as well as extending the Green Line and existing monorail, which will expand the system by a third upon completion.

A complementary aboveground commuter rail system (CPTM) carries about two million passengers per day on seven electrified lines, some of which operate with metro-like frequencies of four minutes. And like the Metro, CPTM operates on a flat fare system with free interchange to the subway, which is very unusual for a suburban commuter rail service. Because CPTM and MetroSP use the same line numbering and color format, they appear as one integrated system on the official transit map.

For my tour of the Metro, I fortuitously had as my guide Luísa Gonçalves, a univesity professor of architecture and urbanism. Luísa's master's thesis and PhD dissertation were on the design of the Metro, and so she was ideally suited to guide me around.

Most of the north–south Metro route (Line 1, now labeled the Blue Line) opened in the late 1970s. Many of the initial-phase stations were designed by Marcelo Fragelli, a midcentury Brazilian modernist architect. Like his world-renowned countryman Oscar Niemeyer (who designed Brasilia and many other famous buildings in Brazil), Fragelli's designs were done in the "brutalist" style—heavy emphasis on showing structural features by using exposed concrete with minimal decoration.

Fragelli paid special attention to the interface between the Metro station entrances and the surrounding neighborhood's streetscape. Several of the stations he designed, such as Plaza Sé and São Bento, feature sunken courtyards planted with lush vegetation where sunlight filters into the mezzanine levels of the stations.

COMPANHIA DO METROPOLITANO DE SÃO PAULO

Left: Plaza Sé station concourse (Blue/Red Line interchange). Marcelo Nitsche's Scrabble sculpture in sunken courtyard. Metropolitan Cathedral in the background.

Right: São Bento station (Blue Line). Plaza and shops within, outdoor seating.

Fragelli used poured concrete in an artistic, highly sculptural way, creating beautiful structures with minimal decoration, such as the elevated station shown below:

Armênia station (Blue Line)

254 | SOUTH AMERICA—BRAZIL

SÃO PAULO

Other architects designed the stations on subsequent lines and extensions and have enlivened the monochromatic concrete with visible and large-scale interventions, such as brightly painted ductwork and color panels and tiles.

Left: Interior walkway at Higienópolis-Mackenzie (Yellow Line)

Right: Luz station, with a skylight oculus reminiscent of New York's Fulton Transit *Center* (Blue, Red, and Yellow Lines)

Although MetroSP's architecture generally does not achieve the level of drama of London's Jubilee Line or Stockholm's T-banan, one of the stations—Sumaré—deserves special mention. The Green Line runs mostly underground, but its alignment required crossing a deep valley in São Paulo's hilly topography. The architects solved the problem by having the subway emerge briefly from its tunnel onto an open-air station suspended from the bottom of a highway bridge spanning the valley below. After traveling lengthy stretches underground, this stop is literally a breath of fresh air! The glass panel walls of this (unexpectedly) outdoor station are finished with forty-four large photo images of ordinary local residents (Paulistanos), and inscribed with Brazilian poetry.

COMPANHIA DO METROPOLITANO DE SÃO PAULO

Left and right: Sumaré station on Green Line

However, the system's signature visual feature is not the architecture but the artwork, and MetroSP has embraced public art as being central to its social mission. The Art in the Metro initiative was launched the late 1980s and has remained an integral part of MetroSP's philosophy. The agency has stated that safety, speed, reliability, and comfort are not enough; the subway also needs to provide its customers with cultural content to humanize the rider experience.

The transit agency refers to the ninety-two large artwork installations in thirty-seven stations as its "collection"—and a very finely curated collection it is! Murals, paintings, ceramic tilework, sculpture, panels—a varied assortment of assemblages. Much of the work is by Brazil's leading contemporary artists. The colorful artwork not only softens but also enlivens the otherwise unpainted concrete spaces—a lesson Washington Metro might learn from. And São Paulo's thought-provoking artwork is intended to challenge the viewer, rather than pacify him, as is the case with, say, Beijing. São Paulo joins the subways in Berlin, Brussels, Lisbon, Paris, and Stockholm in having a Françoise Schein ceramic tile mural celebrating the UN's Universal

SÃO PAULO

Declaration of Human Rights. Some of the artwork is now over thirty-five years old, but it still looks fresh and vibrant. Several examples are shown below:

Left: Odiléa Toscana's painted metal panels at São Bento station

Right: *Four Seasons* mosaic glass tiles by Tomie Ohtake at Consolação station (Green and Yellow Lines)

Left: Panel at Clinicas station (Green Line)

Right: Françoise Schein's Action Light (Luz station, Blue Line)

TRANSIT TOURISM | 257

COMPANHIA DO METROPOLITANO DE SÃO PAULO

Inside the stations, wall posters describe not only the artwork on display there, but also a summary of the installations that may be viewed throughout the system. MetroSP has produced a beautiful coffee-table book, called *Art in the Metro*, describing the artists and their works. MetroSP's commitment to culture extends to temporary art exhibitions along with the performing arts, and its website lists various performances of music, theater, and the spoken word at its stations.

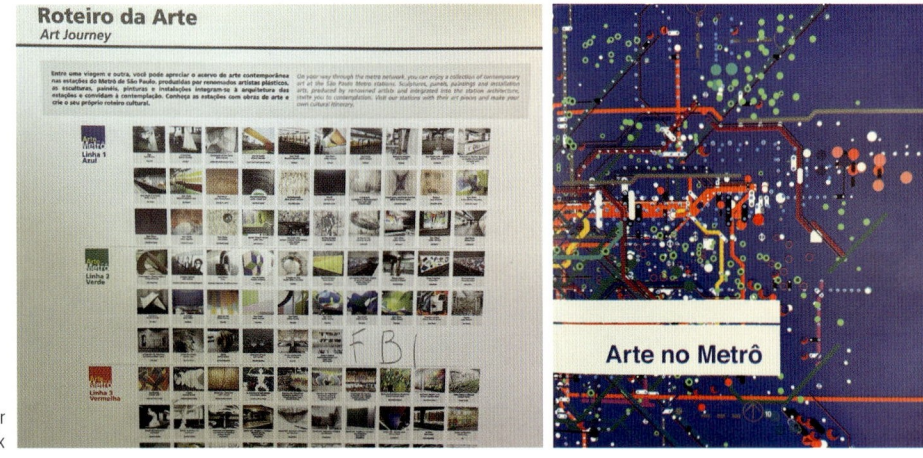

Station poster art guide, and cover of system catalog of artwork

System-wide, station wall graphics are clear, clean, and colorful, and the stations are absolutely spotless. I did not see a piece of litter or graffiti mark anywhere, showing how respectfully the Paulistanos treat their Metro. The only mild criticisms I would make regarding the system's graphics is the paucity of station name indicators on the platform walls viewable from inside the train (in case one missed the PA announcement), and the inconsistency in not having every station entrance marked by Metro pylon indicators at street level.

SÃO PAULO

SUMMARY

The São Paulo metro is a methodically expanding system serving a growing, incredibly busy, and highly congested city. True to the Brazilian modernist tradition, the stations are largely in the brutalist style of unpainted, unfinished concrete. However, the austere architecture is softened by welcoming entrance plazas, excellent graphics, and, above all, superb contemporary artwork, which pairs well with the minimalist design. On par with the art installations used in the Brussels, Naples, and Stockholm metros, MetroSP excels at using public art to achieve its organizational mission of elevating the quality of life for its customers. As a result, the Metro has become a quintessential element in helping convey São Paulo's urban brand identity of a fashion-forward, world-class city.

SELTZER TOKEN RATINGS (SCALE 1–4)

CONVENIENCE	3
EASE OF USE	3
QUALITY OF DESIGN	3
PERSONALITY	4

TRANSIT TOURISM

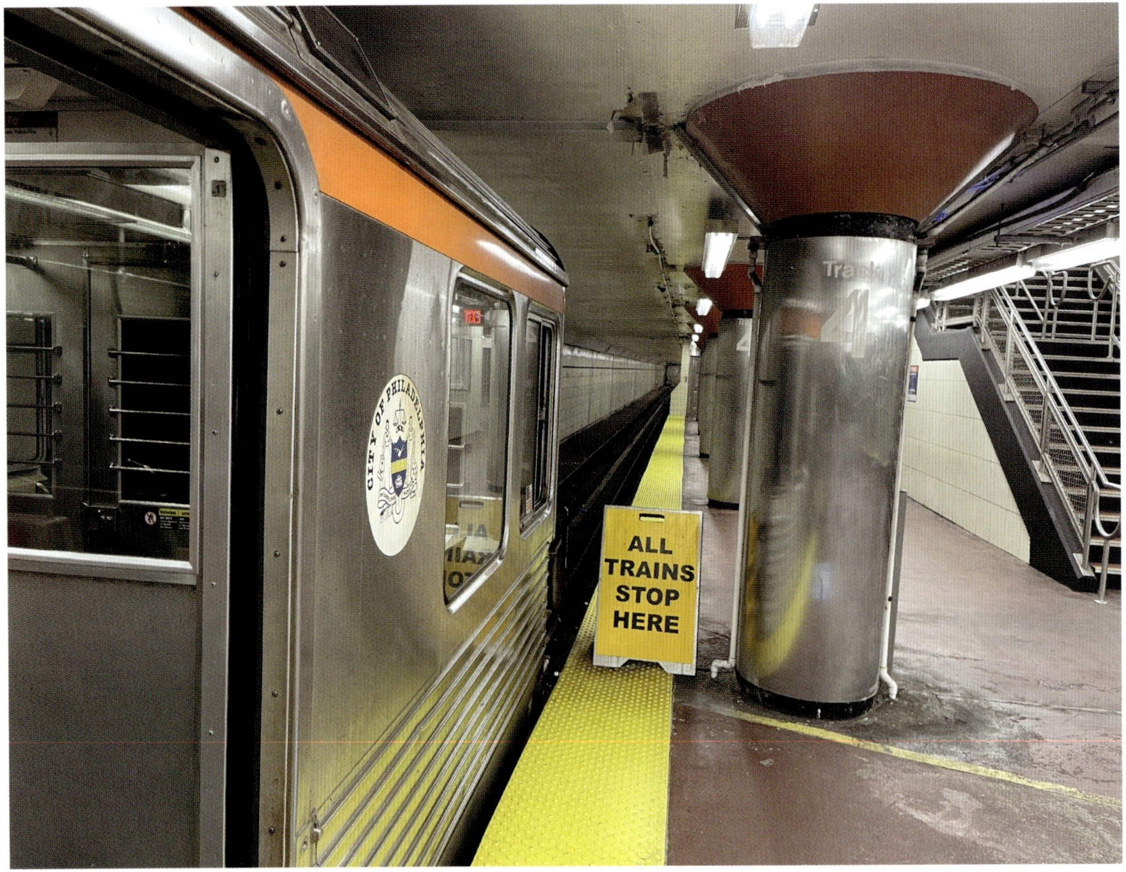
ALL
TRAINS
STOP
HERE

TERMINUS

Terminus! This is the final stop. Terminus!
Please remember to take your personal opinions with you
when you leave the book.

Our travels in the preceding chapters have taken us from some of the world's largest subway systems (Beijing, Tokyo, and New York) to some of its smallest (Naples and Glasgow), and from the very oldest (London) to the very newest (Istanbul). We have seen that subways are much more than infrastructure assets providing a means of urban conveyance. They are important cultural identifiers of a city, reflecting the municipal persona in various ways. The visual culture of the systems—the station architecture, the logo, the map, the typeface—reflects each city's individual character and in many ways presents its self-image to the world at large. The Underground's roundel symbolizes London, just as the art nouveau Metro entrances epitomize Paris, and Manhattan's unglamorous, clamorous stations characterize New York. Thus, the subway represents an iconic marker of the city it serves.

The architecture of subway stations has evolved from largely utilitarian boxes drawn up by local civil engineers in the early twentieth century to daring and sophisticated public spaces conceived by some of today's leading designers and architects. While some systems such as Washington and Beijing generally have hewed to a standardized template, other systems such as Montréal, Munich, and, more recently, Budapest, Naples, and London have shown how involving multiple architectural firms can dramatically enhance the rider experience.

Many world-class *starchitects* have designed world-class subway stations—Tadao Ando, Norman Foster, Zaha Hadid, and Santiago Calatrava, to name a few. However, with the trend toward installing platform screen doors at the train level that form a protective barrier between the tracks and the platform, it is becoming increasingly difficult to appreciate the contemporary station architecture. Most of the newer subways (and many of the older systems whose lines have been renovated) employ either half-high gates or full-height screen doors protecting the passengers but sadly blocking the view. Nearly ninety subway systems now use platform barriers or screen doors on some or all of their lines. One might as well be waiting in an elevator lobby…

Another common theme is the growing aesthetic role that subways play as a platform—literally and figuratively—for public art, or what the Brits call "Art for All." Most major systems have some form of art-in-transit program, and a number of cities exhibit and promote truly museum-caliber contemporary art installations. In Naples, commuters on a daily basis can see provocative contemporary artwork in its spectacular stations—something they might not otherwise be inclined to seek out in a museum. Stockholm and Brussels compete for bragging rights as "the world's longest art galleries" with their bespoke and beguiling contemporary installations throughout their systems, while Moscow's Metro has always made artwork a central feature of its magnificent stations. Numerous cities have even published guidebooks to their underground art collections, outlining self-guided itineraries.

TERMINUS

Some systems also showcase their cities' historical heritage in the stations' decor. The tile murals of Buenos Aires's Subte illustrate the rich history of Argentina. Many of Beijing's subway stations contain art installations depicting the historical events from the immediate neighborhood. Naples has incorporated a first-century Roman-era temple found during construction into the design of its Duomo station, while Paris at its Louvre station displays replicas of famous sculptures housed in the galleries above. Mexico City Metro brags that its excavated Aztec temple at Pino Suárez station is the most visited heritage site in the capital, because of the tens of thousands of commuters scurrying past it every day.

And then there are the graphics, consisting of maps, typefaces, wayfinding signs, and logos. Harry Beck's original, brilliant diagram for the London Underground still casts a long shadow cartographically, since most systems use some variant of that crisp template for their maps (e.g., Boston, Budapest, Istanbul, Madrid). Moscow's subway map may be the most elegant of all, with its beautiful wheel and spokes design. But there are outliers: New York MTA briefly adopted an elegant, schematic design by Massimo Vignelli in the early 1970s. However, on the basis of riders' complaints of excessive abstraction, MTA replaced it less than a decade later with a more geographically accurate (albeit ungainly) map that itself has now become part of New York's visual culture. Mexico City, for unknown reasons, uses rumpled lines to display its subway network, while Buenos Aires shows major streets as well as the Subte lines.

In terms of typeface, with the important exceptions of London and Mexico City, most systems use Helvetica or one of its "grotesk" (to use typographers' terminology) cousins. However, systems are increasingly developing their own, sometimes subtle, house-style lettering variants for signage and corporate communications (Brussels's *Brusseline*, Paris's *Parisine*, Montréal's *Transit*).

TERMINUS

The logos tend toward some riff off the letter "M" for metro or "T" for transit, although I give Class Spirit points to several systems taking a different track: Madrid for its diamond-shaped logo ( ) as an angular version of the London roundel, Montréal's arrow in a circle ( ), and Tokyo Metro's abstract ginkgo leaf ( ). Perhaps the oddest logo of the systems surveyed in this book is Brussels's bloated "M"( ), which looks like it consumed a few too many Belgian waffles with whipped cream.

So, I hope this book has revealed to you a new form of sightseeing—*Transit Tourism*—and that you add a tour of the local metro to the itinerary of your next urban vacation trip. I think you'll find it singularly elevating, even if you remain entirely belowground. As the Cunard Lines advert used to say, "Getting there is half the fun!"

And in the course of your travels, should you come across a late-middle-aged man with his nose pressed up against the front window of the first car peering down the tracks, that likely would be me.

Way out →

IMAGE CREDITS

While gathering images for this book, I made every effort to contact copyright owners and obtain their permission. If I was unsuccessful—or if there are any errors in attribution—I extend my apologies to these owners and thank them for their contribution.

KEY TO IMAGE ABBREVIATIONS
(T) = Top, (M) = Middle, (B) = Bottom, (L) = Left, (C) = Center, (R) = Right

COVER
Rukmal Kivtisinghe, Flickr Creative Commons.

INTRODUCTION
3: Marcos Souza, Dreamstime.com (L). Pingnews, Wikimedia Commons (M). Ben Schumin, Wikimedia Commons (R).

A BRIEF HISTORY OF SUBWAYS IN TWENTY STATIONS
10: Personal collection; **11:** Samuel J. Hodson, Wikimedia Commons (T)., John S. Johnston , Wikimedia Commons (B). **12:** Sunil060902, Wikimedia Commons (T). Author unknown, Wikimedia Commons (M). MBTA (B). **13:** Beyond My Ken, Wikimedia Commons (T). KTo288, Wikimedia Commons (M). Rhododendrites, Wikimedia Commons (B). **14:** Government of Buenos Aires City, Wikimedia Commons (T). TfL, London Transport Museum collection (M). A. Savin. Wikimedia Commons (B). **15:** Fondazione Franco Albini (T). Payton Chung from Chicago, Wikimedia Commons (M). [Duncan] from Nottingham, UK, Wikimedia Commons (B). **16:** N509FZ, Wikimedia Commons (T). Pi.1415926535, Wikimedia Commons (M). poudou99, Wikimedia Commons (B). **17:** Calvin Teo, Wikimedia Commons (T). MusikAnimal, Wikimedia Commons (M). Metrodequito.gob.ec, Guia-uso-prestacion-servicio (B).

BOSTON
20: Massachusetts Bay Transportation Authority (MBTA). **21:** Logo, MBTA. Pi.1415926535, Wikimedia Commons (BL). **23:** Institute of Contemporary Art, Boston; **24:** WardMaps LLC (L). MBTA (R). **26:** Halbergman, iStock **27:** Pi.1415926535, Wikimedia Commons (TR) (BL). Fletcher, Wikimedia Commons (BR). **28:** ROxBo, Wikimedia Commons (L). Chris Sampson, Wikimedia Commons (R) **29:** Fletcher, Wikimedia Commons. **30:** MBTA (T). Hutima, Wikimedia Commons (B).

IMAGE CREDITS

CHICAGO
32: Map, Chicago Transit Authority (CTA); **33:** Logo, CTA. Schwandl (B). **34:** CTA (T). Schwandl (B). **35:** CTA (T). Schwandl (B). **36:** Adam Moss, Wikimedia Commons (L). Schwandl (R). **37:** CTA.

MEXICO CITY
40: System Map, *Sistema de Transporte Colectivo*. **41:** Logo, Hydrox, Wikimedia Commons. ProtoplasmaKid, Wikimedia Commons. **43:** dbrnjhrj, stock.adobe.com. **45:** sahua d, stock.adobe.com (L). Lance Wyman (R). **46:** STC, Wikimedia Commons (L). Hajor, Wikimedia Commons (R). Dave Walker, Adobe Stock (B). **47:** Isaac Greenberg / Alamy Stock Photo (L). Personal collection (R). **48:** Wendy Connett / Alamy Stock Photo.

MONTRÉAL
50: Map, *Archives of the Société de transport de Montréal* (STM). **51:** STM Logo, STM; Metro Logo, STM, Wikimedia Commons. Hugothepinkcat, Wikimedia Commons (B). **54:** Jeangagnon, Wikimedia Commons (TL). Beaumadier, Wikimedia Commons (TR). Anderson (B). **55:** STM (TL). Anderson (TR, B). **56:** STM (L, R). **57:** Jeangagnon, Wikimedia Commons (L). STM (R). **58:** Anderson.

NEW YORK
60: Map, Metropolitan Transportation Authority (MTA). **61:** Logo, MTA. Harrison Leong, Wikimedia Commons. **63:** Minh T. Nguyen, nycsubwayguide.com (L, R). **64:** MTA. **65:** MTAEnthusiast10, Wikimedia Commons. **66:** Personal collection. **67:** MTA (L, R). **68:** Tdorante10, Wikimedia Commons. **69:** Tdorante10, Wikimedia Commons (L). Postdlf, Wikimedia Commons (R). **70:** Personal collection, (L, R). **71:** Rhododendrites, Wikimedia Commons. **72:** MTA, Wikimedia Commons (L, R). **73:** Personal collection.

PHILADELPHIA
76: Map, Southeastern Pennsylvania Transportation Authority (SEPTA). **77:** Logo, SEPTA. Personal Collection. **78:** Personal collection. **80:** Personal collection (L). Michael, stock.adobe.com; **82:** Schwandl (L). Personal collection (R). **83:** Jon Bilous / Alamy Stock Photo. **84:** Personal collection (L, R). **85:** Stuart Rome (T, BL, BR). **86:** Personal collection (TL). Personal collection (TR). Personal collection (BL). Chris Henry / Unsplash.com (BR).

WASHINGTON, DC
88: Map, Washington Metropolitan Transit Authority (WMATA). **89:** Logo, WMATA. AgnosticPreachersKid, Wikimedia Commons (L). **90:** SUSCapitol, Wikimedia Commons (L). Alchetron.com and personal (R). **92:** Andrea Izzotti, Adobe Stock (L). Daderot, Wikimedia Commons (R). **93:** Ben Schumin, Wikimedia Commons. **94:** Ben Schumin, Flickr Creative Commons. **95:** Bohemian Baltimore, Wikimedia Commons (L). Samual Ruaat, Wikimedia Commons (R).

BRUSSELS
98: Map, Société des Transports Intercommunaux de Bruxelles (STIB). **99:** Logo, STIB. Sean Marshall, flickr.com. **101:** Nico Spilt (L). System Map, STIB (R). **102:** Logo, STIB (T). (Logos L-R) wikinight2, Wikimedia Commons. ™/®Los Angeles County Metropolitan Transportation Authority, Wikimedia Commons. Hydrox, Wikimedia Commons. SVG by Ricordisamoa, original PNG by Arbalete, Wikimedia Commons. Orange-kun, Wikimedia Commons. Pb 2001, Wikimedia Commons. WMATA. **103:** Personal collection (TL). STIB (TR, BL, BR). **104:** Schwandl (TL). STIB (TR). STIB © Hergé/Moulinsart - 2022 (BL, BR).

BUDAPEST
106: Map, Budapesti Közlekedési Zrt. (BKV). **107:** Metro Logo, BKV, Wikimedia Commons; Transit System Logo, BKV ZRT. Schwandl (B). **109:** Schwandl. **110:** Schwandl. **112:** Schwandl (TL, TR, ML, BL). FloSch, Wikimedia Commons (BR).

GLASGOW
114: Map, Strathclyde Partnership for Transport (SPT). **115:** Subway Logo and SPT Logo, SPT. Personal collection (B). **116:** Stephan Steinbach, Wikimedia Commons (L). Transitmaps.net (R). **118:** Schwandl (L, R). **119:** Personal collection (T). Garry Cornes (B). **120:** Jaron McNamara, The Transit Camera, Flickr Creative Commons (L). Xabier, Wikimedia Commons (R).

LONDON
122: Map, Transport for London (TfL). **123:** Logo, © TfL. TheFrog001, Wikimedia Commons. **124:** Chris Sampson, Wikimedia Commons; **126:** © TfL. **128:** © TfL from the London Transport Museum collection. **129:** ©TfL from the London Transport Museum collection.

IMAGE CREDITS

130: Eluveitie, Wikimedia Commons (L). TheFrog001, Wikimedia Commons (R). **131:** Jaromir Chalabala/Shutterstock.com (L). Rukmal Kirtisinghe, Flickr Creative Commons (R). **132:** Kim Rennie, flickr.com (L). GrindtXX, Wikimedia Commons (R). **133:** ©TfL from the London Transport Museum collection (L,M,R). **134:** Markobe, Adobe Stock.

MADRID
136: Map, Metro de Madrid. **137:** Logo, Metro de Madrid. Personal collection (L). **138:** Malias, Flickr Creative Commons (L). ©TfL (M). Metro de Madrid (R). **139:** Personal collection (L, R). **140:** PjrTravel / Alamy Stock Photo. **141:** Metro de Madrid. **142:** Tim Adams, Wikimedia Commons (L). Personal collection (R). **143:** Kevin George / Alamy Stock Photo (L). Metro de Madrid (R). **144:** Metro de Madrid (TL, TR, BL, BR). **145:** Draceane, Wikimedia Commons. **146:** Personal collection (L). Metro de Madrid Annual Report (2018) (R).

MOSCOW
148: Map, Moscow Metro; **149:** Logo, Metro1935, Wikimedia Commons. Enso, Adobe Stock (T). JoyNik, Adobe Stock (B). **151:** nskyr2, Adobe Stock. **153:** Anderson (TL, TM, BL, BR). **154:** Alex 'Florstein' Fedorov, Wikimedia Commons (TL). Ludvig14, Wikimedia Commons (TR). Kerimovadzhamila, Wikimedia Commons (BL, BR). **155:** Andrey Kryuchenko, Wikimedia Commons. **156:** Anderson. **157:** Anderson (L, R). **158:** Orange-kun, Wikimedia Commons.

MUNICH
160: Map, Zeno Heilmaier, Wikimedia Commons. **161:** MVG Logo, Redaktion mvg.de, Wikimedia Commons. U-Bahn Logo, 3247, Wikimedia Commons. Florian Scheutz, u-bahn-muenchen.de (L). **163:** Personal collection. **165:** FloSch, Wikimedia Commons. **167:** Radig, Wikimedia Commons. **168:** FloSch, Wikimedia Commons; **169:** FloSch, Wikimedia Commons; **170:** FloSch, Wikimedia Commons (T, B). **171:** Achim Lammerts, Wikimedia Commons. **172:** Jens Grotzke and Christian Stade, Gleisplanweb.de, Creative Commons.

NAPLES
174: Map, Aziende Napoletana Mobilità, (ANM); **175:** Azienda Napoletana Mobilità Logo, ANM. Metro Logo, SVG by Ricordisamoa, original PNG by Arbalete, Wikimedia Commons. Schwandl (L). **177:** Schwandl. **179:** Andrècruz23, Wikimedia Commons. **180:** lingling7788, Shutterstock. **181:** Angelafoto, iStock. **182:** Schwandl. **183:** ANM **184:** ANM (TL). Amtrak, Wikimedia Commons (TR). Schwandl (BL, BM, BR).

PARIS
186: Map, *Régie Autonome des Transports Parisiens* (RATP). **187:** RATP Logo, RATP, all rights reserved. Paris Métro Logo, Pb 2001, Wikimedia Commons. Claude Shoshany, Wikimedia Commons (L). **189:** Maurits90, Wikimedia Commons. **190:** Clicsouris, Wikimedia Commons (L). Steve Cadman, steve@stevecadman.me.uk, Wikimedia Commons (R). **191:** Capitaine AdBlock, Wikimedia Commons (L). UlyssePixel, Adobe Stock (R). **192:** Pline, Wikimedia Common (T). Personal collection (B). **193:** Clicsouris, Wikimedia Commons. **194:** Pb 2001, Wikimedia Commons. **195:** RATP, all rights reserved. **196:** Cameron Booth, transitmap.net.

STOCKHOLM
198: Map, Aktiebolaget Storstockholms Lokaltrafik (SL); **199:** "T" Logo, svg graphics by Kildor, Wikimedia Commons; SL Logo, SL; Personal collection (L). **200:** Anderson. **202:** Personal collection (L). evannovostro, Adobe Stock (R). **204:** EU, Wikimedia Commons (T). Grigory Bruev, Adobe Stock (B). **205:** picture-project / Alamy Stock Photo (L). Pudelek, Wikimedia Commons (R). **206:** Sergiodv/Yayimages; **207:** Ilya Birman, ilyabirman.net (T). Tom Björkstedt, Wikimedia Commons (B). **208:** Arild Vågen, Wikimedia Commons (T). Suicasmo, Wikimedia Commons (B).

BEIJING
210: Map, Beijing Subway Group Company, Ltd. **211:** Subway Logo, pngjoy.com. Personal collection (L). **215:** N509FZ, Wikimedia Commons. **216:** N509FZ Wikimedia Commons (L). N509FZ, Wikimedia Commons (M). Avalon Construction Photography / Alamy Stock Photo (R). **217:** 颐园新居 Wikimedia Commons (T). Brian Salter (BL, BR). **218:** Brian Salter (TL, TR, B).

IMAGE CREDITS

ISTANBUL
220: Map, Metro Istanbul. **221:** Metro Logo, Metro Istanbul. Danbury, Wikimedia Commons (L). **223:** bertilvidet, Wikimedia Commons. **224:** Btian P. Dorsam, Wikimedia Commons. **225:** Btian P. Dorsam, Wikimedia Commons. **226:** Dosseman, Wikimedia Commons (TR). Iznik Foundation (TL, B). **227:** Emrah, Adobe Stock. **228:** Metro Instanbul (L). Wikinight2, Wikimedia Commons (M). Shebejeyebeb, Wikimedia Commons (R).

TOKYO
230: Map, ™/®Tokyo Metro, Wikimedia Commons; **231:** Subway Logo, ™/®Tokyo Metro, Wikimedia Commons; Transit Logo, Pmx, Wikimedia. LERK, Wikimedia Commons (L). **232:** Svetlov Artem, Wikimedia Commons. **234:** LERK, Wikimedia Commons. **235:** Schwandl (L, R). **236:** Schwandl (L, R). **237:** l450v / Alamy Stock Photo.

BUENOS AIRES
240: Map, *Gobierno de la Ciudad Autónoma de Buenos Aires* (BA), Wikimedia Commons. **241:** Subté Logo, BA website. South America / Alamy Stock Photo (L). **242:** BStar Images / Alamy Stock Photo. **244:** Evelyn Proimos, Flickr Creative Commons (L). Schwandl (R). **245:** David Zumbach (L, R). **246:** Ojota, Wikimedia Commons (TL). Personal collection (TR). Schwandl (BL). BA, Wikimedia Commons (BR). **247:** Mauricio V. Genta, Wikimedia Commons. **248:** BA, Wikimedia Commons.

SÃO PAULO
250: Map, *Companhia do Metropolitano de São Paulo* (Metro SP). **251:** Logo, MetroSP; Brigadeiro entrance, personal collection. **252-259:** Personal collection.

TERMINUS
260: Personal collection